One Day That Shook the Communist World

One Day That Shook the Communist World

THE 1956 HUNGARIAN UPRISING AND ITS LEGACY

Paul Lendvai

Translated by Ann Major

PRINCETON UNIVERSITY PRESS
Princeton and Oxford

First published under the title *Der Ungarnaufstand 1956. Die Revolution und ihre Folgen* © 2006 by C. Bertelsmann Verlag, a division of Verlagsgruppe Random House GmbH, Munich, Germany

English translation © 2008 by Princeton University Press

Published by Princeton University Press, 41 William Street, Princeton, New Jersey 08540

In the United Kingdom:
Princeton University Press, 3 Market Place, Woodstock, Oxfordshire OX20 1SY

All Rights Reserved

Library of Congress Cataloging-in-Publication Data

Lendvai, Paul, 1929–

[Ungarnaufstand 1956. English]

One day that shook the communist world : the 1956 Hungarian uprising and its legacy / Paul Lendvai ; translated by Ann Major.

p.   cm.

Includes bibliographical references and index.

ISBN-13: 978-0-691-13282-2 (hardcover : alk. paper)   1. Hungary—History—Revolution, 1956.
I. Title.

DB957.L41213 2006

943.905'2—dc 22   2007026864

British Library Cataloging-in-Publication Data is available

Translation costs from German into English were funded by the Raiffeisen Zentralbank of Vienna and by the Austrian Federal Ministry of Culture and Education

This book has been composed in Dante MT

Printed on acid-free paper. ∞

press.princeton.edu

Printed in the United States of America

10 9 8 7 6 5 4 3 2 1

In memory of Imre Nagy, Pál Maléter,

Géza Losonczy, József Szilágyi,

Miklós Gimes, and all the executed

who have sacrificed their lives

in 1956–1961 for the freedom

and independence of Hungary

Contents

One Day That Shook the Communist World

Introduction

O ne of the most perceptive, if also the most controversial, observers of events before and during the Hungarian revolution of 23 October to 4 November 1956 was Leslie B. Bain, the American journalist of Hungarian extraction. In his 1960 book on Eastern Europe, he wrote: "No event in recent history has been so much lied about, distorted, and besmirched as the Hungarian Revolution."[1]

These words are a very apposite description of the reports and the long-standing debates about the dramatic events that, due mainly to the Kádár regime's disinformation propaganda, have been partly obscured and partly presented in a blatantly deceptive light. The numerous books and studies published prior to the collapse of the Eastern Bloc and the Soviet system in 1989–1991 by Hungarian expatriates and Western historians about the course and consequences of the uprising and the national war of independence could rectify the facts and analyze the motives behind the decisions in Hungary and abroad only to some extent, because the most important documents held in the secret archives in Budapest, and above all in Moscow, were inaccessible to them.

The fact that today we can present by and large reliable conclusions about the fifty-year-old drama and its global consequences is due primarily to the efforts of the Institute for the History of the 1956 Hungarian Revolution, established in Budapest in 1991. Two Hungarian historians, the recently deceased founding director György Litván and János M. Rainer, his successor since 1999, together with their colleagues, have published numerous studies and research papers on the events leading up to the revolution, as well as on its course and its aftermath (admittedly predominantly in Hungarian). It is only thanks to their commentaries and supplements that we can now properly classify and check the veracity of the document collections compiled from the former Soviet archives by Russian historians in 1993 and 1996. The exceptional significance of the three handbooks published in 1996 by the Institute on the Chronology, the Bibliography and Retribution and Recollection, as well as the two-volume biographies of Imre Nagy (by János M. Rainer) and János Kádár (by Tibor Huszár), cannot be overestimated.[2]

Even fifty years after the event, the Hungarian people's uprising, revolution, and freedom fight still attract surprisingly keen interest in Germany, Austria, and Switzerland (as well as in other countries), but by no means only within the ranks of the older generation. Yet in spite of the memory of the world-historical significance of the Hungarian Revolution, the course and background of those events are only sketchily known, probably due primarily to the language barrier.

Although I have only briefly described the revolution of 1956 both in my memoirs and in my book on Hungary's history, the triumph and tragedy of the Hungarian uprising have had, as in the case of so many of my compatriots, a crucially formative influence on my life in a multitude of ways. Even though I left Hungary for good on 13 January 1957, I was able, in the midst of events at the Kilián Barracks, to experience in the flesh how world history was being made and the desire for freedom brutally stifled by a foreign army. Contemporary witnesses could not, of course, perceive the background. Still, up to this day the sense of "having been there," namely the direct personal experience, does play a unique role. I was closely acquainted with some of the key personalities of Imre Nagy's circle, such as Miklós Gimes, executed in 1958, and Miklós Vásárhelyi, sentenced to five years' imprisonment, but also with some of the important political and economic spokespersons of the long-lasting Kádár regime. Thanks to the particularly close relationship prevailing between Hungary and Austria, I was able, during the seventies and eighties—albeit consistently monitored and spied on—to report on Hungary for the *Financial Times* as well as for Austrian, Swiss, and German papers and later on in my capacity as editor in chief and director of Austrian television (ORF). Thus I also had the opportunity by way of many private conversations, encounters, and experiences in Hungary personally to observe the phases of the much-discussed amnesia, the "collective repression," as the psychologist Ferenc Mérei, who was sentenced to ten years in prison in 1959, put it.

This special personal background made me decide to write in depth about those great topics—uprising and revolution, freedom fight and oppression, reprisal and submission—which have kept me under their spell for some fifty years. It is this framework into which the analysis of such complex personalities as of Imre Nagy and János Kádár fits, as well as the dialectic between heroism and treason symbolized by their contrasting roles. The attitude of public opinion then and now is yet another fascinating chapter in contemporary Hungarian history.

Even though there are still some gaps in our knowledge owing to the closed archives of the State Security Service and the Interior and Defense Ministries in Moscow and to some extent in Budapest, on the basis of the currently available sources, we can shed light on such previously fiercely disputed questions as the responsibility for the "cry for help" to the Soviet Union; the siege and capture of the Radio Building by the insurgents; the background of the first Soviet military intervention; the delay and the turnaround in the attitude of Imre Nagy; the "disappearance" of Kádár and his attitude before and after the second Soviet intervention; the zigzag course taken in the Kremlin; the controversial broadcasts by the U.S. radio station Radio Free Europe in Munich and the American aloofness during and after the revolution; the duplicity and betrayal by the Tito regime of the group around Nagy during the three-week asylum in the Yugoslav Embassy; and, finally, the role played by Kádár in the trial of Nagy and his associates.

Above and beyond documents and personal impressions, I was also able to draw for my research for this work on interviews carried out in Moscow with the former head of the KGB, Vladimir Kryuchkov; the long-serving Soviet expert on Hungary and until the end of 2005 Russian ambassador in Budapest, Valeri Musatov; the former U.S. secretary of state Henry Kissinger (with the assistance of the ORF office in Washington); as well as prominent Hungarian personages, such as Árpád Göncz (president, 1990–2000); member of Parliament Imre Mécs; the recently deceased poet Istvan Eörsi; the widow of General Pál Maléter, Judit Gyenes; the former chairperson of the Federation of Political Prisoners, Jenő Fónay; and Ödön Pongrátz, one of the legendary brothers (who is still fostering the tradition of the Corvinists in his museum).

The Hungarian Revolution was the greatest challenge to Soviet hegemony in post–World War II Eastern Europe and at the same time a widely visible symbol of the bankruptcy of Soviet-style socialism. It was an international event, which to this day has engendered a profoundly positive image of Hungary in the eyes of the world. It was a "victorious defeat,"[3] an authentic "anti-totalitarian"[4] revolution, and perhaps above all a "fantastic story."[5] It is a paradox, yet true: The ethical significance of this Revolution of Hopelessness has been, and is, better perceived and more appreciated abroad than in Hungary.

No one would have thought, on that radiantly beautiful, memorable fall day as Budapest shone in a resplendent light, that 23 October 1956 would go down in history and be documented as a major world event. Historians and journalists have been arguing for decades about that elemental episode, which on that day opened the way in Hungary for a revolutionary process of dramatic and bloody events, often without any apparent logic. In his *Reflections on History*, Jacob Burckhardt writes about historical crises: "Developments which otherwise take centuries seem to flit by like phantoms in months or weeks, and are fulfilled.... Only the study of the past can provide us with a standard by which to measure the rapidity and strength of the particular movement in which we live."[1]

On the face of it, the "unexpected revolution"[2] began on that Tuesday with two mighty student-organized protest marches. One of them proceeded from the building of the Faculty of Arts on the Pest side to the Petőfi Monument on the banks of the Danube, the other from the Technical University (TU) in Buda to the monument of the legendary Polish general Joseph Bem, who had led Hungarian forces to victory in several engagements with the Habsburgs and the czarist interventionist army in 1849. That morning the student leaders had already coordinated their deployment plans. The students of the TU, the Sports School, and eight hundred cadets from the Petőfi Political Officers' Training Academy marched at first in silence, linking arms. Those from the Faculties of Philosophy and Law chanted demands for freedom, marching to the Petőfi Monument carrying signs and banners proclaiming: "Poland is our example, let us follow the Hungarian path!" When the famous actor Imre Sinkovits began reciting Petőfi's stirring poem *Talpra magyar, hív a haza* (Rise Magyar, the Country Calls!), the refrain rang out from ten thousands throats from the neighboring narrow streets as well: "God of Hungarians, we swear unto Thee, we swear unto Thee that slaves we shall no longer be!"

The spontaneous, grassroots demonstration, originally called as a show of solidarity with the Polish reformers threatened by the Soviets, was something unheard of in the eyes of the Communist Party leadership, accustomed as they were to officially organized mass marches. For the past eight years or more, ever since the Communist takeover, there had been but a single spontaneous demonstration of displeasure by soccer fans embittered over the lost championship in Bern in 1954. And even that had been shamefacedly hushed up by the media. Other than that, mass rallies and marches in the capital had been organized solely by the powers that be. Thus it was a totally novel experience for the students, as it was for everyone else! The frequently screened TV pictures demonstrate how happy, excited, and elated the young people were in their role as successors of the 1848 revolutionary youth.

However, most people found out only through the contradictory radio announcements that something unusual was afoot. At 12:35 p.m. a Gypsy music program was interrupted on the radio, and a demonstration prohibition, decreed by the interior minister, was broadcast. The students themselves, however, paid little attention either to the prohibition or to its withdrawal, which was announced on the radio at 2:23 p.m. That news seemed to them like a first victory.

The spark that ignited the tinderbox of old grievances was the breakthrough of the reformers in Poland. The traditional friendship between the two countries—the joint kings of old, Hungary's more recent support when over 100,000 Polish refugees fleeing from Nazi occupation found asylum there in 1939–1940, their shared post–World War II fate, and the common threat of Soviet hegemony to their simultaneous reform movements—provoked an added dynamism of revolt against Hungary's own discredited regime. The ongoing tension received a further impetus when it became clear that despite all the Soviet threats, Władysław Gomułka, who had been imprisoned for many years, was going to make a triumphant comeback as head of the Polish United Workers' Party—which actually came about on 21 October 1956. The speech made by the victorious Gomułka to the Central Committee of his party was printed in full in all Hungarian papers on the day of the solidarity demonstration.[3]

All politically involved Hungarians were fully aware that their own future was also at stake. The dam had already been broken the night before during a stormy meeting of over five thousand students of the Budapest Technical University. The then student and today's liberal member of Parliament Imre Mécs, who was sentenced to death in 1958 for his part in the resistance movement, vividly remembers the passionate discussions, whose direction soon slipped out of the hands of the Communist youth functionaries.

> We discussed the sixteen points of our program in a passionate, and in the end euphoric, mood. First we wanted to resolve the establishment of an independent student association in line with that of our brothers-in-arms at the University of Szeged, and then to make the appointment of Imre Nagy as the head of a new government the main point of our program. Students of several other universities and from the Petőfi Military Academy were also present. And then, in the midst of the discussion, in stormed József Szilágyi, a previously convicted prewar Communist, who at age 39 attended a correspondence course at the TU. In an impressive speech he described the dramatic situation in Poland, and called on his enthusiastic audience to put political rather than educational matters in the forefront. Then we unanimously resolved to organize a demonstration as a show of solidarity with the Poles on Tuesday, the 23rd.[4]

The fact that several versions of the TU's legendary points, formulated on the model of the 1848 revolutionaries' twelve-point program, were circulating was due to the spontaneous character of this unique event. As the evening wore on, delegations from other universities and workers from a number of large firms also joined the proceedings. As it was, the program went far beyond all previously discussed reforms, and the demand for the withdrawal of Soviet troops moved to the top of the list. The other core points were calling a party congress and the election of a new Communist Party leadership; a new government under the leadership of Imre Nagy and the removal of all criminal Stalinist leaders; free elections, that is, a multiparty system, freedom of the media, and removal of the Stalin Monument; and the reintroduction of Hungarian national holidays and symbols of state.

Something incredible came to pass: Typewritten leaflets, mimeographed by the thousands during the night on the few copying machines available in the university offices, for the first time spelled out in black and white the call for the withdrawal of Soviet troops and for free elections. At 7:30 p.m. the suggestion was born amid an atmosphere of exuberant enthusiasm to have the demands read out over the radio during the eight-o'clock news. István Jankovics, a senior lecturer, promptly drove with three students to the radio station in his 1938-vintage Topolino. On the way it transpired that the demands had not even been written down yet. While still in the car, Jankovics and the students quickly summarized the TU meeting's demands in ten points. That is how the "Topolino-Points" (as the *Corriere della Sera* later called them) came into being. However, the officials at the radio station were willing to broadcast only five points, and definitely not the demands for the pullout of the Soviet troops and for free elections. The correspondents of the Communist youth association who were present also refused to disseminate the highly explosive document. That is why the indignant students resorted to calling a demonstration for the following day as a show of solidarity with the Poles.[5]

In the early hours of Tuesday mimeographed appeals or small posters with the TU students' demands appeared on walls, trees, and advertising pillars. Some contained 10 or 12, others 14 or 16 points. The fact that several versions were being circulated demonstrates the impulsive and spontaneous nature of both the TU meeting and the preparations made by the representatives of the various faculties for the great rally.

Everyone experienced this memorable, radiantly beautiful fall day in a different way. It happened to be my second day at my new job for the evening paper *Esti Hirlap*, in the same press building that also housed the editorial office of the party's principal organ, *Szabad Nép*. After fifteen months of military service, eight months' imprisonment, and a three-year professional ban, that is, altogether five long (wasted) years, I was at last permitted, since the previous day, to work as a completely rehabilitated journalist. When some of my colleagues decided to have a look around to see what was happening in the city, I too went along with them. For the time being the atmosphere was deceptively calm but somewhat tense. Still, here and there we already noticed young people wearing rosettes of red, white, and green in their buttonholes. Some were already putting up posters on advertising pillars. All of us, who were on the side of Imre Nagy and the reform movement that he represented, were hoping for a democratic restructuring of the Socialist model. We were deeply impressed by the changes in Poland, and above all by the experiments in Yugoslavia, the only Communist country in Eastern Europe that had seceded from the Soviet sphere of interest. "We," at least everyone that I knew, were reformers and not revolutionaries.

The marches began in the early afternoon. At first the students sang not only the Hungarian national anthem, but also the "Marseillaise," followed by various revolutionary and folk songs. Wherever the huge throng passed by, life came to a standstill. People waved from the windows, and the streets reverberated with slogans. The demonstrators carried Hungarian and in some cases Polish national flags. They marched through the inner city and the boulevard in Pest, across Margaret Bridge to the Buda side (Elizabeth Bridge, destroyed during World War II, had not yet been rebuilt at the time) to the Bem Monument. By then the crowd numbered in the tens of thousands.

In the meantime, however, the character of the demonstration had changed. Many sympathizers, mainly young workers and other passersby, joined the students. The slogans became increasingly radical and patriotic: "Russians go home!" "Go home and take your Stalin [meaning the behemoth statue] with you!" "Rákosi into the Danube, Imre Nagy into power!" "Don't stop halfway, sweep Stalinism away!" "If you're Hungarian, you're with us!" More and more flags appeared from which the red star had been ripped.

Since our paper had already been printed and released with its optimistic headlines about the Polish reformers' peaceful victory and the impending, or rather already launched, student demonstrations, I tried with some of my colleagues to catch up first by car and then on foot with the march, which had reached the Bem Monument by late afternoon.

Nobody was in a position to channel the spontaneous demonstration or to influence the dynamics of its progress. Nowhere was there even a loudspeaker in working order. The unprecedented, immense grassroots outpouring swamped both the representatives of the Petőfi Circle, the discussion forum of intraparty rebels (whose vehicle with its loudspeaker was lost somewhere in the milling crowd), and the official Communist youth functionaries and party activists who had been hastily mobilized. The speech of the president of the Writers' Union was drowned out by the noise, as was Mihály Vörösmarty's poem *The Call*, recited by a famous actor.

The Abandoned Masses is the title of a brilliant essay collection by the contemporary Hungarian historian László Varga. It is a most appropriate portrayal of what happened in Budapest that day, 23 October 1956, a natural political phenomenon without a focus, without a concept, and without any coordinated leadership. That the close to 900,000-strong Hungarian Workers' Party (MDP), the "vanguard of the working class," was but a colossus with feet of clay was proven within the next few hours. It was thus absolutely logical that the demonstrators and the immense human mass that had joined the students in Pest and Buda should surge from Bem Square over Margaret Bridge in the direction of Parliament House on the banks of the Danube. They wanted to hear the "great white hope" of the opposition, the sixty-year-old Imre Nagy, who had been toppled by the Stalinists in early 1955 and readmitted to the party only ten days earlier.

But how did I, for my part, live through the rest of that day? After the imposing rally at the Bem Monument, I went home. I did not know anything about the crowd assembled in front of the Parliament Building, nor of the demonstration that was under way in front of the radio station. First of all I had to attend to a personal matter. My friend Endre Gömöri, at the time special radio correspondent, had phoned me from Warsaw, asking that I look in on his wife and baby daughter. "For safety's sake," he said. Obviously he was better informed through the international news agencies and Polish correspondents in Budapest than I was. At any rate, I took the tram to his place and found both of them safe and sound.

By nightfall, around 6 p.m., some 200,000 people had gathered in front of the Parliament Building and in neighboring streets—students, workers, white-collar workers, pensioners—all of whom were calling for Imre Nagy. The path to an uprising could no longer be blocked by the time-tested methods of Communist "crisis management": intimidation and misinformation. By the early hours of the evening it became obvious that the regime, installed by the Soviet occupation force and controlled from Moscow, had lost its foothold.

For the leaders in party headquarters, right next to the Parliament Building, it was a ghastly situation. Although fearing the worst from the commotion, they were totally isolated from the masses, even from their own party members. Since the Kremlin-endorsed dismissal—imposed in the presence of Politburo member Anastas Mikoyan on 18 July—of Mátyás Rákosi, Stalin's hated "best disciple," the process of the party's disintegration had continued inexorably. In a conversation on 12 October with Soviet ambassador Yuri Andropov, Rákosi's successor Ernő Gerő, the almost-as-unpopular and inflexible Muscovite, described the situation as "exceptionally grave."[6] The "extremely nervous" and hesitant first secretary added that it was more than likely that it would deteriorate further. The former mayor of Budapest and economic boss Zoltán Vas, also a Muscovite, but henceforth a follower of Imre Nagy, bluntly warned the ambassador of an "impending national catastrophe," which "the Soviet comrades do not see, because they are listening to people who are supported neither by the party nor by the people."[7] Even the highly intelligent Andropov, who was to be elected secretary-general of the Communist Party of the Soviet Union (CPSU) in November 1982 after a long career as head of the KGB, had seen the answer in a "crackdown" on the Hungarian party leadership, "else we regard it as entirely possible that Imre Nagy could become the leader of the party and the country."[8]

However, the authorities, and especially Gerő himself, underestimated the danger. Despite the domestic warning signals, he wanted to savor the Moscow-initiated conditional "reconciliation" with President Tito, who until recently had counted as the revisionist archenemy. The party and government delegation, including almost half of the Politburo—First Secretary Gerő, his deputy János Kádár, Prime Minister András Hegedüs, and the Budapest party secretary István Kovács—happened to be on an eight-day state visit to Yugoslavia. While they exchanged amicable words with their hosts, chatted with them about the different paths to socialism, and even went hunting with them, the regime at home came progressively undone. In a joint interview the blissfully ignorant Kádár and Hegedüs declared to the Belgrade journal *Politika*: "Matters are proceeding in a healthy direction." After signing a completely trivial bilateral communiqué, the delegation arrived by train on the morning of 23 October at the Budapest East Station. All the remaining Politburo members, as well as two Central Committee secretaries, showed up at the station to warn the home-coming leaders of the situation's serious nature. The entire group drove immediately to party headquarters to start a virtually uninterrupted series of crisis meetings at ten o'clock.

This day was the actual turning point in the process of disintegration of a broken-down "apparatus," whose controllers were hesitant, ineffectual, and above all inflexible. In the light of an increasingly dramatic situation, not only did the headless "apparatus" have nothing with which to neutralize the situation, but it added fuel to the fire by a series of fatal miscalculations.

During the midday hours a steady stream of enraged delegations of writers and student leaders, party organizations, and journalists of the party organ Szabad Nép beat a path to the door. Shouting matches between the rebellious party journalists, who had enthusiastically embraced the student movement in their editorial entitled "New Spring Review of Troops" and the "hawks" in the Politburo, who demanded not only the prohibition of the demonstration but if necessary the order to shoot, clearly demonstrated the hitherto inconceivable loosening of the hallowed dogma of party discipline. The then thirty-five-year-old prime minister András Hegedüs, one of Rákosi's and Gerö's minions who had replaced the popular Imre Nagy in the spring of 1955, described in his memoirs thirty years later that at the time the Politburo was no longer the country's collective leadership, but a heap of bewildered people who were capable of making diametrically opposed decisions every half hour. Thus the demonstration was at first prohibited by the Politburo, to be followed by the lifting of the prohibition, only to be banned once more and yet again authorized, depending on whether the hard-liners or the followers of the more flexible line happened to have gained the upper hand.[9]

The fact that the ban on public meetings and demonstrations was lifted in the end was the result of the high-ranking army, police, and security officers' unanimous opinion that they had no "suitable means" available for dispersing the demonstrators. Colonel Sándor Kopácsi, the police chief of the capital, who sympathized with the intraparty opposition, had assured the students in the morning that the police would not proceed forcefully against the demonstration. During these hours news of the "apparatus's" and especially the highest leadership's weakness and panic spread like wildfire.

In this chaotic situation the party bigwigs chose the worst imaginable solution: Party Chief Gerő was to broadcast a speech that same evening at 8. While tens of thousands were gathered in front of the Parliament Building, and other groups of demonstrators proceeded to the radio station and the Stalin Monument at the edge of City Park, the first secretary retired to his office to work on his radio speech. What, for instance, did the official number two, Prime Minister Hegedüs, do at that point? According to his statement in an interview released much later, he was in his office working on files accumulated during his ten days' absence. He had not listened to the radio and was not aware of what was happening in town. However, some years later Hegedüs, who in the meantime had developed into an antiestablishment thinker, contritely admitted that he had completely forgotten that he was chairing a meeting of the Council of Ministers on 23 October! The minutes published after the change of regime in 1989 show that the prime minister reassured his colleagues regarding Gerő's forthcoming speech and acquainted them with the Politburo's decision to convene a meeting of the Central Committee for the following Wednesday, the thirty first. It would then present a clear program for the further building of the Socialist democracy as well as the uninterrupted perpetuation of the bonds of friendship with the Soviet Union. However, contrary to Hegedüs, several important ministers were worried about the critical situation and demanded an earlier date for the Central Committee meeting. This was an absolutely classic example of Freudian repression, of "amnesia as a survival remedy!"[10]

While the completed text of Gerő's speech was being presented for approval to another session of the Politburo meeting, things were happening at breakneck speed in the city. In the square in front of the Parliament Building the streetlights were turned off in the hope that the darkness would dampen the spirits of the people and that the immense crowd, impatiently waiting for Imre Nagy, would disperse. It was worse than a provocation—it was a crass tactical error. The infuriated people did not disperse; instead they ignited their newspapers. In the end the parliamentary guards gave in and turned the lights back on in the square. From 5 p.m. onward more and more demonstrators appeared in front of the radio station, and their demands to have the students' sixteen points put on the air during the newscast became increasingly vociferous. Having consulted party headquarters, the officials at the radio station refused to the last to broadcast the demands for the pullout of the Soviet troops and for free elections for a multiparty system. Later, thousands of extremely incensed people tried to force their way inside the building. Almost at the same time thousands of impatient demonstrators, beside themselves with anger for having waited for hours in vain before the Parliament for Imre Nagy, assembled at the edge of City Park to topple the eight-meter-tall and eighty hundredweight Stalin Monument off its pedestal. Quite a few trucks flying Hungarian national flags were by now speeding around in the city filled with young factory workers, some toward the radio station or the Stalin Monument, others, however, already on the lookout for armaments factories and ordnance depots.

The slogan "Now or never!" echoed everywhere. In this feverishly tense atmosphere Gerő's fifteen-minute speech, which had been announced over and over again, acted like a detonator that set off the accumulated explosives.[11] The address elicited general outrage. Basically it was a rambling and boring defense of the alleged achievements of the people's democracy and the eternal friendship with the Soviet Union based on a completely equal footing. This, however, was followed by offensive and provocative threats against those "who try to spread the poison of chauvinism among our youth, and who use the democratic freedom which our state has assured the working people for nationalistic demonstrations. However, not even this demonstration shakes the resolution of our party to proceed on the road to developing Socialist democracy." Admittedly there is no trace in the text of the assertion that was circulating then and has still some credence to this day that Gerő had called the young demonstrators a "rabble" or even a "Fascist rabble." In the dramatic situation, his arrogant speech with his hackneyed phrases and threats had a catastrophic effect, especially on the demonstrators who were besieging the radio station. It unscrupulously poured oil on the flames. The speech had been prerecorded at party headquarters, and many of the demonstrators, who had wanted to confront the hated party chief with their manifesto in front of the radio station, were utterly affronted. Although events in the capital were of considerable significance, one must not forget that the students had organized meetings in the more important regional towns as well. It is little known that the first casualties in the early evening hours were in Debrecen in eastern Hungary. There a total of thirty thousands students and workers had demonstrated during the day. When they threw stones at the building of the Interior Ministry's regional administration, three of the demonstrators were shot by the security forces.

The explosion of pent-up hatred evident that evening and in the ensuing days was directed last but not least against the intolerable and cynical insult against the people and the nation. The Leninist party dictatorship never consisted merely of the use of force. Alexander Solzhenitsyn expressed this aptly in his acceptance speech when presented with the Nobel Prize: "Force can only shroud itself by lies, and lies can only be upheld by force." In their unbridled rage the people first attacked the symbols of dictatorship and of foreign rule. That is why the furious demonstrators' prime target was the colossus on Parade Square, where the powers that be, agents of a foreign power, used to wave from the marble platform to the hundreds of thousands marching under duress on 4 April (the official day of liberation) and 7 November (the day of the Russian Revolution). At precisely 9:37 p.m., skilled laborers managed to topple the hated Stalin Monument off its base with the help of trucks and blowtorches. The waiting people then fell upon this symbol of the system with great gusto to smash it into smithereens with hammers and hatchets. Gaudy red stars were removed from more and more government and party buildings. During the late evening hours of that first day, the crowds also burned pictures of and books by and about Marx, Lenin, and Stalin.[12]

Even before Gerő's infamous radio address, even before shots were fired on the demonstrators in front of the Radio Building, and even before the appearance of the first Soviet tanks, it was a popular uprising by young students and workers that was under way. The Kádár regime's numerous propaganda efforts between 1957 and 1988 were far from the truth precisely as far as the basic questions were concerned. Instead of an alleged insurrection instigated and organized by "Western intelligence agencies"—with the occupation of the essential centers of power and communication, the telephone and telegraph exchanges, police stations, ministries, and party buildings—what the world witnessed was an elemental outbreak of the Hungarian people's rage against dictatorship and foreign rule.

We know today from original sources that, due to the pressure of the rebellious streets and the subsequent armed resistance, the situation in the centers of power in Moscow and Budapest changed not merely from day to day but often from hour to hour. Members of the CPSU's Politburo, in particular the main protagonist, Nikita Khrushchev, wavered in their opinions, which changed even within the very same session (just as their henchmen's did in Budapest) as they strove not to jeopardize their own positions. In this political milieu events took an uncontainable course, especially in the capital, but later, of course, in the entire country.

The so-called Leninists experienced thus a revolutionary situation that, according to their taskmaster, displayed three criteria: first, the inability of the upper strata to maintain their authority, which also involved a rift within the ruling class itself; second, a revolutionary situation characterized by the escalation of the social disparities between the ruling class and the downtrodden masses of the populace beyond the usual extent; third, a significant increase in the populace's political activities, a rapid increase in the fighting spirit of the revolutionary classes, and the inclination toward revolutionary actions.[13] In other words, it is not sufficient for the outbreak of a revolution that the "lower strata" no longer have the will to carry on in the old manner; it is also essential that the "upper strata" should no longer have the ability to do so.

The only Hungarian politician who might have had a ghost of a chance to avert the outbreak of the armed uprising with the right words at the right time was Imre Nagy. Where was he? What did he and his like-minded friends and advisers do on that memorable day?

Ever since June 1953, most Hungarians considered Imre Nagy the symbol of new departures. He was installed as prime minister on the orders of the Soviet leadership in the face of the powerful party boss Mátyás Rákosi's temporizing opposition, who as Stalin's man of confidence had until then possessed total power as party and government head. Yet this staid man, who gave the impression of a jovial professor and—in contrast to Rákosi—spoke to the people in a lucid, pleasant-sounding Hungarian, managed to implement a new moderate course, at least for seventeen months until November 1954. In the last four and a half months of his incumbency, he was already powerless due to the change of policy in Moscow and the intrigues of the Rákosi-dominated party apparatus. Although a lifelong Communist who had spent twenty years in Soviet exile, after his downgrading he was not willing to perform the ritual of self-criticism. He lost his professorship and his party membership, but remained not only popular but also a latent danger to the Stalinist clique around Rákosi. After the Twentieth Congress of the CPSU, the de-Stalinization initiated by Khrushchev, and Rákosi's downfall, the cautious and mistrustful Nagy, albeit merely a "private citizen" without any function, once again became a key figure of the true events. All that happened between 23 October and 4 November 1956, nay, during the last twenty months of his life, can be viewed only in conjunction with his personality, his career, and the subsequent inner transformation of the reform Communist and patriot.

János M. Rainer, the author of the first comprehensive biography of Imre Nagy,[14] estimates that in the summer of 1956 the circle of Nagy's partisans and active sympathizers respectively comprised two hundred to three hundred people. Many of them had read his secretly circulated writings on political theory, which were in part aimed at the party leadership. These intellectuals, predominantly writers and journalists, prewar Communists, and reformist party functionaries, as well as youth representatives, formed not an organization but "a loose informal political pressure group." The reformers, most of all Nagy, who adhered strictly to party discipline, wanted a correction, not the abolition of the political system. No one from his closer circle or the thousands of committed supporters of reform knew or suspected that in the Hungary of October 1956 a correction was already tantamount to the abolition of the system.[15]

According to the opinions of his closest companions, Nagy himself was the most wary and skeptical of all of them. Above all, he was a procrastinator and not a determined politician. Suffering from a heart condition and prone to occasional bouts of depression, he frequently underwent inexplicable periods of passivity in crucial situations. That was also the case during the days after his readmission to the party. On 22 October, for instance, he went to Badacsony on Lake Balaton to attend a grape harvest, although his closest adviser, the journalist Miklós Vásárhelyi, advised him against it in view of the tense situation. However, the exciting news of events in the Polish party caused him to drive back to Budapest sooner than he had planned. That same evening two of his influential friends, both of them Central Committee members, called on him, followed by several phone messages urging him to talk to the students at the Technical University. Shortly before midnight, during a lightning visit to his apartment, a professor known to him from the Moscow emigration and two assistants from the TU implored him to appeal to the students for moderation, particularly as their demand for the pullout of Soviet troops was by now at the top of their list. Nagy refused all requests, with—among others—the rationalization that not knowing the party's up-to-date standpoint, he would not be able to answer the students' questions. He was not in favor of the demonstration.

On the morning of 23 October, Nagy at first looked after his sick grandchildren while his son-in-law and closest friend, Ferenc Jánosi, went to get some medicine for them. Jánosi, was a former Protestant pastor who, after an anti-Fascist indoctrination as a POW in the Soviet Union, made a political career as a high-ranking officer, deputy minister for culture and general secretary of the Popular Front. After his father-in-law's downfall, he too was shunted to an insignificant post, and his wife was fired from her job as a translator at the Russian-language monthly *Vengriya*. During the ensuing turbulent days, Jánosi was constantly at the side of Nagy. Thus, too, late that morning Nagy and his closest circle of friends met to confer in the apartment of the publicist Géza Losonczy. Losonczy, at the time editor of *Magyar Nemzet*, the Popular Front's daily, was a prewar Communist and for a time political state secretary at the Ministry of Popular Education. He was arrested on trumped-up charges in 1951 and sentenced to ten years' imprisonment, but was released in view of serious illness in the summer of 1954. Oppositionist writers and students considered him Imre Nagy's respected spokesperson. The following also attended the conference: the journalist Sándor Haraszti, Losonczy's father-in-law, a prewar Communist who had been sentenced to death by the Stalinists and subsequently released after four years on death row; his former codefendant Szilárd Ujhelyi, who had shared his fate; as well as two prominent reform Communists journalists: Miklós Vásárhelyi, chief press officer of Nagy during his prime ministership, and Miklós Gimes, the most radical mastermind of their intimate circle.

In view of the dramatic turnabout in Poland and the return of Gomułka to the head of the party, they all shared the opinion that Imre Nagy too could soon become prime minister again. That is why they discussed contingency plans for the essential comprehensive changes in the composition of the Politburo and the Central Committee. The most important conclusion they reached was that, whatever the outcome, Nagy should accept an invitation to return to the top only after all his personnel and political conditions were met, first and foremost Gerő's resignation as first secretary. They had no political or economic program. That summer Nagy had told a visitor: "In the fall power will drop into my lap." His critical biographer aptly remarked: "If he really believed that, then it is almost incomprehensible why he did not consider how he would use that power."[16] As a close friend later noted, regrettable though it was, they never actually discussed fundamental issues.

However, the opinions about the student demonstrations were varied. Nagy rejected the demonstration, as well as his friends' suggestion that he appear at the mass rally now held with official approval at the Petőfi Monument. On leaving he told them that the demonstration could have serious consequences. He then proceeded to go home with his son-in-law. While the latter went to town, Nagy ate his midday meal, after which he took a nap. Considering the turmoil taking place in the city, his biographer was hard put to explain this flabbergasting fact. He tried to do so by mustering a number of reasons, such as habit, the "restful life-style" prescribed by his cardiologist, the previous day's agitating discussions lasting well into the night, and possibly even a certain subconscious desire to escape from responsibility.

Later in the afternoon eyewitnesses of the demonstration turned up at the house. Writers such as old friends Tibor Déry, Péter Veres, and others gave their accounts over the telephone about the huge crowds waiting in front of the Parliament. Not only his followers but also a smaller group of students pressed him to proceed to the Parliament. The president of the radio station, Valeria Benke, phoned twice between 6 p.m. and 7 p.m. asking for his advice on whether to permit the students' sixteen points to be put on air. Nagy said that she should ask the Politburo, and later added that if it would placate the angry crowd in front of the Radio Building, then the manifesto should be broadcast. Meanwhile three desperate deputy prime ministers, two of them Politburo members, called Nagy from the Parliament; thus far he had been totally opposed to making a public appearance. When he was told at 8 p.m. that they were transmitting the Politburo's request that he should come immediately to the Parliament Building to speak to the waiting crowd, Nagy finally gave in and composed a short address. Before leaving, he read out the text to the few friends and followers who were present in the apartment. All of them regarded the draft poor, insubstantial, and inappropriate. Yet Nagy did not alter anything in the text. The leader of the Council of Ministers' secretariat picked him up in the prime minister's large, black, armor-plated limousine. His son-in-law, Jánosi, and a journalist friend, György Fazekas, accompanied him in the car.[17]

It was already 9 p.m. when Nagy appeared in a window of the Parliament to address the vast and impatient crowd, estimated at anywhere between 150,000 and 200,000. The overcautious, ponderous old Communist, ever toeing the party line, who was unable to improvise, who precisely during these days feared a huge provocation from the besieged Gerő, was suddenly confronted with "an unknown force," namely the people themselves.[18] It was, like so many things during those days, an incredible scene. Fazekas was worried that the corpulent Nagy would fall from the window, and so he was held fast by Fazekas and Deputy Prime Minister Erdei. After some hecklers shouted "We want to see Imre Nagy," Erdei lit his face with a flashlight. That moment Nagy realized that the speech he had prepared was inappropriate and that he had to improvise. When he began his speech with the normal address "Comrades!" it was answered by whistles and chantings of "We are not comrades!" and his appeasing, pedestrian comments, by overt disappointment. He omitted entire passages from his brief prepared speech, yet what he said still contained only cut-and-dried repetitive promises of democratization by way of the Central Committee's forthcoming decisions, time and time again interspersed with calls for sobriety and discipline. His only successful gesture was that in conclusion he asked his audience to join him in singing the national anthem.[19]

By this time news had already been received about a gun battle at the radio station; the ambulance service reported the first fatal casualties at 9:37 p.m., and at the same time the Stalin Monument was torn off its pedestal. A quarter of an hour later, enraged demonstrators attacked the building of the central party organ, *Szabad Nép* (Free People). They brought along the corpse of a demonstrator, wrapped in a national flag, who had probably just been killed near the Radio Building. A bookshop was set on fire. What happened next was not a planned attack; demonstrators did not even attempt to occupy the composing room. As the compositors had earlier refused to print Gerő's provocative speech, and also due to the general chaos, the paper had not appeared at all. Incidentally, the editorial office, or more precisely, the overwhelming majority of the editors, had in the past months formed the vanguard of the intra-party opposition.

While throughout the night the battle was raging around the Radio Building, the outside world was informed of the gripping atmosphere of these hours only through the dreary reports about the date of the next Central Committee meeting. After Gerő's speech, the next Central Committee meeting was supposed to be convened on 31 October. At 8:23 p.m. the music program was interrupted, and a convocation was announced for the days ahead. Until 4:30 a.m. there was only a two-line report about the uprising in the capital: "Budapest youth marched this afternoon to the Parliament: in the evening Comrade Imre Nagy spoke to the young people. Comrade Nagy is at this moment negotiating with representatives of the young people and with several members of Parliament." Then at 10:22 p.m. an "extraordinary communiqué" was read out: "The Politburo has called an immediate meeting of the Central Committee in order to discuss the existing situation and decide upon the measures to be taken." At midnight too there was only foreign news.[20]

In the meantime Imre Nagy went with his son-in-law from the Parliament Building to party headquarters, which was within easy walking distance. Entering Gerő's office before 10 p.m., he found that virtually the entire Politburo was holding a meeting there. A few minutes after the arrival of Nagy, Gerő was on the telephone with Khrushchev in Moscow and was apprised of the decision of the Soviet party's Presidium—which was just sitting—about the deployment of Soviet forces stationed in Hungary to put down the insurrection. In fact by that time the first Russian tanks were already en route to Budapest from their nearby bases. That night the appearance of Soviet tanks and the deployment of Soviet troops transformed the already inflamed uprising against the Stalinist dictatorship into a national war of independence.

By now formerly top-secret documents are available from Soviet and Hungarian archives that present an authentic picture and clarify the vexed questions of who asked for armed Soviet intervention and when and how decisions were reached in Moscow. Before we turn to this gripping set of questions and the course of the armed uprising, let us briefly deal with the attitude of Imre Nagy, which to many of his followers was incomprehensible and deeply disappointing. The disastrous decision about the military intervention was reached after a lengthy process through no fault of his own; he did not belong to the top leadership. The assertions of the Kádár regime's propagandists that Nagy had taken part in the decision making were just as unfounded as the myth circulating during the revolution that he had been forced into various actions with a machine gun pointed at his back by Gerő's men or by the Russians. Still, the prelude to his failure during the first five days, namely his silence regarding the Soviet intervention, remains a mystery. "Why did he not speak up against it?" asks his biographer János M. Rainer.

Even at his trial during the last days of his life Nagy tried to explain—perhaps for posterity—his incomprehensible reaction: "I was present for a while in Gerő's room during the telephone conversation regarding the call for help from Soviet troops. . . . I did not agree with the involvement of the Soviet troops. Yet there was no indication that I would be given any position. Gerő did not discuss the matters with anyone. I left like someone who was not affected by this question."

He sat in the corridor in an armchair—weary and almost detached from the hustle and bustle around him. Why did he not take a firm stand against the intervention? Rainer, his perplexed biographer, mentions five possible, partly interrelated, reasons. First, it might have been due to a sort of breakdown, a feeling of impotence after the confrontation with the crowd. Second, he had seen only the relatively friendly crowd and might not have grasped the significance of the armed conflict near the Radio Building and the appearance of Soviet tanks in the streets of Budapest. Third, he fell under the influence of the panic-stricken mood reigning in party headquarters. Fourth, his well-known tendency for passivity in tense situations caused him to take a position of "aloofness." Fifth and last, he might have acted consciously, even demonstratively, in an atmosphere in which he felt the mistrust, animosity, and even hatred that were directed against him. Whether all this was part of a deliberate political consideration cannot, of course, be established in hindsight.[21]

What did the other protagonists of the intraparty opposition movement, who were later tried and sentenced to long prison terms as the "general staff of the counterrevolution," do during these hours? As a result of President Benke's desperate telephone calls, Géza Losonczy and Miklós Vásárhelyi went to the Radio Building, where there was no shooting yet, but a large crowd was more and more stridently demanding that the sixteen points be broadcast. Losonczy was asked whether he could not pacify the protesters from the balcony, but he did not think that was feasible. They returned to the editorial office of *Magyar Nemzet*, and later met for dinner with prominent oppositionists in the recently reopened Café Hungaria (previously, and also today called the New York). Also present in addition to a few composers and journalists was the eminent historian Domokos Kosáry. Forty years later he stated in an interview: "That dinner is so memorable for me, because it was a historical alibi for the fact that the Imre Nagy group was not prepared for any organized action, and how surprised they were about all that was happening."

The scene was Kafkaesque. Some fifteen to twenty minutes' walking distance away, the armed battle for the Radio Building was already in full swing. Also, a belligerent crowd was gathering in front of the even nearer editorial office of the party's central press organ. Quite a few trucks filled with young people were dashing around the inner-city boulevard. Groups of agitated people were standing around everywhere discussing the day's happenings. But in Café Hungaria black-clad waiters were briskly serving food and drinks to guests sitting at tables set with white damask tablecloths. One of the reform-Communist journalists found the guests in a depressed mood; the followers of Nagy sensed that "the whole story would have dire consequences ... that the Communist reformers let the events pass them by." Then suddenly "an unknown man appeared, a deranged expression on his face, and asked us: you are journalists and you don't know that there is blood flowing in Hungarian streets?" The eyewitness of this scene, the political scientist Peter Kende, does not say how the members of the dinner party reacted, apart from bewilderment. Losonczy tried, unsuccessfully, to reach Nagy at party headquarters. At 11 p.m. everyone went home without realizing that by that time an armed revolution was in progress. Almost all of the leading reformers went to bed, even those with whom Nagy had conferred in the morning and afternoon, and all of them slept through the first dramatic night of the Hungarian Revolution.[22]

I met a few colleagues for dinner at the restaurant Kulacs (The Flask), just a few steps away from Café Hungaria. We argued heatedly about the political situation, and then I went home. I had just as little idea as the followers of Nagy nearby that at that very moment the revolt in front of the Radio Building and the Stalin Monument, and soon after also in front of the newspaper building, was already in full swing. At any rate, I went calmly to bed and missed, as did the leaders of the opposition, the beginning of the end of the regime.

Why was it that in October 1956 an uprising broke out in Hungary, and only there, against the Communist regime that within a few days engulfed the entire country, and which, unlike events in Berlin in June 1953 and in contrast to the peacefully proceeding and limited contemporaneous reforms in Poland, immediately developed into a revolution and a national war of independence? Undoubtedly the circumstances of the takeovers in all of the Eastern Bloc countries by the local and the Kremlin-appointed Communist leaderships, supported by the presence of Soviet troops, were more or less similar. Equally so were the great stepping-stones on the path to party dictatorship and to Soviet colonization: liquidation of the other parties, nationalization of the economy, promotion of the heavy and armaments industry at the expense of consumers, expulsion of ethnic Germans, arrests of real or alleged opponents (many of whom were executed), as well as economic exploitation and complete control and domination by the Soviet occupying forces.

If one were to pose the question, therefore, why there was a popular uprising in Hungary, and only there, while the situation in the other Eastern Bloc countries (apart from Poland) remained calm, then one has to look for the causes, against the backdrop of general developments from the de-Stalinization initiated by the Twentieth Congress of the CPSU to the reconciliation with the heretic in Belgrade, in the interplay between the general instability after the death of Stalin and *three* special factors in Hungarian history.

First: The tragedy of Trianon and the nationalities question. Since the partition of Poland, no other country was treated by the Great Powers so mercilessly and so unjustly as historical Hungary. In the Trianon Palace, in the park of Versailles, the Allies issued the death certificate of the thousand-year realm of Saint Stephen, and two representatives of Hungary had to sign the dictated settlement on 4 June 1920. After the breakup of the Danube monarchy, the now-independent "Kingdom of Hungary" was left with only 93,000 of the 282,000 square kilometers of the old prewar kingdom (together with Croatia, it had even covered 325,000 square kilometers). According to the 1920 census, the population now numbered 7.6 million inhabitants compared with the earlier figure of 18.3 (with Croatia, 20.9). The victors distributed the booty among the three neighboring states: Romania, Czechoslovakia, and Yugoslavia. Austria, herself dismembered, was promised today's Burgenland with 4,000 square kilometers and almost 300,000 inhabitants. More than 3 million Magyars lived henceforth under foreign rule, although half of them inhabited homogeneous communities on the borders of the three successor states. The only question on the minds of the overwhelming majority of Hungarians on both sides of the new borders during the subsequent years and decades was whether the revision of the treaty could be attained by peaceful means or only by a victorious war.[1]

The fateful military alliance with the Third Reich and Hungary's entry into the war were connected with the recognition by the government and Regent Miklós Horthy that the only possible way to achieve a restoration of the pre-1920 borders was with Hitler's help. The reannexation of 40 percent of the territories lost at Trianon (by way of the Vienna Awards granted by the Allied Powers) between 1938 and 1941 and the increase of the population by 5 million (albeit only 2 million of whom were Magyars) to almost 15 million were greeted with indescribable jubilation in Hungary. Under strong pressure from the German high command, Hungary soon had to give up hope of being able to conduct a war, so to speak, from the sidelines and was forced to send a whole army to the Russian front by mid-1942. After the military catastrophe at Voronezh in January 1943 (40,000 solders were killed, 35,000 were wounded, many disappeared, and 60,000 were taken prisoner), a moderate and pro-Western government tried to make contact with the Allies. Yet the majority of the Hungarian leading classes and above all the officers still gambled on a German victory. There was no military or civilian resistance when on 19 March 1944 Hungary was occupied by the German Wehrmacht.

Up to the bitter end in the spring of 1945, tens of thousands of senselessly sacrificed soldiers died, as did Resistance fighters and deserters, Catholic anti-Nazis and Social Democrats, members of the nobility and Communists. Tens of thousands of Hungarians, soldiers and civilians, perished in Soviet captivity. Twenty thousand people died in bomb attacks, which began in April 1944. There is no doubt, however, about the validity of the comment made by Elie Wiesel, the Nobel Peace Prize winner from the formerly Hungarian, now Romanian, township of Sighet in Transylvania: "Not all victims were Jews—but all Jews were victims." Under the supervision of Adolf Eichmann and his thugs, Hungarian gendarmes and detectives proudly reported to their German masters that between 15 May and 7 July 1944 they had expedited 147 trains to Auschwitz containing 437,402 Jews (and those Christians who, according to the race laws, counted as such). The Hungarian historian György Ránki pointed out that nowhere else in Eastern Europe had the Jews identified so strongly with a nation as they did in Hungary, and therefore the tragedy of the Jews was also a tragedy for Hungary.[2]

In contrast to Romania, Hungary did not manage to change sides. After a failed, comic opera–style defection attempt, the aged regent was even forced to legalize the reign of terror by the German-appointed Arrow Cross. An astounding fact was the flight, before the total collapse, of the entire military and civilian administration to the West. A total of approximately 1 million civilians fled, the majority of them members of the middle class. Many returned later, but about 100,000 remained permanently in the West. The war damage amounted to five times the national income for 1938 and about 40 percent of the nation's total wealth. It has been estimated that some 900,000 people, or 6.2 percent of Greater Hungary's 14.7 million inhabitants (1941), among them more than 564,000 Jews, died. The estimate of Jewish victims amounts to a total in the Greater Hungary of 1941 to 297,000 from Trianon Hungary (over 100,000 in Budapest). About 600,000 Hungarians fell into Soviet captivity, including 100,000 to 120,000 civilians, and 300,000 soldiers capitulated to British and U.S. troops. The fact that approximately 100,000 soldiers took the oath to Szálasi should not be disregarded in this context. Twelve Hungarian divisions fought to the bitter end on the side of the Germans.[3]

Because of the sad legacy of Trianon and because of the nationalities question, Hungary was in a far more difficult situation than the other Eastern Bloc countries; in spite of its Russophobe resentment, Poland was still regarded as a victorious power, as was Czechoslovakia; Bulgaria was traditionally Russophile, and while Romania, which had opportunely changed sides, could thank Stalin for the return of northern

Transylvania, Hungary lost all the territories regained during the war from Czechoslovakia, Romania, and Yugoslavia. On top of that, the country had to bear the odium of having been "Hitler's last satellite."[4]

The conduct of the "liberators," by the way—as in all Soviet-occupied territories, even in Yugoslavia—was not exactly conducive to arousing amicable feelings toward the Soviet Union. Rape, plunder, and brutal interference in domestic policy led to the naked hatred of the Soviets becoming even stronger than before the defeat. In addition, there was the uncertain fate of more than half a million prisoners of war, the abduction of tens of thousands of civilians impressed to forced labor, and the Soviet-supported Communist offensive to undermine and finally destroy the young Hungarian democracy. Let us not forget the enormous burden of war reparations, the takeover of some four hundred firms and landed estates that were deemed to have been German owned, and the consequences of the establishment of so-called joint companies (until 1954) in air transport and shipping, as well as in the oil and aluminum industries. In the decade after 1954, Hungary had to pay to the Soviet Union, in one form or another, not the $200 million as laid down in the treaty, but at least $1 billion, a sum that in today's prices equals more than $10 billion![5] All that contributed to the fact that in contrast to the convinced democrats and the few resistance fighters, as well as the Jews and deserters in fear of their lives, the large and later overwhelming majority of Hungarians regarded the collapse not as a liberation but as the beginning of a new bondage. Incidentally, ever since their defeat in the initially victorious War of Independence of 1848–49 against Austria, the Russian armies have been considered in Hungarian historical consciousness as traditional enemies.

The explosive impact of Sovietization, carried out without any regard for national sensibilities, should be seen against this backdrop. Thus, for example, between 1945 and 1959 more than half of all books translated into Hungarian were of Russian, or rather Soviet, origin.[6] Symbols such as national holidays and the flag, the country's coat of arms and uniforms, made the supremacy of Soviet communism and the suppression of hallowed national traditions manifestly clear to all. The disruption of the symbols was epitomized by the change of Saint Stephen's name day to the Day of the Constitution, the Holiday of the New Bread. Between 1949 and 1956, the editorials about 20 August always emphasized these metaphors and consistently failed to mention the country's founder. New laws decreed the introduction of the new holidays; thus 4 April became a national holiday, declared as the Day of Hungary's Liberation, and 7 November a state holiday. On the other hand, 15 March, which had been traditionally celebrated as the day of the Hungarian revolution of 1848, lost its status as a national holiday. At the same time the red star, the symbol of Soviet communism, became omnipresent on flags and uniforms, on roofs and walls, as shop-window decorations and stand-alone monuments.[7] When on 23 October the star was cut out from the flags and removed from roofs and public buildings, it was a matter of a symbolic act against the oppression and against the disrespect for national traditions. That is why the students (and not only they) demanded the reintroduction of the Kossuth coat of arms, the emblem of the revolution of 1848. The demand for the abolition of obligatory Russian-language tuition also fitted into this framework. They were protesting not against the Russian language as such but against the compulsion that Russian be taught in the schools as the only foreign language. The gleeful burning on 23 October of Russian classics, together with books by Lenin and Stalin, was the people's reaction to the nation's profound and long-lasting humiliation by the unbearable cult of Stalin and the Soviet Union.

Second: The particular character of Hungarian Stalinism. All historians of Hungary's postwar history agree that as first man of the Communist Party, Mátyás Rákosi was the driving force behind the political dictatorship and the bloodiest purges in the Eastern Bloc before and after Stalin's death.

Born in 1892, the first child of the grocer József Rosenfeld (Magyarized to Rákosi in 1904), he grew up in humble circumstances in southern Hungary. After passing his high school exams with distinction, Rákosi studied at the Oriental Academy in Budapest and spent a year in 1912 in Hamburg on a scholarship. In 1913 he went to London, where he worked as a commercial correspondent, returning to Hungary at the outbreak of war. After three years as a prisoner of war in Russia, he became the youngest commissar in the top leadership of the short-lived Hungarian Soviet Republic. During the 1920s Rákosi crisscrossed Europe with six forged passports on the behest of the Comintern in order to advise the various Communist parties. He spoke not only German and English, but also Russian and Italian and allegedly French and Turkish as well.

Arrested in Budapest in 1925, Rákosi was sentenced at a second trial to life imprisonment in the face of protests from all over the world. After 15 years and 39 days, he was exchanged for the Hungarian flags seized by czarist Russian troops in 1849 and allowed to leave for the Soviet Union, where the legendary comrade was received and honored as a hero.[8]

During his period in office from 1945 to 18 July 1956, "Stalin's best Hungarian pupil" proved to be one of the most evil politicians in Hungarian history. Without doubt he was the ugliest. He had no passions. Love and hate, human emotions, did not play a part in his life, according to his few biographers. Rákosi, whose wife, eleven years younger than him and a prosecutor, came from Yakutsk in northern Siberia, lived only for power. The tactic and strategy of handling power in Hungary depended, as everywhere else in the Eastern Bloc, on the incumbent's personal relationship with Stalin. Between 1945 and 1947 a reliable party comrade installed a direct radio communication with Stalin's office in the attic of Rákosi's villa. Rákosi always spent his holidays on the Black Sea, and no one, not even his inner circle, knew whether and when he met Stalin. The secretary-general discussed every politically significant decision with the "Soviet friends" on the spot (the "advisers" were constantly present in all important institutions) or sought consent by telephone or by a letter sent by special courier to Stalin's personal secretary Alexander Poskrebyshev. The decisive maneuver that dealt the deathblow to the young democracy was the arrest in February 1947 by Soviet security police of the secretary-general of the Smallholders' Party, the deputy Béla Kovács. Although his immunity had been explicitly confirmed by the parliamentary majority, he was abducted to the USSR on the pretext of "setting up armed terrorist groups and spying for a Western intelligence service against the Soviet Union," and he was released (critically ill) only in 1956.[9]

In a famous speech delivered after the "Year of Change," Rákosi invented the term that was to become a well-known adage, "salami tactics," to describe the slice-by-slice attrition of political rivals. Having eliminated the bourgeois politicians and condemned them as conspirators, Rákosi turned to the church. Within a few weeks 225 Catholic priests were arrested. Show trials were organized against Cardinal József Mindszenty (February 1949) and two years later against Archbishop Grösz of Sopron, resulting in sentences of life imprisonment and fifteen years respectively. Numerous other repressive measures became important building blocks of the totalitarian system's rapidly intensifying reign of terror. In the end they all had their turn: the real opponents of the Communists, right and left Social Democrats in the coalition, and many others who did not fit in with Rákosi's concepts.[10]

The Rajk trial in the fall of 1949 was the prelude for the great bloody purges within the ruling party. The open declaration of war on the heretic "Titoists," the excommunication of the Yugoslav Communists from the Cominform, the so-called Communist information bureau founded in the fall of 1947, were the starting signals in the entire Soviet Bloc for the witch hunt for "Titoists" and agents of imperialism disguised as Communists: "enemies with party cards." We know today that the whole of the indictment against the former Hungarian minister of the interior and later foreign minister Rajk, as well as the death sentences, were authorized by Stalin. Soviet "specialists" under the direct supervision of General Fyodor Byelkin, chief of the Soviet State Security Service in Eastern Europe, then named MGB, with headquarters in Baden near Vienna, were in charge of implementing the most sophisticated and brutal physical and psychological torture methods.

Yet Rákosi and his right-hand man, defense minister and party representative for the Secret Police Mihály Farkas, together with Chief of Police Gábor Péter, were much faster and more avid tools of repression than the other leaders in the satellite countries. One evening, when Rajk remained unyielding even after the most brutal treatment with rubber truncheons, his successor as minister of the interior, János Kádár, and Farkas tried to persuade him to make a comprehensive confession of having been an agent of the "Titoists," the "Fascist Horthy regime," and the "American Secret Service." Rákosi had the whole bizarre conversation taped. The transcript was later used in the acute phase of the intraparty power struggle as a weighty means of pressure against Kádár. Secret documents published since show the hatred and eagerness with which old accounts were being settled during the course of the following years between the torturers, fighting for their own survival. In the event, it was Rákosi himself who, despite his cunning, put his foot in it in his notorious speech after the trial to a howling crowd of activists in the Budapest Sports Stadium: "I had many sleepless nights before the plan of the implementation was finalized." All later attempts to shift responsibility onto others were thus condemned to failure from the outset.

As far as László Rajk was concerned, he was by no means a convinced "National Communist" or revisionist. As minister of the interior, he had played an evil role as a merciless destroyer of the bourgeois parties and the architect of the disgusting show trial against Cardinal Mindszenty. In the trial of Rajk, Stalin's classic method, the so-called amalgam—the linking of quite differing elements—was employed. Hungarian Communists who had been living abroad for long periods, especially veterans of the Spanish Civil War, right and left ("Trotskyites"), Social Democrats, "Fascists" (for example, prewar officers who had joined the resistance), and "Zionists" (that is, Jewish Communists) were potential targets of the vigilance campaigns. Of the 93 persons convicted directly in connection with the Rajk trial, 15 were executed, 11 did not survive their jail sentences, and 39 were interned.[11]

But that was only the beginning of the ever-faster-gyrating fiendish merry-go-round of purges. In the spring of 1950 the head of state Árpád Szakasits—former secretary-general of the Social Democrats, now united with the Communists—was invited with his wife to dine with the party chief. Afterward Rákosi had his guest—at least nominally first man of the state—arrested on the evidence of crudely forged records proving his activities as an alleged informer for the Horthy police. He was arrested there and then by General Gábor Péter, who had been waiting next door, and locked in the cellar of the Rákosi villa for a few days, before being taken to prison. The verdict was a life sentence, and according to usual practice, his entire family were exposed to continual harassment. Szakasits was set free six years later, in 1956—incidentally, at the same time as his predecessor as head of state, the erstwhile head of the Smallholders' Party, Zoltán Tildy. Tildy had been forced by the Communists to resign in July 1948, and his son-in-law, a diplomat, was executed for alleged corruption. Tildy and his wife were placed under house arrest for eight years. In a total of twenty political trials, 180 leading Social Democrat politicians were sentenced to long prison terms and 276 former Social Democrats (including me, twenty-three years old at the time) were interned. Right- and left-wing Social Democrats, who fought bitter battles among themselves, suffered the same fate almost without exception.[12]

It is still impossible to determine whether Rákosi's evil, cruel, and even diabolical conduct should be attributed to his long imprisonment, whether it can be explained by his inferiority complex and the consequent dislike of his luckier or better-looking comrades, or whether it was his slavish devotion, mixed with fear, of Stalin that decisively molded his attitude. Stalin did not like Rákosi for several reasons: first, he was a Jew; second, he talked far too much after his arrest in 1925; third, in Stalin's eyes he could have been an American spy. This absurd reservation was due to a famous photo showing President Harry Truman chatting away genially with the similarly laughing Rákosi in Washington. The solution is simple: Rákosi was the only one in the Hungarian government delegation who spoke fluent English.[13]

Rákosi's fear of Stalin was all too understandable, especially in view of the purges that had taken place within the Soviet apparatus. Yet Stalin appreciated slaves who were not only boundlessly devoted to him but were also clever and efficient. The so-called homegrown Communists, who had sacrificed their freedom in their own country for the cause of the party, were, of course, a tiny group. Kádár himself admitted many years later that during World War II there were only a few hundred (never more than a thousand) members, and after a wave of arrests in 1942–1943, only seventy to eighty party members remained. Incidentally, it was a political and statistical miracle that by the end of 1945 the number of Communist Party members had grown to half a million.[14]

In the spring of 1951, Deputy Secretary General János Kádár, who eighteen months earlier, as minister of the interior, had tried on Rákosi's orders to persuade his friend Rajk to make a "confession," was arrested and later tried for having been a "police informer," just as Rákosi's chef de cabinet Ferenc Donáth and Foreign Minister Gyula Kállai were, as well as the top journalists Sándor Haraszti and Géza Losonczy. Prior to that, Kádár's successor in the Interior Ministry, Politburo member Sándor Zöld, also a home-based Communist, after sharp criticism of his work in the Politburo, drove home without a word and with his service revolver shot his mother, his wife, his two small children, and then himself. Zöld knew what awaited him in the torture chambers of the Secret Police. Thereupon the party chief had the other home-based Communists arrested, led by the best-known top functionary Kádár, "in order to impede their flight," as reported in a radio message to Stalin.

The search for enemies of the party and agents of foreign powers launched the chain of mysterious causes and incalculable effects, both nationally and internationally in 1949, which even decades later can be only partly clarified. The basic method was always the same: false accusations; intimidated witnesses; torture by hunger, light, water, sleep deprivation, and if necessary electric shock; and mistreatment by the traditional rubber truncheons. The role change of perpetrator-victim was often writ in blood. Rákosi, Nagy, Kádár, and Rajk played different roles at various times in a bizarre drama, which could perhaps best be likened to an odd mixture of theater of the absurd (Ionesco or Beckett), passages from Shakespeare, and cheap thrillers. In the first part it was Rákosi who acted as producer and leading man, and in the final act it was János Kádár. Over time all four of the key figures were transformed from hunter to hunted, from jailer to victim; Kádár was the only one to perform a triple role change, culminating in insanity.[15]

However, it would be erroneous to believe that only the hated Communists were settling accounts with one another. Although between 1948 and 1951 a total of 400,000 members, preponderantly former Social Democrats, but also "minor Arrow Crossites" and "passive petit bourgeois," were purged from the party, when all is said and done, the dynamics and dimensions of the purges and reprisals affected almost a third of all Hungarian families in one form or another.

Between 1949 and 1952, real wages and salaries shrank by 20 percent instead of the promised 50 percent increase, the result of an unbridled and mindless industrialization that aimed at transforming Hungary, within only four years or even less, into a "land of iron and steel." Small enterprises were virtually liquidated, and as a countermove temporary rationing was introduced during the early 1950s. Barely a few years after the land reform, the regime set in motion collectivization and cooped up the peasants into cooperatives. Officers and some 75,000 public servants from the Horthy era, as well as almost 300,000 merchants, lost their livelihoods.[16] Most of them were forced to find employment in factories or on building sites as unskilled laborers. It sufficed for a workman or clerk merely to utter "suspicious" views about the pressure of ever higher working norms or the unequal relationship with the Soviets, a simple rumor about antiparty or "nationalistic" resentments, a denunciation, or the whim of a functionary, for him to be put "on record."

It is almost unimaginable from today's perspective that during the 1950s the omnipresent ÁVH (the security service) held records on over a million persons ("antidemocratic elements"), or 10 percent of the total population. Between 1951 and May 1953 alone, around 850,000 police convictions were recorded; between 1950 and the first quarter of 1953, 650,000 people were arraigned, of whom 387,000 were sentenced (most of them fined). In addition (as of 1 June 1953) there were 40,734 inmates in prisons and internment camps (of these, some 28,000 were in forced labor), and during the spring of 1951, 15,000 "bourgeois" and "unreliable elements" were moved from the capital to remote settlements, where they frequently were made to perform agricultural work under the harshest conditions. The black humor of the time divided the population into two groups: those who were already under arrest and those who would be next in line behind bars.[17]

What made life even more intolerable was the cult of Stalin and the Soviet Union, as well as of his Hungarian governor. Thus in March 1952 the entire nation had to celebrate the sixtieth birthday of "Stalin's best pupil." The highlight of the festivities was a gala performance in the Opera House. There he sat under his own giant likeness, flanked on the right by a similarly huge image of Stalin and on the left by that of Lenin, "modestly" accepting the untold number of homages paid to him and the singing of a song specially composed for the occasion. The poets' and writers' eulogies (later these were extremely embarrassing for their authors) written for the birthday were subsequently immortalized in a special publication. In addition, he gave his name to 3 streets, 1 university, 2 factories, 31 cooperatives, 1 honorary decoration, 1 kindergarten, and 1 cultural center.[18] In the so-called parliamentary elections of 17 May 1953, the unity ticket celebrated an overwhelming victory: 98 percent of the electorate voted, and 98.2 of the votes cast were in favor of the MDP. Rákosi, since the summer of 1952 both party chief and prime minister, appeared to have arrived at the height of his power.

During the next few months that late fall and winter the persecution mania of Stalin reached a new zenith. The notorious Slánsky trial in Prague (eleven of the fourteen accused were Jews) and the Moscow conspiracy of the "murderers in white coats" (nine top doctors, six of them Jews, were said to have tried to murder the Soviet leader on the orders of the American-Zionist espionage services) sounded the alarm bells for the Jewish members of the almighty Hungarian "troika"—Rákosi, Gerő, and Farkas. In this tense situation a personal messenger of Stalin's turned up in Rákosi's office at the beginning of January 1953; General Fyodor Byelkin from the Soviet Ministry of the Interior had been unmasked as a British spy. During an interrogation, he had revealed that Gábor Péter, head of the ÁVH, with whom he had staged the whole Rajk trial, was also a British spy and traitor. In the tried and tested manner, Rákosi invited the police chief and his wife—who ran his whole secretariat—to dinner for the following evening. On their arrival, the commander of the host's bodyguard handcuffed both of them. They were then locked for safety's sake in the icy cellar of the villa, while eighteen high-ranking security officers were dismissed from the ÁVH. Only after the purge was over were Péter and his wife transferred to the special jail.[19]

Péter (alias Benö Eisenberger) had been an NKVD agent prior to the war and was regarded as the Soviets' and Stalin's most important instrument.[20] That a man such as the Communist secretary general Slánsky, who had spent the war years in the Soviet Union, or a top agent like Péter, with whom at a reception in the Kremlin in 1948 Stalin clinked glasses as a special sign of esteem, could now be sacrificed to the anti-Semitic persecution mania of the aging dictator showed that now *all* party chiefs of Jewish origin, including Rákosi, were under threat. Elias Canetti's reflections on power are also applicable to Rákosi (and naturally his master in the Kremlin): "For the true goal of the real power-wielder is as grotesque as it is incredible: He wants to be the *only* one. He wants to survive them all so that no one will survive him."[21] To prove his reliability and indispensability to Moscow, Rákosi did not let any time elapse and ordered the arrest of prominent Jewish Communists, top doctors, and members of the Jewish community.[22]

Then on 5 March 1953, in the midst of the totally unpredictable last great wave of purges from Moscow to Prague and Budapest, Stalin died. The collective leadership immediately adopted a new course. Thus the anti-Semitic witch hunt ordered by Stalin was discontinued, the doctors were rehabilitated, and top functionaries of the Interior Ministry were arrested or dismissed; first and foremost, though, an amnesty was declared. The leadership examined the situation in the satellite countries and came to the conclusion that Hungary was potentially the most dangerous trouble spot. We know today that Stalin's heirs fought each other like scorpions in a glass bottle, but they were united on one question: that a purge had to be instituted in Hungary and that Mátyás Rákosi, the man responsible for the highly disquieting situation, should immediately resign. A large Hungarian party and government delegation—its members "chosen" by the "hosts" (!)—was summoned to Moscow. As a prelude to the three-day meeting, Secret Police Chief Beria and Prime Minister Malenkov, but also Party Secretary Khrushchev and Foreign Minister Molotov, attacked their hitherto top man in Budapest with unprecedented sharpness and biting irony. The collective leadership decided unanimously that the fifty-seven-year-old Imre Nagy, deputy prime minister and Politburo member, should become Rákosi's successor.

They broached all critical subjects, from the catastrophic consequences of the forced promotion of heavy industry (naturally on Soviet orders) and the exploitation of agriculture, to the despotism and mass arrests by the ÁVH and Rákosi's autocracy; and over and over again there were references to the fact that more "cadres of Hungarian nationality," meaning fewer Jews, should be in the top leadership.[23] The respective Russian records, as well as the Hungarian Central Committee's astoundingly unreserved resolution, were first published in full thirty-three and almost forty years later respectively. It was thus a command of the extremely worried Soviet leadership that made it possible to embark on the road of reform under Imre Nagy, then to a retrogression under Rákosi, and eventually to a three-year power struggle within the party.

Third: Three years of intraparty ferment against the background of the political and moral crisis had prepared the ground for the uprising.

- Hungary was the only satellite where—four months after Stalin's death, on the initiative of the Soviet leadership—Stalinism was openly condemned and a new reform course proclaimed.
- Only there did two factions, two diametrically opposed concepts in the party, battle on from June 1953 to October 1956 over the direction to be taken in the future.

The popular uprising could occur only when the party, in the first place its leading cadre, became so divided on the question of de-Stalinization that it could no longer assert its power. In no other Eastern Bloc country was there a political development that seemed to indicate a prospect of the system's reformability and humanization (fifteen years *before* the Prague Spring!). One could, of course, demur that it was incomprehensible for the head of a government in a sovereign state to be unseated and another appointed by a decree from the Kremlin. However, this was the political reality—and in this particular case it was a boon. Without Soviet authority, Nagy could not have been appointed, nor could the "baldhead" (as Rákosi was called in opposition circles) have been banished.

From Moscow's viewpoint Imre Nagy seemed to be an ideal solution. He was one of the very few non-Jewish Muscovites. After his long stay in Soviet emigration, the agrarian expert first held the position of minister for agriculture in 1945 and carried out the popular land reform. Some 660,000 farmhands and indigent peasants received an average of three hectares of farmland. Afterward he was minister of the interior for a short while, and subsequently president of Parliament. Although this fact was not widely known to the public, Nagy had temporarily to step back into the second ranks in 1949 because of his opposition to the overhasty collectivization of agriculture. Yet barely two years later, he was reinstated in the top leadership both in the government and in the Politburo. Nagy evidently had backing from Moscow. Now the Soviet leadership explicitly confirmed the correctness of his former opposition over the agrarian question and condemned his expulsion from the Politburo.

The congenial, reassuring, and informal Nagy was willing to adopt a "new line," based on the trust of his Soviet patrons. At a closed meeting of the party's Central Committee on 27 June 1953, the new prime minister–designate made an epoch-making speech, which, however, became public knowledge just as little as the significant party resolution that followed. Nagy held Rákosi primarily responsible for the deplorable state of affairs, and not only him, but also the other three members of the notorious "quadriga" (Mihály Farkas for breaking the law, Ernő Gerő for his adventurous economic policy, and József Révai for the poor state of education and culture). He spoke of "intolerable conditions characteristic of a police state." Rákosi performed political and personal self-criticism before a totally flabbergasted Central Committee. The resolution (published only thirty-three years later in a small-circulation party journal) was a sweeping indictment of the Rákosi clique: "It was improper that Comrade Rákosi gave the ÁVH direct instructions how to conduct their investigations, whom to arrest, and it was improper for him to order physical mistreatment of the arrested, which is against the law."[24]

Despite Nagy's good intentions and changes of personnel, power over the political machinery still remained in the hands of Rákosi and his colleagues. The fact that another infamous Muscovite, Ernő Gerő, was appointed minister of the interior was not really conducive to encouraging faith in "Socialist legality." And yet, the speech given in Parliament by Nagy as the new head of government on 4 July 1953 came as a bombshell. The promise to end police despotism, disband the internment camps, decree an amnesty, and revoke deportations immediately enabled tens of thousands, including me, to return to normal life. Work norms were also lowered, and the forced collectivization of agriculture was stopped. The standard of living rose, and important reforms considerably improved the atmosphere. The people breathed a sigh of relief and could draw hope once again.

However, appearances were deceptive. After the riots in East Berlin and the GDR on 17 June and the fall of the chief of security, Lavrenti P. Beria, the divided and hesitant collective leadership in Moscow went into reverse gear. Molotov had phoned Nagy personally to prohibit publication of the "exaggerated" resolution. A wall of silence surrounded the dramatic events in Moscow and Budapest. Rákosi's promptly launched unscrupulous counterattack during a mammoth meeting of party activists in Budapest on 11 July restricted the room for maneuver of Nagy and his comrades in arms from the outset.

The main issues in the struggle between Nagy and Rákosi were the scrutiny of the secret trials and purges, the priorities of the economic policy (light versus heavy industry), and the revival of the People's Front, not as a "transmission belt" for the party's instructions, but as a means of winning the confidence of the people. In every Communist-controlled country—thus in Hungary too—the party took absolute priority over the government. The apparatus, just as the security service, obeyed Rákosi and his clique until the bitter end. The great majority of the leading cadre in Hungary rejected the limited reforms. Nagy enjoyed the sympathy of public opinion, but he had no real access to the power structure. His "power base" consisted of the surviving victims of the trials—writers, journalists, and artists, especially the former standard-bearers of the Stalin era—who felt betrayed by the Rákosi clique and, plunged into conflicts of conscience, gathered around the once-again-isolated Nagy. They dictated the tempo of the reform movement.

In no other Eastern Bloc country was there such a fierce political battle. It was not about ideological hair splitting but about the freedom, the well-being, and the personal future of hundreds of thousands of oppressed, disenfranchised, and in part, even up to the autumn of 1956, imprisoned people. Nagy had few allies in the party leadership and committed crude errors in his personnel policy, in part on the advice of the sympathizing Soviet ambassador J. D. Kiselev. Thus he enabled the (temporary) readmittance to the Politburo of one of the Rákosi era's most evil figures, Mihály Farkas. Next to Rákosi, the former minister of defense was the most culpable for the bloody purges in the party and the army leadership. When it later came to "working through the past," Farkas—as one would expect—promptly stabbed the prime minister in the back.

The ups and downs of the power struggles in Moscow and of the relationship with Yugoslavia were closely connected with the murderous jockeying for positions, feelings of bitter resentment, and paranoia of the leading cadres in Hungary. Rákosi, the crafty and unscrupulous tactician, cleverly exploited the power struggles in the Kremlin and Nagy's heart condition, above all the fall of Beria in June 1953 and of Malenkov in the spring of 1955, both of whom had strongly supported Nagy against Rákosi. At that time Rákosi, and more than thirty years later János Kádár and his followers, deliberately spread the rumor that Nagy was "Beria's man," and later even that he was an NKVD agent. There is no doubt about the fact that the émigré Nagy, who was under arrest in 1938, admittedly only for four days, had regularly transmitted information about his comrades, also in the form of lists of names, at least between 1936 and 1940, perhaps even earlier. The former Secret Service chief General Vladimir Kryuchkov personally confirmed to me in September 2005 in Moscow the same statement he had conveyed in the summer of 1989 to the leadership of the Hungarian Communist Party, which was fighting for its survival: Nagy's information had led to the execution of twelve and the arrest or punishment of two hundred. The Russian expert on Hungary and until recently ambassador to Budapest, Valeri Musatov, does not doubt Nagy's contacts with the NKVD, even though, in contrast to Kryuchkov, he acknowledges Nagy's political role in 1956 and his human tragedy. His biographer János M. Rainer also concludes that Nagy, like so many others, rendered "modest service" to the "organs," but definitely not as an "agent." Be that as it may, neither genuine nor forged documents can alter or detract from the status of Imre Nagy in Hungarian history between 1953 and 1958.[25]

Between the fall of 1954 and the spring of 1955, the pendulum of Nagy's "new course" swung into the opposite direction. There was a change of tune in Moscow too. In a rebellion at the editorial office of the central party organ, *Szabad Nép*—unprecedented under the prevailing conditions—80 percent of the party members attending a three-day conference argued for Nagy's course and against the top leaders, Ernő Gerő and Mihály Farkas, in charge of economic policy and the media respectively. The effect of the one-hundred-page shorthand minutes was enormous, because it was sent not only to the Politburo but also to the party organizations of other newspapers and important institutions. This and reports of a speech by Nagy during the founding congress of the Patriotic People's Front, regarded by the Kremlin as nationalistic, as well as intrigues by Rákosi, who was on a two-month "convalescent holiday" in the Soviet Union, had provoked a turnabout. However, Nagy refused a comprehensive self-criticism and the renunciation of the June resolutions.[26]

At the beginning of March 1955, the same Central Committee that in October had unanimously supported his course branded him just as unanimously as a "right deviationist." In April he was expelled from all party bodies and toppled from the prime ministership. The Stalinists' campaign of vengeance reached its peak in early December with Nagy's exclusion from the party. Dozens of journalists and writers, public servants, and party functionaries who appeared suspicious to Rákosi were fired or banished to the provincial backwaters. The Soviet ambassador Yuri Andropov and his third secretary, Vladimir Kryuchkov, both of whom spoke and understood Hungarian, shared this assessment of the situation.

After Khrushchev's historic secret speech during the Twentieth Congress of the CPSU about the crimes of the Stalin era, which was known in abridged form and read at closed party sessions in full, the dams that the apparatus had raised against the reformers quickly burst. Rákosi was jeered simultaneously from various sides: by the outraged Communist intellectuals, the unmoved victims, but also by Marshal Tito, who was only willing to normalize his relationship with Hungary after Rákosi's resignation, the public rehabilitation of Rajk, and the retraction of anti-Yugoslav accusations. The pressure from below became increasingly intense. The Soviets adopted a zigzag course that had grave consequences. Between May and December 1956 the Presidium of the CPSU's Politburo dealt with the topic of Hungary twenty times, and at least seven times it reached important decisions. However, these were almost always chronically late, according to the Russian historian and copublisher of the most important document collection Vjacheslav Sereda.

The Russian-Hungarian document collections published after the change of regime contain insightful reports by Andropov and his predecessors about the broad spectrum of denunciations and warnings from their Hungarian interlocutors. The Soviets realized too late that Rákosi had become an encumbrance. Anastas Mikoyan, Khrushchev's closest confidant in the party's Presidium, was sent to Budapest, where for weeks he carefully prepared and took part in the decisive meeting of the Central Committee on 18 July 1956. The news of Rákosi being stripped of power was a political bombshell. The public was delirious that straight after the Central Committee session the dictator disappeared in the direction of Moscow "for health reasons"—as the official wording had it. The rehabilitated Kádár's reentry into the Politburo was also welcome. However, the reformers and the young people were disappointed that Rákosi's place was taken by another Muscovite, Ernő Gerő, and that Hegedüs remained the prime minister. The call for Imre Nagy became increasingly strident. Knowledgeable observers claim in hindsight that the last chance to avert an explosion of bottled-up hatred of the unbearable and cynical offenses against the people and their nation would have been a genuine changing of the guard—Nagy's reappointment as head of government and the election of Kádár as first secretary of the party. Without that, however, the situation became, if anything, more acute.

As so many times before in Hungarian history, a funeral set the masses in motion. In this case it was the public burial of the rehabilitated victims of the first great show trial, Rajk and his companions; what is more, it took place on a profoundly symbolic date: 6 October, the day of mourning for the thirteen martyred generals of the revolutionary army executed by the Habsburgs in 1849. A crowd estimated at 200,000 persevered in the cold, drenching rain and howling winds to pay their last respects to the dead. As well as the mourning, there was also a palpable sense of threatening determination. Although a week later Nagy was readmitted to the party, that was all. Nothing further happened on the political scene.

Alexis de Tocqueville pointed out in his book *The Old Regime and the French Revolution*, published in 1856: "Experience teaches us that, generally speaking, the most perilous moment for a bad government is one when it tries to mend its ways. Patiently endured so long as it seemed beyond redress, a grievance comes to appear intolerable once the possibility of removing it crosses men's minds." Politicians are often overthrown when—for whatever reason—they are deemed unworthy of fulfilling their tasks. These lines precisely describe the situation in Hungary one hundred years later, on the eve of the armed uprising.

The chaos that—as we have seen—ruled in the evening hours on the streets of the capital, the looming collapse of the old order, and the fear that the unrest in Budapest would draw the other Eastern Bloc countries into the vortex of violent changes called the Soviet power early and inexorably into action. The old Communist order with its absolute, ideologically structured claim to power still ruled in Moscow. As the Hungarian regime introduced by the Soviets between 1953 and 1956 had eroded itself and feared the worst from the revolt, it had to be propped up as fast as possible by way of military and political clout. That is why the first and in retrospect the most disastrous political decisions were made during the evening session of the Soviet party presidium. The written and telephone reports by Soviet ambassador Yuri Andropov and by the commanders of the Soviet troops stationed in Hungary since 1955 as a result of the Austrian State Treaty, had, of course, prepared the ground for those disastrous decisions that ultimately sparked off the War of Independence.

To clarify the historical connections, it has to be pointed out that the prehistory of Soviet military intervention had already begun in July 1956. At the time, Lieutenant General Lashchenko, head of the Special Corps (consisting of four divisions, one sapper regiment, as well as appropriate units of the antiaircraft and rear echelons) stationed in Hungary since September 1955, received the order to work out a plan "for the maintenance and reestablishment of the Socialist public order in Hungary" in case of political unrest. Among others, the guarding and defense of the most important sites in Budapest as well as the rules of conduct in case of emergency were determined under the code name Volna (Operation Whirlwind). After the plan was approved, it was given the name Kompass. Hungarian military experts have pointed out that the planned deployment of Soviet troops to maintain order with the option of employing force of arms constituted an a priori flagrant breach of the Warsaw

Pact and all the other agreements concluded up to 1956. At any rate, the plans for intervention three months in advance demonstrated the Soviet leadership's determination to resort to unlimited force in order to bring a political crisis in Hungary under control.[1]

In October 1956, after initial threatening gestures, the collective leadership of the CPSU had argued for a political solution in Poland. The Presidium of the party held a meeting in the Kremlin on 23 October at 11 p.m. Moscow time (at 9 p.m. Budapest time). According to the brief notes of the keeper of the minutes, Marshal Zhukov, minister of defense and candidate of the caucus (that is, with no voting right), reported: "Hundred-thousand-strong demonstration in Budapest. The Radio Building on fire. The headquarters of the county party committee building and the county chief department of the Ministry of the Interior occupied in Debrecen." Khrushchev and all the other members and candidates agreed that troops should move into Budapest. However, there was one weighty dissenting vote. Anastas Mikoyan, the collective leadership's authentic expert on Hungary, expressed his doubts regarding a military intervention: "Without Nagy, the movement cannot be controlled. In that way it will be cheaper for us, too. What can we lose? Let the Hungarians themselves do the job of restoring order. If our troops intervene, we will only make things worse for ourselves. Let us make an attempt at political action first, and have the troops move in only afterward."[2]

His warnings were not heeded. All the speakers, Marshal Zhukov included, emphasized that Hungary could not be compared with Poland. Khrushchev concluded the half-hour debate with the unanimously accepted suggestion that two members of the Presidium, the moderate Mikoyan and the tough Central Committee secretary Suslov, should immediately be sent to Budapest, together with Deputy Chief of Staff Malinin and the head of the KGB, General Serov. Khrushchev agreed to Mikoyan's suggestion inasmuch as—although he endorsed Nagy's involvement "in political action"—he added verbatim: "But for the time being, let us not make him prime minister." These words throw a significant light on how the so-called cadre matters were treated in an officially independent "fraternal country." Incidentally, there was no reference in the minutes of the meeting to any request from "the Hungarian comrades" or from Gerő as a basis for the military intervention. It has been proved meanwhile that the military preparations were in full swing prior to the Presidium's formal political decision with or without Khrushchev's knowledge.

Hence, two mechanized divisions of the Special Corps were brought to full combat alert as early as 8 p.m. Hungarian time—and not at 9 p.m. as stated in the official report by Zhukov and Chief of the General Staff Sokolovski to the Central Committee. Sokolovski personally gave the marching orders by telephone for the troops to start off for Budapest, to establish control over the most important sites in the capital, and to restore order. Some of the forces were to seal off the Hungarian-Austrian border. Two divisions stationed in the Transcarpathian District and one division from Romania were redeployed earlier—at 7:45 p.m.—toward the Hungarian border. Their task was to occupy eastern and southern Hungary, first and foremost the important towns of Debrecen and Szolnok, Szeged and Kecskemét. The core members of the Special Corps's staff arrived at midnight in the Ministry of Defense; the first tanks reached the capital's outskirts by 2 a.m.

What happened during those hours in Budapest and what were the factors that influenced the Hungarian party leadership's decision-making process? We have already discussed, at the end of the first chapter, the reasons why Imre Nagy could not (or would not) yet act as an active politician on this fateful night. Who, how, and why set the course for the Soviet party Presidium's decision briefly outlined above? During a hastily convened meeting on 24 October in Moscow, Khrushchev informed his East German, Czechoslovak, and Bulgarian counterparts about recent developments in an arguably afterward "fudged" report. According to this version, Khrushchev invited Gerő by phone on the twenty-third to put him in the picture at the conference about the developments and the settlement of the crisis in Poland. However, Gerő informed him that the situation in Budapest was bad and for that reason he would rather not come to Moscow. As soon as the conversation was over, Marshal Zhukov informed Khrushchev that Gerő had asked the military attaché at the Soviet Embassy in Budapest to dispatch Soviet troops to suppress the hostile demonstration that was reaching an ever greater and unprecedented scale. This version is rightly regarded by Hungarian historians as unlikely or downright "absurd." After all, Gerő had already conferred with Ambassador Andropov—and it is entirely possible that the military attaché was also involved in the crisis talks.

Gerő had spoken at least twice with Khrushchev that day, and it is certain that Andropov himself was the driving force in favor of the intervention. It is also probable, although not confirmed by documents, that Gerő had initially still hoped that the situation could be brought under control without outside help. Later Gerő informed the members of the Hungarian Politburo that such a step would create a difficult situation for the Soviet Union internationally. According to Khrushchev's later version, in the course of the evening Gerő had requested an intervention after all. In keeping with Marshal Zhukov's alarming report about the situation in Budapest, the Kremlin decided on sending in troops without waiting for a formal or written resolution by the Hungarian government. Incidentally, before the decision, Khrushchev had also consulted with Rákosi, who had been living in exile in Moscow since July. He, as would be expected, had recommended an immediate intervention.[3]

At any rate, it is known that all the Hungarian Central Committee (CC), which met only at 11 p.m. at the party's headquarters to try to "manage the crisis," could do was to acknowledge the fait accompli of the intervention. Only later, in view of international protests, was it necessary to have a formal request by the Hungarian government to legitimize the Soviet deployment. As Imre Nagy had several times categorically refused the retrospective signature, András Hegedüs, who had meanwhile been relieved of his post, had to sign the request to the Soviet government on the twenty-sixth, predated to the twenty-fourth. Although Khrushchev had instructed Gerő not to convene a CC meeting and not to make any decisions about personnel changes before the arrival of the Soviet emissaries Mikoyan and Suslov, the hard-pressed party chief was bound to ignore this advice, simply because he needed the Central Committee's retrospective agreement to legitimize such a weighty decision as the call for help to Moscow. Gerő and the other top functionaries had to endorse this momentous step for several reasons. Due to the fact that, because of the panicky situation at party headquarters, no records were kept of the Politburo and Central Committee meetings, or at least none could be unearthed, the historian Zoltán Ripp had to rely on the written and oral recollections of the participants for his excellent analysis of the "last days of the party leadership." From these and other interviews with important functionaries and military individuals, as well as from the Moscow documents that have since been published, one can identify the motives of the enormous miscalculations of this night.[4] The first disastrous experiences with the deployment of the Hungarian Army at the besieged Radio Building confirmed the doubts about their capability and reliability. In addition, the total ineptness of Minister of Defense István Bata—who had been promoted from tram conductor to his position after a Soviet crash course—as well as of his chief of the general staff and the top political commissars, was obvious already during the first hours of the unrest. The Hungarian Army consisted of 120,000 soldiers, and at that time 4,500 soldiers with 65 tanks and some 2,500 armed workers' militiamen responsible to the Interior Ministry were available in the capital.[5]

The military and political leadership, evidently in consultation with the Soviet Special Corps' commander, presumed that the tactical threat of force used during the June 1953 unrests in East Berlin and the GDR, where the march-past of Soviet tanks relatively quickly put paid to the workers' rising without any significant bloodshed, would be successful also in Hungary. However, three years later this did not work. The Soviet troops were not prepared for the strong resistance in Budapest. The 6,000 soldiers with 290 tanks, 120 armored personnel carriers, and 156 cannons did not suffice to defend the most important sites and to break up the groups of armed freedom fighters. Apart from the heroic courage and the determination of the insurgents, it was the botched military tactic that was responsible for the fact that, in spite of their numerical superiority, the Soviet troops could not put down the rebellion speedily. The deployment of Soviet tanks did not "sober up" the rebels as the politicians had hoped; on the contrary, it only increased their fury. Analysts today believe that the long delay in giving the firing order to the defenders of the Radio Building was due to the consideration that the quick arrival of Soviet tanks would promptly lift the siege.[6]

By playing up the counterrevolutionary danger, Gerő and his people also wanted to fend off the intraparty push for fundamental reforms. The party chief tried to stall until the arrival of Mikoyan and Suslov by presenting a broad overview of the situation and the measures taken so far. Yet the thick fog thwarted his efforts: the plane carrying the two Soviet emissaries could not land at the military airport in Budapest. They arrived, together with Malinin and Serov, only on the morning of the twenty-fourth in the Ministry of Defense and then in party headquarters, that is, *after* the decisions. The fog also delayed the eagerly awaited Soviet tanks.[7]

Never since the Communist takeover has the state party's Central Committee convened at such short notice and under such chaotic circumstances. Instead of the 105 full members and candidates of the CC, only 54 took part; most of the functionaries from the provinces were absent. After Gerő's above-mentioned speech, in which he branded the events as counterrevolutionary, the impression prevailed that the Soviet tanks would quash the rebellion within a few hours. Other Politburo members suggested the arming of workers and functionaries, the announcement of martial law, the occupation of all printing presses, the closing of the universities, and the affirmation of the ban on a multiparty system. While the majority of those present accepted the view that they were dealing with a counterrevolution, Márton Horváth, editor in chief of the party organ *Szabad Nép* and a long-standing top functionary, rejected Gerő's line as catastrophe politics and demanded his immediate resignation and János Kádár's election as first secretary. They eventually elected a nominating commission, and the personnel decisions were reached during the early hours of the morning. In the meantime they also established a so-called military council to maintain contact with the Soviet and Hungarian armed forces and to ensure the political coordination. In fact, the creation of these bodies merely hastened the disintegration of the leadership structure. A further problem was the question of the government. The measures adopted that day were announced in the name of a nonfunctioning government. There was no debate in the nominating commission about Imre Nagy's assuming the post of prime minister. Hegedüs, the incumbent head of the government, did not raise any objections; he was willing to cooperate with Nagy as the latter's deputy. However, initially Nagy stipulated several conditions; his first condition was that his reform notions be accepted as the government's program and the cabinet be composed accordingly. The majority's only concern, of course, was that Nagy's person should pacify the fury of the people. The formation of the new government was adjourned, the more so as the decision about the person of the new head of government had to be cleared with Moscow. Yet Nagy was not willing to assume the post of prime minister without the clarification of his conditions regarding personnel. First and foremost he wanted to accomplish the replacement of Gerő as first secretary by Kádár. In the event, the question was decided by Kádár himself, who declared that he was now prepared to act as number two in the party next to Gerő. Given the dramatic deterioration of the situation in the capital, Nagy finally acquiesced, although only two of his closest associates—Géza Losonczy as candidate of the Politburo and Ferenc Donáth as secretary of the CC—were admitted to top positions in the party.[8]

By daybreak the various commissions had finished their work. The CC approved Nagy's appointment to the prime ministership and confirmed (with four dissenting votes) Gerő in his position as first secretary. The road to a peaceful "Polish" solution was thereby barred. Everything that happened that night and during the ensuing days in the fantasy world of the party committees in their headquarters at Academy Street, soon-to-be hermetically sealed by Soviet tanks, became increasingly irrelevant to the "Pest Street," the young people who had taken up arms. While during that night the party functionaries were haggling over the redistribution of power, the armed conflict around the Radio Building was reaching its climax. Reports about the first fatal casualties were the actual signal for the outbreak of the general uprising. "Who fired the first shot" in the evening of 23 October at the Radio Building has been a contentious question for decades. For the Kádár regime's propagandists it was the "counterrevolutionaries." According to the research conducted by the historian László Varga, it was a case of a misunderstanding, an accident. Soldiers of a signal corps wanted to disperse the crowd at 9 p.m. when two tanks, sent there as reinforcements, inadvertently broke through their cordon. The crowd poured back, whereupon the commander pulled back his unit to the nearby garden of the National Museum and let the soldiers—in order to restore morale—shoot two salvos into the air. The defenders inside the building "returned" the fire. The first bodies fell in the street. According to research by the author László Gyurkó, who relies on data from the hospitals, the first reports of State Security militiamen wounded by stones thrown at them arrived around 8:45 p.m.; besiegers hit by bullets were reported at 9:36, and the first fatal casualty among them at 9:37 p.m. The first death of a defender was reported at 10:14 p.m.

The course of the battle for the Radio Building clearly showed both the incompetence of the highest military command and the strong sympathy of the army for the overwhelmingly young insurgents. According to their own accounts, the minister of defense and his chief of staff ordered three thousand soldiers during the course of the evening and the night to the Radio Building. The building was positioned in a narrow street and was at the same time part of a large complex with its back entrance next to the museum garden. The various army units were not even informed about that back entrance. They tried for the most part to fight their way through the angry and increasingly large mass of people in the narrow lanes to reach the Radio Building. They were either disarmed while on their way or regarded by the defenders as turncoats and now and then shot at. Some units did not even attempt to obey the orders, and a considerable number of officers and soldiers joined the insurgents. During the night rebel groups stormed several armaments factories, police stations, and army barracks, returning to the Radio Building already armed. Meanwhile the first Soviet tanks arrived in Budapest. A member of the CC's military council, the erstwhile partisan László Földes, who was in the Ministry of Defense at the time, vividly described the army command's disintegration that night. Thus a mechanized regiment was ordered to the Radio Building from the provinces without the knowledge of the regional commander. When the soldiers, without any ammunition, finally found the building complex through the thick fog, a number of them merged with the crowd, while others sought refuge in a nearby barracks. At 3:30 a.m., at a joint meeting of the general staff, General Malinin promised that a Soviet tank unit would immediately proceed to the Radio Building to break through the besiegers' cordon. After the route was marked on the map of the city, the general requested that a Hungarian liaison officer escort them. At 9:30 a.m. the tanks had still not arrived at their destination. In Földes's view, what happened is not clear to this day, nor whether the liaison officer perhaps led the tanks in the wrong direction.[9]

At 10 the insurgents occupied the Radio Building, released the soldiers and the radio employees, and arrested the militiamen of the Ministry of Defense; they shot four of them on the spot, but many managed to escape. Hungarian soldiers retook the building the following day, supported by Soviet tanks, and found fifty militiamen who had managed to hide in the labyrinthine and badly damaged office complex. The siege of the Radio Building was the crucial spark that ignited the powder keg, although its occupation had no practical consequences, as the programs were recorded in an improvised studio in Parliament and broadcast from a strongly guarded facility at Lakihegy, thirty kilometers away. This night marked also the beginning of the end of the regime, although the heads of the dictatorship and their Soviet patrons were not yet as aware of the gravity of the situation in Hungary as those people who—in one way or another—were directly carried along by the dynamics of the events. The farsighted and significant reform Communist mastermind Ferenc Donáth, who was on the go all during that night, later commented: "Already that evening it was evident that the workers played the most important role. It was also evident that the revolt was aimed primarily against the humiliation of the nation, and that the working class recognized and felt that humiliation just as keenly as the intellectuals."[10]

As dawn broke, Hungarians and the world learned from radio news-casts what had happened during the night—at least according to the official version. At 4:35 a.m. a communiqué of the Council of Ministers announced: "Fascist, reactionary elements have launched an armed attack against our public buildings and have also attacked our police. For the sake of restoring order and until further measures are taken, all gatherings, meetings and demonstrations are banned. The forces of order have received instructions to apply the full strength of the law against those who break this order." The announcement was repeated every half hour; however, by 5 a.m. the "Fascists" had already become "counterrevolutionaries." At 8:13 the appointment of Imre Nagy as prime minister was announced, together with personnel changes in the Politburo. Barely half an hour later Prime Minister Nagy declared that martial law would be put into force for the whole country; all crimes falling under martial law would be punishable by death. At 9 a third communiqué announced the call for help to the Soviet formations stationed in Hungary to assist in restoring order because of the "extremely serious situation created by the dastardly armed attacks of counterrevolutionary gangs." At noon Nagy himself spoke on the radio and promised that martial law would not apply to those who laid down their weapons by 2 p.m. He invoked the reform program of June 1953 and called for order, calm, and discipline.[1]

I too woke early in the morning to the noise of caterpillar tracks. On Üllői Avenue a Soviet tank column was moving slowly toward the inner city. Our house on the corner was in a strategically important position, since only the narrow Liliom Street separated it from the nearby Kilián Barracks. A few hundred meters away on the other side of the street, which no longer belonged to the Ferencváros District but to the Józsefváros, small streets led to the Corvin Passage, a building complex constructed in 1928 on the corner of Üllői Avenue and József Boulevard. Exactly in the middle there was a large cinema set back from both major roads that formed this crossroads, accessible only through narrow side streets from either and sheltered on all sides by the buildings that fronted onto the boulevards. During my childhood and high school years I used to spend my time in these familiar narrow streets around the Corvin Passage and the barracks. It was precisely in this neighborhood that the resistance groups installed themselves. Before I even heard the first shots, I knew instinctively that an entirely new situation had arisen: the emergence of Soviet tanks had turned an uprising against the Stalinist dictatorship into a national war of independence. During the following four to five days the inhabitants of the houses close to the armed action were to all intents and purposes cut off from the outside world. I could not even think of going to the editorial office. We had to flee to the cellars.

The condemnation of the popular movement as a counterrevolutionary attack, the declaration of martial law, and the call for help to the Soviets discredited Imre Nagy's promises in the eyes of many people, who less than twenty-four hours earlier had demonstrated for his reappointment as head of the government. The erstwhile bearer of the people's hope remained at first a prisoner of his past and his surroundings in party headquarters. As he too appeared to carry the Soviet-dictated hard line, he began to lose his popularity among the intellectual reformers. His closest associates Losonczy and Donáth immediately refused their election into the party leadership because of the lack of a decision on reform measures and the confirmation of Gerő in the position of first secretary. Isolated from the "Pest Street" and his friends, Nagy the vacillator, exhausted and suffering from a heart condition, was being crushed between the grindstones of his loyalty to the party and the Soviets, his deep-rooted patriotism, the pressure from the streets, and the personal urgings of his closest advisers.

Meanwhile, what had begun on 23 October as a spontaneous uprising developed, after the appearance of the first Soviet tanks, into a national protest against foreign rule. Even if the trailblazers of the revolution were—just as in 1848—the intellectuals and eventually the students, the decisive armed conflict was led by young workers, apprentices, and representatives of all social groups. In her appreciation of the Hungarian Revolution, Hannah Arendt wrote "that never before has a revolution attained its goals as fast, as thoroughly and with so little bloodshed."[2] A few thousand young people, without central leadership or a coordinated plan and organized in small groups, exacted this victory virtually within five days because they were committed to a struggle to the death and enjoyed the moral and in many cases the practical support of the population.

All the documents and research reports, as well as my personal experiences, bear out what an unnamed professor of philosophy (one of III witnesses) testified before the Committee of the United Nations after his flight in 1957: "It was unique in history. The Hungarian revolution had no leaders. It was not organized; it was not centrally directed. The will for freedom was the moving force in every action.... There was no difference made among those fighting in the revolution as to their Party affiliations or social origin. Everybody helped the fighters."[3]

Just as during the siege of the Radio Building, during the first nights, and especially on Wednesday the twenty-fourth, small fighting groups formed at lightning speed and spontaneously, whose composition and size changed from day to day, sometimes from hour to hour. They acquired their weapons from the armaments factories and weapons depots in the ninth district, which were often barely guarded, from police stations, and from army barracks, but also from soldiers and policemen, many of whom handed over their weapons or were relieved of them. It also came to combat, with casualties on both sides, when, for instance, some insurgent groups wanted to raid the Kossuth Artillery Officers' Academy or an army printing press.[4]

During the five-day battle against the Soviet formations and sometimes also against the armed units of the internal militia and the frontier guards, both under the command of the Interior Ministry, or against individual, weak police or army units, the center of resistance was formed in the eighth and ninth districts.

Although the deadline for laying down weapons was extended several times on the twenty-fourth and then during the next few days, the freedom fighters would not give in. On the contrary, their number grew from day to day. In the Józsefváros and the Ferencváros (eighth and ninth districts) young workers, apprentices, and vocational school students, including young girls, streamed from the local worker and apprentice barracks, as well as from factories and the poorest districts, to join the fighters. The insurgents recognized early on the strategic significance of the blocks of buildings at the junction of those main roads that fan out from the Danube and that served as the indispensable routes for the

Soviet tanks. The fact that they were in control of the intersection of Üllői Avenue and the Great Boulevard (Nagykörut) revealed itself time and time again as a deadly trap for the Soviet troops. That was where one of the bastions of resistance was situated: the Corvin Cinema in the Center of an inconspicuous inner courtyard surrounded by four-and five-story houses. The passage was originally named after the famous poet Kisfaludy but has been officially named Corvin Passage since 1991.

In a report by an agent, its position was compared to that of Gibraltar: just as impregnable. One can attack from four streets without tanks or other attackers coming dangerously close, because everything can be covered from the windows of the cinema. The two likely accesses from Üllői Avenue and the Great Boulevard are far too narrow for tanks or armored cars. It was a particularly lucky fact for the insurgents that there was a convenient gasoline pump behind the cinema with inexhaustible reserves for the famous Molotov cocktails. Observers posted on the top floors of buildings on the side streets signaled the approach of Soviet vehicles. At the signal, the preparation of Molotov cocktails began. Any kind of bottle was filled almost to the brim with gasoline, then loosely corked and a piece of cloth wrapped around the cork. At a second signal, indicating that the tank was drawing nearer to the Corvin Cinema, the bottle would be turned upside down so that the gasoline could seep into the cloth. At the third signal, the cloth would be ignited and the bottle hurled at the tank. As soon as the loose cork fell out, the bottle would explode.

The predominantly young fighters had learned from the many Soviet partisan movies how to disable the armored vehicles with their openings on the top by attacking them with burning bottles. The insurgents split up into small groups in the upper storys of the surrounding houses of the Great Boulevard and Üllői Avenue. Opposite one of the narrow streets leading to the Corvin Passage on the other side of Üllői Avenue stood the massive gray-stone barracks erected in 1845–1846 according to the plans of the famous architect József Hild. The structure, built around three inner courtyards, was originally named after Maria Theresa, but after the Communist takeover it was renamed after Kilián, who had fought in Spain. Four stories tall and with a red-tiled roof, it was a massive stronghold in the heart of the city. The building, with its extremely thick walls, controlled the strategically important intersection of Üllői Avenue—which formed the most important route for the Soviet tanks from the easterly direction toward the center of the city—and the Great Boulevard between the insurgents' various bases. The latter had tried on several occasions to invade the barracks in order to capture weapons. However, there was no arms depot there. Most of those stationed in the middle section of the barracks, some thousand unarmed so-called auxiliary soldiers, were engaged in labor service on various building sites, while the two side wings housed workers' hostels. There were sporadic exchanges of fire on the twenty-fourth and twenty-fifth between the guards and the insurrectionists from the Corvin Passage; the commander asked for reinforcements from his superiors in the Ministry of Defense.

The immense building was rich in tradition for our family, since my father had to attend the same barracks as an officer candidate in the reserve prior to the First World War. I too had to appear there in November 1951 before the draft board. For us, there was no getting away from the neighborhood of the mighty barracks. It was a paradoxical situation. We, that is my father, my mother, who had been suffering from a nervous disorder since 1944, and I, were caught in the focus of events. It was above all here, around the Corvin Passage and the barracks, as well as in several squares on the Buda side, that a few thousand young people were committed to a struggle to the death, thereby forcing a turnabout in the entire political scene. Our own lives, as it turned out later, depended on whether the concentrated attack on the Corvin Passage by cannons and aircraft demanded by the party's hard-liners and the military commission would take place or not. We knew nothing about what went on in town, and especially not about the decisions made at party headquarters.

During the following days numerous small groups came into being that operated in the most important side streets. László Eörsi, the outstanding historian of the insurgent groups' activities and organization, has described thirty-three different groups actively involved in the resistance in the Józsefváros and the Ferencváros alone.[5] Although most of the independent units with their own commanders acted autonomously, the so-called Corvinists remained by far the most significant fighting formation because they had ample space at their disposal in the relatively large cinema, and because they were able to set up a largish kitchen in the neighboring houses, an improvised first-aid center with nurses, and even a cellar for prisoners. However, the main reason for their prestige, in spite of internal tensions, was the unfaltering fighting spirit and tactical ability of their group leaders.

Who were the freedom fighters? Above all, they were very young, some not yet out of childhood: the average age of the Corvinists was eighteen. Under the chaotic circumstances and due to the constantly changing composition of the fighting groups, there were, of course, no representative data. Still, the résumés of 235 insurgents from the Józsefváros gathered by László Eörsi in his study are informative. The overwhelming majority, 88 percent, had only primary school education. Nine out of ten insurgents were manual workers. Only 9 percent were engaged in an intellectual or administrative profession, and 29 percent came from an intellectual or public official background. Exactly five-sixths of the respondents came from the poorer sections of society. The proportion of those who had graduated from high school or who had military experience was higher among the group leaders. According to this compilation, 29 percent had criminal records, although a third of the cases (illegal border-crossing attempts, shirking work, and so on) would no longer count as criminal offenses today.

Hatred of the Rákosi dictatorship was the common political denominator. Within that framework the motives were diverse. Some aspired to the realization of the students' sixteen-point program. Others hoped for an improvement in their living conditions. Still others were influenced by Hungarian broadcasts of the Munich-based U.S. Radio Free Europe. Yet others joined the insurgents for emotional reasons. Thus, for instance, István Asztalos (subsequently sentenced to six years' imprisonment) explained that the sight of a youngster allegedly wounded by the State Security militia had motivated him to join the fighters.

The number of insurgents in the Corvin Passage rose from the initial seventy or eighty within two to three days to fivefold. The first commander, László Iván Kovács, estimated the number of fighters on 28 October at 800, and on the twenty-ninth at 1,000 to 1,200. Eventually, on the eve of the second Soviet intervention, their number is supposed to have reached 4,000.

Who was László Iván Kovács? Born in 1930, after completing his secondary education he was not admitted to study law at the university on account of his father. His father had been a professional soldier, a senior noncommissioned officer, and returned to Hungary only after having spent the year 1944–1945 in Landsberg am Lech. The young Kovács worked as a civilian army employee. Dismissed after two years for having concealed his "Westy" past, he was employed in various administrative jobs, mainly because of his talents as a soccer player. In 1955–1956 he studied for one year as an evening student at the Free University. On 23 October he too marched to the Bem Monument, to the Parliament, and was present at the dismantling of the Stalin Monument. Outside the Radio Building Iván Kovács took part in the protest against the militia's firing at the people, and on the afternoon of 24 October he joined the insurgents at the Corvin Cinema. He managed to gain the confidence of most of the young fighters by his circumspect conduct, his organizational talent, and his bravery.

Early tensions arose within the closer leadership of the Corvinists between Iván Kovács and Gergely Pongrátz, the dynamic spokesman of the group of the four Pongrátz brothers. The twenty-four-year-old agronomist, known to everyone by his nickname "Bajusz" (Mustache), arrived in Budapest from the country only on the twenty-fifth. The Pongrátz family (nine children) came originally from Transylvania, and Gergely's brother Ödön, ten years older, had taken part in the fighting from the outset. Through his radical stance and his determination, Gergely Pongrátz came across as totally uncompromising. "We never asked anybody, Where do you come from, Who are you? We did not ask about nationality or religion. Whoever had a weapon and fought for the students' 16 points was a comrade in arms," Pongrátz recalled. The fact that the Corvinists and the affiliated groups refused to lay down their arms until the very end and insisted on the withdrawal of Soviet troops until the end of 1956 was largely due to Pongrátz's determination to resist and to endure. However, behind the unbending bearing was a sensitive nature. Witness a dramatic incident on the evening of 26 October. After a day of fighting and the annihilation of several Soviet tanks, Pongrátz suddenly became involved in a murderous gun battle. In a hairdresser salon close to the Great Boulevard, two insurgents were wounded by Russian soldiers. With six of his comrades, Pongrátz hastened to their help. Within a few seconds all hell broke loose in the dark shop. Shots churned up the ground; he heard a machine-gun barrage. Several dead comrades, hit while trying to flee, lay at his feet. Who knew who was shot here and

why? Pongrátz could not look for cover under the broken window. He
had to run for his life along the boulevard. He found shelter in the door-
way of the fourth house, and with a last effort shot a lightbulb to pieces
so he could wait in the darkness. Three of his comrades eventually found
the trembling "Bajusz." When he saw that in front of the hairdresser
salon fourteen corpses and seriously injured people, among them his six
comrades, as well as Soviet and militia soldiers, were being removed by
ambulances, Pongrátz broke into an uncontrollable crying fit, and his
brother Ödön had to take him to the hospital, where he spent the night.

The heaviest fighting against the Soviet tanks had been raging since
the morning of the twenty-fourth around the Corvin block and the Kilián
Barracks. In her testimony of 1 March 1957, Éva Kovács, a fifteen-year-old
high school student, told how she observed, from her apartment, two
approximately twelve-year-old boys, each with a gasoline bottle in hand,
concealed behind a telephone booth at the intersection of Üllői Avenue
and József Boulevard. She saw them running to a Soviet tank that was
turning from Üllői Avenue into the boulevard, and from close by toss-
ing the two bottles at the slowly proceeding tank. The tank exploded in
an enormous fireball. Kovács did not know what had happened to the
soldiers because she quickly left her position at the window. Sometime
later she witnessed an armored car being blown up on József Boulevard.
She also described her third burned-out tank; three or four dead Soviet
soldiers were lying there, who, as she was later told, had been hit by
snipers from the Corvin Passage.

For many of the young fighters, the often daredevil attack against
the Soviet troops was also an adventure. They discovered that the open
armored personnel carriers, the so-called open coffins, could easily be
put out of action by small arms, and that the gas tanks of the T-34 armored vehicles could easily be set on fire from the back. At other places
they smeared the main roads with soap and oil or threw pots and packing
cases at the monsters, pretending they were mines. When the soldiers
left their cover to examine the suspicious objects, they were attacked
from the windows of nearby houses or from the Corvin Passage. Time
and time again the young people fought against the Soviet tanks with
the most primitive resources, such as handguns and Molotov cocktails,
sometimes with hand grenades. There was little if any contact between
the diverse, loosely associated groups, yet their style of fighting was

remarkably similar. The following true accounts by several eyewitnesses will serve as illustrations.

In the evening of the twenty-fourth, fifty meters away from Üllői Avenue and the József Boulevard, the insurgents attacked a Soviet munitions transport from four directions and set two trucks alight by fierce target-oriented firing. Between 10 and 11 p.m., yet another six trucks laden with munitions were exploded. At the crack of dawn, at 3 a.m. on the twenty-fifth, the young guards heard the rattle and squeak of approaching caterpillar tracks as a column of Soviet tanks proceeded along Üllői Avenue in the direction of József Boulevard. Two of the four tanks were blown up; seven to eight Soviet soldiers, among them a first lieutenant, lost their lives. At this junction and at other locations controlled by the fighter groups, a unit of the Kossuth Artillery Officers' Academy was forced to retreat with casualties, and a police company was also attacked. On József Boulevard rebels forced a twenty-five-man police unit finally to capitulate after a fierce exchange of fire. At noon on the twenty-fifth or twenty-sixth, five groups of insurgents attacked an artillery battery consisting of eight cannons on the corner of Üllői Avenue and the József Boulevard, destroying five or six cannons. Fifteen Soviet soldiers died. An officer and three soldiers were taken prisoner the following day. Although the insurgents were still only fighting with small arms and Molotov cocktails, on the twenty-seventh they managed to capture two 155-mm cannons on self-propelled gun carriages and later two antitank guns, thereby inflicting even greater losses on the Soviets. There were, of course, blunders and accidents, sometimes fatal ones, caused by inexperience and lack of discipline.

Because of the wrecks, it became increasingly difficult for the Soviet trucks, tanks, and semitrailers to move about. At the big intersection next to the Kilián Barracks, a long motorized column of Soviet antitank guns, semitrailers, and personnel carriers was gunned down. Their burned-out torsos covered Üllői Avenue during the entire time of the fighting. All the while the neighborhood's residents were subjected to gruesome sights. In the center of the crossing one or two tanks were burning, lighting up the gloomy streets. Everywhere there were dead bodies and wrecked vehicles. Some wounded soldiers were moaning and wailing, trying, on hands and knees, to reach the other side of the street or any vehicle that was still able to move. Now the Soviet tanks were driving along faster, attempting to smoke out the rebel strongholds in the eighth and ninth districts. However, they failed. They shelled the houses surrounding the intersection. It was not long before the entire neighborhood was in ruins. Yet they could not get close to the Corvin Cinema until the very end. As fast as the young fighters dispersed, they regrouped at a different spot.

At any rate, in his documentation László Eörsi reckons that during the fighting in October, that is, until the cease-fire, the Soviets lost at least 120 soldiers and 20 to 25 tanks; that corresponds to an entire armored battalion. The Corvinists are said to have lost 30 fighters, and some 210 to 230 noncombatant civilians lost their lives during this period in the Józsefváros. However, it has been emphasized in recollections that the general populace provided the insurgents with very definite assistance.

In light of the dogged resistance shown by the Corvinists and the other loosely associated fighter groups in the eighth and ninth districts, the Soviets and their Hungarian accomplices assumed a "planned action directed by trained soldiers and general staff officers" (thus Janza, minister of defense in the second Nagy government).[6] Hegedüs, the former prime minister, opined at the 28–29 October meeting of the Politburo: "Very clever army officers are leading the military resistance. For example, Dezső Király in the Corvin Passage. He used to be a general staff officer."[7] General Serov, head of the KGB, who was in Budapest at the time with Mikoyan and Suslov, informed the two CPSU Presidium members: "The commander-in-chief is a certain Berlaki, a former colonel in the Horthy army; his military deputy, responsible for distributing weapons, is called Porcsalmi; the leader of the resistance groups, Banyasz, is a former active nationalist. The liaison man for the insurgents is the priest of the local church, Domján."[8] He listed these names, quoting as his source agents of the Interior Ministry and stressed that the Corvin Passage was the hub of the entire insurrection in Budapest. Similar information was also discussed at the Soviet party Presidium's sitting on 28 October. Since these alleged colonels and other names do not appear in any sources, not even in the list of army and gendarme officers from the year 1944, it is most probable that they were pure inventions by Hungarian police informants. The Soviets and their Hungarian collaborators simply did not have any reliable information available regarding the actual size of the fighting group, and they exorbitantly overestimated the number of the exceptionally mobile insurgents around the Corvin

Passage, who frequently changed their positions. Bearing in mind the unbroken resistance, plans for attacking the Corvin Passage were again and again floated at the highest political and military levels.

The "hawks" in the divided Politburo (Gerö und Hegedüs), the military commission of the CC, and most of all the Soviet-Hungarian commanders, led by General M. S. Malinin, deputy chief of staff of the Soviet Army, who had been sent to Budapest together with Mikoyan, Suslov, and Serov, had discussed various options for bringing the matter to an end on 25 and 26 October. Thus, for instance, a Hungarian general suggested dropping bombs from helicopters in order "to reduce the number of civilian victims." László Földes, a member of the military commission, put forward a plan of attack to blow up the Corvin Cinema via the underground canal system.[9]

Meanwhile there were also various attempts at direct negotiations with the Corvinists. Although this reflected the disintegration of the regime's central political and military leadership, it also led to a split in the heterogeneous fighting groups, and later to open conflict between Iván Kovács, the leader of the Corvinists, and the rival Pongrátz group. Until the declaration of the cease-fire and the political turnaround on 28 October, the question of action to be taken against the insurgents in general and the Corvinists in particular was constantly on the agenda of the political and military bodies. Thus one of the charges against him in the secret trial of Imre Nagy after the defeat of the revolution was that he had thwarted the decisive attack against the Corvinists by a personal directive. It is an established fact supported by numerous testimonies that Nagy had indeed repeatedly spoken up against the deployment of artillery and the bloodshed in the residential quarter around the Corvin Cinema. Still, whether he had actually stopped the decisive attack on 28 October by threatening to resign must be left as a moot question, since he himself has denied it in court.[10] It is a fact, though, that the offensive initiated by General G. I. Obaturov, commander of the Thirty-third Mechanized Division, involving Soviet tanks, to be followed by three hundred Hungarian soldiers, dismally backfired from the word go. When the three T-34 tanks sent at 8 a.m. of 28 October to reconnoiter the area did not return after an hour and a half, three heavy T-54 tanks were dispatched after them. It soon transpired that all three T-34s had been torched, and of the three T-54s only one managed to return unharmed. Nagy then prohibited a second attack.

Despite the cease-fire, fighting continued in the Corvin Cinema's vicinity until 29 October. Yet these skirmishes could no longer change the fact that the motley crew of young insurrectionists had won an internationally significant political and symbolic victory. During the repeated negotiations with representatives of the army, they steadfastly refused to lay down their arms. In spite of their internal conflicts, the Corvinists kept up their demands until the political turnabout for the withdrawal of Soviet troops, a declaration of neutrality and independence, a multiparty system and free elections, the disbanding of the State Security forces, and an amnesty for the insurrectionists. The integration of the Corvinists and their leading representatives on 31 October into the newly formed National Guard signified the crowning recognition of their outstanding role.

Still, it would be wrong to regard the "Pest Street," these heroically fighting youngsters, as the only crucially decisive force.[11] One should not underrate the extension of the revolutionary uprising to the country towns and the larger communities, the significance of the self-governing bodies of the quickly arisen revolutionary committees, as well as the workers' councils and their growing pressure on the party and government and also personally on Imre Nagy. Throughout the weeklong struggle for the choice between bloody confrontation with the entire populace or the acceptance of the central revolutionary demands, the oppositionists within the party—the writers, journalists, and scientists among the followers of Imre Nagy—also played a considerable role in the background. But more about them later.

There are moments in a person's life when everything becomes different. In the case of Imre Nagy the great story of the Hungarian Revolution and all the contradictions, the grandeur and the procrastination, the conflict and the vacillation between loyalty to the party and patriotism, became the experienced and endured biography of an individual. In the course of the night of 23 to 24 October, the same CC members who a year and a half ago had chased him out of office, eventually stripping him even of his party membership on a specious pretext, appointed him prime minister under the most inauspicious of circumstances. The politician, wary and cautious by nature, was neither the instigator nor the supporter of a revolutionary transformation. Buffeted hither and thither in the Communist movement both at home and in Soviet emigration, the prime minister was a dyed-in-the-wool reformer, who during the first days wanted in the truest sense of the word to move toward the future in reverse gear. In his first speech as head of government and then in his second one after the replacement of Gerő, he combined threats with promises about the continuation of his June 1953 program and the democratization in the framework of the Patriotic People's Front. The retrospective description by the resistance fighter and poet István Eörsi, a steadfast admirer of Nagy, is apposite: "He was an unhurried man, shaped by doubts and also by deep-rooted party discipline, who simply needed more time to make decisions than one should or could afford in a revolution. He was always two, three days behind in his decisions."

The personnel changes—Nagy instead of Hegedüs, Kádár instead of Gerő—did not satisfy anyone. While fighting proceeded in Budapest and the news from the capital mobilized people across the whole country, the prime minister kept quiet for the first seventy-two hours. For all intents and purposes, he was still a head of government without a government. As had been done before, decisions were still made by the highest party bodies. The haggling for positions in Nagy's new government took up an important part of the internal power struggles. The old guard around Gerő and Hegedüs tried to hang on to their people. While the central state power became increasingly paralyzed in the entire country, during the debate about the person for the office of minister of culture, for example, the functionaries discussed seven different possibilities.[1] That happened on 26 October, the same day that at Mosonmagyaróvar, near the Austrian border, the Interior Ministry's frontier guards opened fire from their barracks on a peacefully demonstrating crowd. According to official statistics, fifty-eight people were killed, among them women and small children, and eighty-five were wounded. A few hours later a furious mass of people returned; they occupied the barracks, and several officers were lynched.[2]

The army was divided. The total failure of the minister responsible for the event and the chief of the general staff led to a disintegration of the central command structure in the ministry. The majority of military units in Budapest and the countryside remained passive, and the local commanders as a rule did not show much enthusiasm for the use of weapons. Yet in the few days between 24 and 29 October, there were seventy-one cases of armed clashes between army units and the populace in fifty towns and communities. In considering these figures, it has to be kept in mind, of course, that they include the defense of attacks on civilian and military objectives, as well as fighting with the insurgents and, last but not least, barrages against the unarmed civilian population.

Much depended in each case on the attitude of the commanding officer. The bloodshed in the town of Kecskemét in the Great Hungarian Plain was an appalling example. On the twenty-sixth there were demonstrations in front of the office of State Security and in front of the jail. Subsequently some groups of armed insurgents were also active. On the orders of the infamous commander of the Third Corps, Major General Lajos Gyurkó, the following day summary justice was exercised: the organizers of the demonstrations were arrested, seven of them shot, and in four townships fighter planes deployed to put an end to the unrest. First they fired warning shots and then shot directly at the people. In the community of Tiszakécske, a fighter plane strafed a crowd demonstrating before the town hall, killing 17 and wounding 117. The ruthlessly acting general, who fled with his political commissar to the Soviet troops on 31 October, was also rumored to have been the Soviet military circles' favored candidate as town commander of Budapest in case of a "military solution." The muddle-headed idea of a kind of "military dictatorship" was, incidentally, mooted by some members of the military commission. To this day it is not known to what extent the hawks in the party leadership and the Soviets were involved in the planned disempowerment of the Nagy government.[3]

During the two-day session of the Central Committee on 25 and 26 October, the various trends clashed in the course of fierce discussions.[4] The distinct majority of the party leadership and the military commission represented the hard line: first the suppression of the uprising by way of a curfew, martial law, use of military force, newspaper censorship, and so on. Only after these measures were taken should the demands of the rebels be examined. The representatives of this line were motivated partly by the fear of the threat of a restoration of the Horthy regime. The workers, they assumed, could be misled only for so long and sooner or later would side with the party. However, the increasingly unambiguous reports about the true attitude of the workers eventually elicited doubt even in some members of this group.

A second group, among them initially Nagy himself, inclined toward a tactic of limited reconciliation. Simultaneously with the war against the "counterrevolutionaries," the "misguided, decent working people" should be won over through political and social concessions. This goal was served by the nonapplication of martial law, the repeated extensions of deadlines for laying down arms, promises of amnesty, and last but not least the announcement of the formation of a so-called national government. The appointment of Kádár as first secretary of the party also fitted into this framework. The decisive role in this phase was eventually played by Géza Losonczy and Ferenc Donáth, the two reform Communists who from the very beginning argued for a clear line: radical political concessions by recognizing the uprising as a democratic national mass movement; after all, not only students but the working classes took part in it too. They demanded immediate negotiations with the leaders of the various insurgent groups.

During the long meeting of the Central Committee, which was adjourned several times, the pent-up tensions exploded into an inconceivably vociferous and dramatic confrontation. More than ever the issue was the alternative between a military and a political solution. In the early morning of the twenty-sixth, Prime Minister Imre Nagy could at least stop two irreparable decisions: through his personal intervention, he managed to have the curfew that was announced at 4:30 for the entire day between 10 a.m and 3 p.m lifted, and the intended concerted attack on the Corvin Passage, which would have involved scores of civilian casualties, was stopped.[5]

However, for the time being Nagy could not achieve any break-through as far as the fundamental questions were concerned. Most of his candidates for ministry were, after, all not accepted in the various party bodies. Even worse was the fact that after a passionate intervention of members of the party's military commission, established on the twenty-fourth, the stance of the Central Committee altered radically. The "hawks" in the commission and the CC accused Donáth and Losonczy and implicitly Nagy of throwing in the towel. Instead of the draft resolution on which work had begun earlier, a disappointing resolution containing nothing new of any substance was accepted and published. Besides vague promises, it repeated the threat that anyone not laying down his arms by 10 p.m. would be "mercilessly liquidated."[6]

All this was in glaring contrast to the demands published on the same day by the National Council of Trade Unions and the Writers' Union. The two important groups demanded the withdrawal of Soviet troops, an immediate cease-fire, a complete amnesty for the insurgents, the formation of a national government, and the establishment of workers' councils in the factories. Nagy behaved passively during the important session of the Central Committee, and he was absent most of the time because of discussions with the Soviet representatives and the delegations of students and writers. His vague replies had a rather disappointing effect on the delegates. At the end of the meeting with these delegations, Losonczy and Donáth informed the prime minister about the disheartening results of the CC meeting. Since they had suffered a defeat and had been accused of treason, they were forced to decline endorsing such a policy with their names.

Nagy was visibly shaken and dejected. "Even though he totally agreed with our situation, he stared wordlessly ahead. . . . Meanwhile his wife phoned him several times . . . she spoke apprehensively of how those who trusted him would now judge his behavior. . . . He remained silent, sunk in himself. Tears rolling down his cheeks, he gave the impression of a man who served his people, his country, and the cause of socialism, who was full of the best of intentions, but who, in a very difficult situation, was at a loss in the face of events," wrote Donáth in his later recollections.[7] That same day or the next, Nagy had a similar telephone conversation with his daughter Erzsébet. She told him: "Fighting is going on here at the Petőfi Barracks; this is a revolution." He replied: "I know." The family's opinion, above all that of his wife, whom he had married thirty-one years earlier in their hometown, had always strongly influenced the introverted Nagy, although—or perhaps because—she was never politically active. She was not a party member, neither during their stay in the Soviet Union nor after their return to Hungary.[8]

Nagy's mood fluctuations caused by his hesitation were manifest that day. The behavior pattern of the sixty-year-old suffering from heart trouble was of course also affected by the fact that since 23 October he could get neither any rest nor any sleep in the crowded conditions of party headquarters. Going home to rest was out of the question. The following day, during an interval in the three-hour-long Politburo session with Mikoyan and Suslov, Nagy suffered a dizzy spell and passed out. Aided by a doctor and thanks to a medication, Validol, proffered by Suslov, Nagy quickly regained consciousness.[9] Prior to this breakdown, he had experienced a disturbing scene, which Hegedüs described in his memoirs: "I can still picture it: with paper in his hand, Gerő tries to influence Nagy to sign the predated request for help to the Soviets. With ever-quickening steps, in the end almost running, Nagy moves away from him." Eventually Hegedüs signed the rewritten letter, which the Soviet leadership urgently needed as an alibi for the United Nations Security Council's session convened for 28 October, and which Ambassador Andropov immediately dispatched to Moscow.[10]

Imre Nagy—cut off for days from the happenings, but contacted by a number of individuals and delegations both in writing and on the telephone, some even in person at party headquarters—increasingly came to realize the true situation. The deciding nudge for the prime minister was probably his three-hour meeting in the afternoon of 27 October with a group styled the Budapest Angyalföld District Workers' Delegation. In fact, this was a clever ruse. Although two young workers were also present, they served only as "decorative door openers," so that the ten-man delegation, as the voice of the workers, could be admitted to the prime minister in the strongly guarded party headquarters. The "Workers' Delegation" was none other than a deputation of his most radically like-minded friends, who, in the almost lost battle for the soul of Nagy, put all their eggs in the basket of a personal encounter.[11]

Sándor Kopácsi, chief of the Budapest Police, played a key role in the preparation of this meeting, just as he had since the beginning of the uprising. This former partisan, who came from an old Communist working-class family, had already assured the organizers of the student demonstrations on 23 October that the police would not be used against peaceful demonstrators. During the fighting, only about 200 of the 2,500 Budapest policemen were in action in the eighth and ninth districts. They were instructed to negotiate with the insurgents, to withdraw to the police stations in case of emergency, and if it came to a confrontation, to lay down their arms. Some policemen also joined the insurgents. Part of the latter's weapons came from police depots.[12]

Kopácsi's friends and political advisers in the centrally situated police headquarters played a special role in shaping this levelheaded attitude of the Budapest Police. These were his brother-in-law, the oppositionist journalist György Fazekas, the former police chief József Szilágyi, who had been booted out because of his courageous stance, and the prominent reform Communist journalists of the central party organ, Miklós Gimes and Pál Lőcsei. They were all staunch followers of Nagy, and Fazekas several times conveyed telephoned situation reports to him and particularly to Nagy's son-in-law, Jánosi.[13] Incidentally, one of the bizarre facts, hardly mentioned in Western literature, was that during those chaotic thirteen days the telephone, electricity, and gas services functioned quite adequately!

After an accidental encounter with the two young workers from the thirteenth district (Angyalföld), Nagy's friends at police headquarters came up with the idea of calling on the prime minister with the two of them and escorted by a colonel of the police to—as it were—present "the authentic *vox populi*." In the course of their conversation in party headquarters, Gimes and Szilágyi harshly criticized Nagy on account of the martial law, the deployment of Soviet troops, and the composition of the new government. They warned him that his prestige was increasingly being gambled away; they even showed him leaflets about "the Russian hireling Imrov Nagy." They sought to persuade him to recognize and accept the movement as a national democratic revolution. Nagy showed them the unsigned draft letter with the plea for help to Moscow, but his explanations about an intended political solution with reference to "the counterrevolutionary danger" did not cut any ice with them and were unreservedly rejected. They called on him finally to distance himself from the decrepit party leadership and to move to Parliament or even to police headquarters, to proclaim an immediate cease-fire, and to act on the basis of his own political platform.

Nagy's conversation with his friends lasted three hours and naturally took place in a tense atmosphere. Nagy suffered a further breakdown, this time a mental one, and, according to Gimes, wept almost incessantly. However, in the end he finally took a determined stance. The government would in the course of that day take decisive steps. All he asked from his friends was support and patience. Shaken and deeply moved, they took their leave from Nagy, who was wrestling with his own doubts. This encounter, in the opinion of the greatest Hungarian experts on contemporary history, helped Nagy at last to overcome the "deadlock." The concurrently received memorandum to the government by prominent writers and artists in favor of a cease-fire, the extension of the amnesty, and the creation of a reconciliation commission helped to reinforce his stance.[14]

His notes in preparation for the next meeting with the Politburo and with the Soviet functionaries bear out his determination to implement a change. The thoughts scribbled in his handwriting on a piece of paper were discovered again in his trial documents.

> We cannot govern. We cannot liquidate the armed conflict.
> There is nothing else left but to rely on Soviet troops. We are losing the support of the people. We have come into conflict with public opinion. The salami tactic was caused by the insecurity of the leadership. If we can ensure order with the help of the working people, we shall remove the Soviet troops.... Political steps and measures. The situation is critical and deteriorating. Political reasons trigger it off. The key question: further political steps, effective military action. If the decision is put off, everything stagnates and the provinces will also get going.

He added the following either during or after the discussion: "Seminal political measures necessary. Earlier demands. Independence."

Nagy recognized at last the depth of the moral and political crisis of the state party, and with it the collapse of the political system and the counterproductive political effect of the attempts at a military solution. But could he at the same time convince the profoundly suspicious Soviet functionaries of the necessity for an extensively perceptible political change? In the evening he first met with the five members of the newly formed Directorium (later called the party Presidium)[15] and subsequently with Kádár for an "unofficial friendly conversation" together with Mikoyan and Suslov. During that night the course was set for those political changes that the party bodies in Budapest and Moscow then approved on 28 October.

Many details of those negotiations are unknown to this day. What is known is that Nagy threatened to resign if the new line were not applied. According to the foremost expert on party history, the historian Zoltán Ripp,[16] the support of Kádár and of Interior Minister (and Directorium member) Ferenc Münnich perhaps also played a decisive role. Two factors influenced Kádár's attitude: he was never wholeheartedly in favor of a solution by resorting to violence, and he saw in the joint statement of the trade unions, the University Revolutionary Students' Committee, and the Writers' Union supporting the recognition of events as a "national democratic revolution" the danger of a potential second political center. Nagy's determined attitude was also evident at the session of the Politburo in the early hours of 28 October. When Mikoyan spoke about the limits of the concessions and parenthetically mentioned Nagy's vacillating nature, the head of government replied with unusual clarity: "Turning to me, Comrade Mikoyan said that one should take a firmer stand. I will not stop and stand firmly where the party's interests demand a forward move."[17]

Deadlocked

6

The first secret report—released decades later—sent by the Soviet emissaries Mikoyan and Suslov on the afternoon of the twenty-fourth from Budapest to the party Presidium reflected a completely unrealistic picture of the situation. While official statistics registered 250 dead and numerous wounded for 23 and 24 October alone, and during the course of the day repeated clashes took place between armed insurgents and guards at armories and military institutions, the pair reported at 3 p.m. Budapest time that—apart from the Radio Building, largely destroyed by the rebels—all centers of the uprising had been annihilated, and that the Hungarian comrades, especially Gerő, had overestimated the enemy's strength and underestimated their own. The top functionaries, including Nagy, reassured Mikoyan and Suslov that they were of the same mind, were masters of the situation, and were convinced that they could deal with the problems.[1]

Against this optimistically portrayed background, the Politburo then held another meeting in the evening of the twenty-fourth, at which the two Soviet politicians naturally also took part. In their fantasy world, isolated from reality, all of them, probably Nagy as well, counted on an impending political normalization. Accordingly the curfew was lifted, and at 6:23 a.m. the radio broadcast an official government communiqué, announcing that during the night "the attempted counterrevolutionary coup" had been liquidated. Public transport, factories, and businesses should carry on with their work; only the schools and universities were closed until further notice.[2] This announcement was a tragic miscalculation, whose consequences became evident within a few hours. Prior to the Politburo meeting called for 9 a.m., Géza Losonczy and Ferenc Donáth, who the previous day had categorically declined their election to the Central Committee as a protest against Gerő's confirmation as first secretary, called on Nagy at party headquarters. They told him that what was happening was a great national uprising and by no means a counterrevolution. The two of them stressed that "we did not agree with the government's present attitude, nor with the Russian intervention, the martial law and the other measures," and they tried to induce Nagy to resign. Nagy was probably tired, exhausted, and brusque. "Comrades, I do not have any time now! We are in the middle of an important Politburo conference; the Soviet comrades are here too. I must go back to the meeting." He did not even cast a glance at their petition. The meeting of the friends was a bitter disappointment for both sides. Nagy felt they had left him in the lurch by their radicalism and resignation, whereas they believed that Nagy had not kept their original agreement of 23 October.[3]

While the party leadership was making its last-minute arrangements for the session of the Politburo, Deputy Prime Minister Erdei and Nagy's son-in-law, Jánosi, appeared in the meeting room. Alerted by telephone calls from the university, they informed the party leaders that the students were preparing a demonstration. It should be prevented in order to avoid any fatal casualties, they said. Gerő told them edgily that he was fully informed about events. They should not get into a panic and annoy the Politburo.[4]

Meanwhile huge crowds were milling around in the streets of the city. In the morning some seventy thousand commuters came to the capital from the provinces. However, public transport was not working properly in town. At 9 a.m. thousands of students assembled to hold renewed demonstrations. In front of the Hotel Astoria some Russian-speaking students fraternized with the crews of three Soviet tanks. They then set off for Parliament perched on these tanks, flying the Hungarian tricolor. Thousands of passersby joined the students. They chanted slogans, such as "Shit Gerő," "We are not Fascists," "The radio is lying," and "The Russians are with us." Improvised processions of demonstrators approached from other directions, led by people carrying tricolor and black flags. They all marched toward the Parliament. Eleven Soviet tanks and three armored cars were stationed in the square, guarding the building. The nine to ten thousand demonstrators were unarmed, and they sent a three-man delegation into the Parliament Building with their demands. All of them wanted to see Nagy. However, the prime minister happened to be at the session of the Politburo with Mikoyan and Suslov at party headquarters in 17 Academy Street, a mere couple of hundred meters away. General Serov of the KGB was also attending, but he left the meeting when he heard of Soviet soldiers fraternizing with the Hungarian demonstrators.[5]

All of a sudden a barrage of machine-gun fire rang out from the roof of the Ministry of Agriculture. The confused Russian tank crews began to shoot, probably in the direction from which the shots had come, that is at the roofs of surrounding houses. The reports of surviving eyewitnesses are contradictory. Some claim that the shots were fired from the Parliament Building. Most of them blamed the unknown snipers of the security forces. Others even had the impression that the Russians fired at each other across the large square with cannons and MGs. When the shooting stopped, the square was littered with dead and dying men and women. A few minutes later, three Soviet tanks came rattling from Academy Street in the direction of the Parliament and aimed at the fleeing crowd with grenades and machine guns. Unimaginable scenes took place as the crowd sought shelter in the entrances of ministries and in a burned-out restaurant. Two American correspondents, John MacCormac from the *New York Times* and Endre Marton from the Associated Press, described the ghastly carnage. They thought it possible that it had all been a tragic misunderstanding. "The most credible version is that the political policemen opened fire on the demonstrators and panicked the Soviet tank crews into the belief that they were being attacked.... The total number of casualties has been estimated at 170. This correspondent can testify that he saw a dozen bodies." A British diplomat claimed to have seen twelve trucks with bodies. The most recent research speaks of 75 dead and 284 wounded. According to the official statistics, 120 dead were counted in the capital, while the historian Eörsi estimates the victims in front of the Parliament at 200.

Numerous hypotheses have been published on the course of the massacre and its possible motives. In his book *The Abandoned Masses*, the historian László Varga suggested a mass murder prepared in cold blood. In 2003 the military historian Miklós Horváth revised his assumption published in 1996 that all of the dead and wounded were victims of firing from Soviet tanks. Now he argues that the tragedy was caused by the fusillades of border guards fired at the crowd from the roof of the Ministry of Agriculture. He notes, however, that among General Serov's documents released so far, the report of 25 October 1956 is missing—obviously it is still being treated as a secret document.

There is no doubt whatsoever that because of the slaughter between 11:15 and 11:30 a.m., this "bloodiest day" became a turning point in the turbulent history of the revolution. The U.S. correspondent Leslie B. Bain, who was an eyewitness of the "bloody Thursday," described in his book, just as John MacCormac did in the *New York Times*, that far from deterring the demonstration, the firing embittered and inflamed the Hungarian people. They wanted to take revenge on the Russians for this barbarity perpetrated at the Parliament. The laughing revolutionaries became solemn, angry-faced men ready to go to war, wrote Bain, who a few hours earlier had himself experienced the fraternization between the Soviet tank crews and the young students. He even compared those scenes to the reception received by American liberating troops in Paris. From then on, however, the journalist, a fluent Hungarian speaker, could palpably sense "the feverish desire for revenge." "Thus the revolution became a blind, merciless war between half-armed people and the Soviet Army. The ÁVH was temporarily forgotten. This was a war between Hungarians and Russians."[6]

What a day! The news of the massacre swept across the city at lightning speed. Brandishing black and bloodstained Hungarian flags, people marched that day in groups in the inner city. A few minutes later and only a few blocks from the scene of the massacre, the surviving demonstrators reassembled in Szabadság (Liberty) Square. A crowd assembled before the United States legation in the square and shouted: "The workers are being murdered! Help us!" The chargé d'affaires explained to them that their case was one for decision by his government and the United Nations, not for the legation. The British ambassador had received a deputation and given it the same message. Another group was able to have not only the students' famous sixteen-point program printed in a large printing plant under army control, but also a new leaflet. It demanded a new revolutionary national government, the withdrawal of Soviet troops, the abrogation of the Warsaw Pact, the dissolution of the armed State Security Service, and the punishment of those responsible for the massacre at Parliament Square. The young intellectuals who had composed the leaflet and who, as signatories, had invented a "Provisional Revolutionary Government" and a "Defense Committee," even telephoned and asked for an appointment with the prime minister, who received them in the late afternoon.[7]

Earlier, around lunchtime, a drastic change had occurred in the party leadership after some dramatic happenings. At the time of the bloodbath a session of the Central Committee with the two Soviet functionaries had been in progress for quite some time in party headquarters, which was closely guarded by Soviet tanks, soldiers, and members of the State Security forces. Suddenly the dumbfounded party leaders heard machine-gun rattle, shell fire, and even cannon shots. The noise came from close by. Then an MG fusillade shattered the large window of the conference room and hit the wall barely a meter above the heads of the Politburo members. Gerő jumped up nervously from his chair. Suslov, in his second report to the Central Committee, later wrote that the falling plaster threw the leading Hungarian functionaries into a panic. They strode in single file down to the cellar, which, however, was not suitable for a meeting. So they went up again to another office. Indescribable confusion reigned in the entrance hall. Wounded soldiers were being brought in and examined, shouting could be heard from outside. That is where in those few minutes Zoltán I. Tóth, dean of the faculty of history of Budapest University, breathed his last breath. Together with two other professors (who were also wounded), he was about to hand a petition from the students to the leadership, and in the exchange of fire was fatally hit by eight bullets.

What had happened in Academy Street? A company of border guards from Pécs in Southwest Hungary had been ordered to reinforce the guards at party headquarters. To get through the throng of demonstrators, the border guards, hated for being part of the Interior Ministry, removed their green-striped uniform caps and green epaulets as a precautionary measure. As their truck emerged in Academy Street, the Soviet tank crews and other guards promptly opened fire at the assumed insurgents. Four— according to other statements 10—of these Hungarian guards were fatally hit and a further 28 to 30 seriously wounded.[8]

At its hastily continued meeting after the bloody midday incident, the Politburo yielded to the demands of the crowd. At 12:32 p.m. the radio announced that the Politburo of the state party had replaced Ernő Gerő as first secretary with János Kádár.[9] That was a political bombshell and an extremely visible concession to the Hungarian people: the hated Gerő had been sacrificed. Still, Hungarian historians of the period are split on the question whether the bloodbath gave the crucial impetus for the changing of the guard or whether his dismissal had been previously decided in the Kremlin.[10] Be that as it may, the fact remains that all of the most important decisions during the first week of the revolution came too late. The radio speeches by the newly elected Kádár and by Imre Nagy that were broadcast three hours after the announcement of the change did not achieve any sustainable effect. Although Nagy had for the first time promised that the government would initiate negotiations with the Soviet Union about the withdrawal of Soviet troops from Hungary, the hoped-for political change failed to materialize.[11]

While the Hungarian public, more than ever outraged and agitated, gave every necessary moral and political support to the insurrectionist groups that sprang up like mushrooms after a spring rain, the announcement by Nagy, at least in the beginning, fell flat practically without any echo.[12] On the other hand, the two Soviet leaders in Budapest were furious, as they had not been told of this in advance, and because previously they had argued against such suggestions from some Politburo members on the specious grounds that such a step would mean an invasion by American troops.[13] The next day they were informed by a contrite Gerő and Kádár that they too had agreed to the announcement made by Nagy, because the working masses and some important party organizations had also demanded the withdrawal of Soviet troops.[14]

The following days showed that genuine changes in politics were taking place long before they were visible to all. The fact that the Communist Party leadership in a historically very short period, barely five days, underwent a seemingly absurd metamorphosis from damning the "counterrevolutionary" (at first even "Fascist") rebellion to acknowledging it as a national and democratic popular movement would not have been possible without the demands from below, the pressure from the armed insurgents and the revolutionary self-governing bodies spread all over the country. On the other hand, the revolutionaries could not have achieved the political victory without a turnabout in the power center of the party. Although the emerging dichotomy of power reflected the balance of power, yet one constant remained: Hungary was basically a part of the Soviet empire, and its mighty machinery of repression could theoretically be called into action anytime for the preservation of the power structure. At the same time, the Kremlin's agreement had to be won over and over again for making concessions to the rebels.[15]

During the first five days of the uprising, the party's leading bodies were practically permanently in session. The first and foremost question under consideration was the character of the revolution itself as a process of radical, even violent changes. Next were the causes and effects of the changing balance of power, which were not always easy to see through. And finally, the risk of remedying grievances in a dictatorial system and in a critical situation, which could backfire and accelerate the fermentation.

The conflict of opinions and power struggle were not merely about individual ambition and personal power. At issue also were trendsetting political notions: the question of whether reforms in the framework of a proletarian dictatorship would still be possible, or whether these processes, under pressure from the revolt of the street, the public emotions, and fear of treachery, would break through the framework set from above and outside—the Soviet factor!

During the decisive meetings of the party committees, which usually took place at night and in the morning in the presence of Mikoyan and Suslov, Imre Nagy managed to achieve a political breakthrough with the help of Kádár, who had been elected chairperson of the newly formed party Presidium. The most important concessions could already be broadcast on that 28 October, a Sunday. Supported by the radical oppositionists (Gimes, Donáth, Losonczy, Szilágyi, and so on) and as a result of the slow but inexorable transformation of Nagy's attitude, the armed uprising managed in 120 hours to force a change that hitherto had appeared almost impossible.

At 1:20 p.m. the prime minister announced an immediate and general cease-fire, which was confirmed on the radio by the ministers of defense and the interior. The new, so-called national government that had been sworn in, meanwhile, differed from the previous one inasmuch as it included two well-known persecuted politicians of the former Smallholders' Party: its former secretary-general Béla Kovács, who had been abducted nine years earlier by the Soviets and released only in April 1956, as minister for agriculture, and the former president of the republic, Zoltán Tildy (who for eight years was under house arrest), as minister of state. The government also comprised two popular Old Communists disciplined by the Stalinists: the internationally renowned philosopher György (better known in the Germanized form: Georg) Lukács as minister of culture and Zoltán Vas, in charge of supply. Of course, the demands of the freedom fighters and the revolutionary intellectuals went far beyond such cosmetic personnel changes.

Yet the speech,[1] whose text had already been composed in part by Nagy's close associates gathered in party headquarters, signified the beginning of a historic turnaround:

1. to assess the uprising not as a counterrevolution but as a "great, national and democratic movement";

2. the announcement of an unconditional general cease-fire; an amnesty for participants in the uprising;

3. negotiations with the insurgents;

4. the dissolution of the State Security forces after the consolidation;[2]

5. the establishment of a national guard; and

6. the immediate withdrawal of Soviet troops from Budapest and negotiations for the withdrawal of Soviet troops from Hungary.

In addition, Imre Nagy promised that the government would introduce a bill in Parliament to have the Kossuth coat of arms reinstated as the national emblem and the fifteenth of March declared a national holiday. This program essentially complied with the Technical University students' sixteen points. However, since 22 October, developments had gone way beyond this framework. That is why what Nagy did *not* mention was so important. He did not say anything about a multiparty system and free, secret elections. And it was precisely these and full Soviet withdrawal from the entire country that the newly formed Revolutionary Council of Hungarian Intellectuals demanded.

With the dissolution of the party's top bodies and the Soviet-organized departure to Moscow that same evening of the leadership's most dangerous Stalinists—with Gerő and Hegedüs in the fore—Nagy gained more room to maneuver. With his move from the Academy Street party headquarters to Parliament, central power effectively passed from the party leadership to the government. Besides, now his closest associates took over the organization of his secretariat and the most important staff positions.

At any rate, in the morning of the twenty-ninth, according to his first biographer and eyewitness, Tibor Méray, Nagy appeared "bright, relaxed, confident—and impatient." He urged the delegation of the revolutionary intellectuals to restraint. The fact that for the first time since the twenty-third he was able to spend the night at home, change his clothing at last, and recapitulate with his wife—his only real intimate—the turbulent events of the past five days palpably stabilized his bearing, both mentally and physically.[3] The prime minister's expectations that the political breakthrough would herald a fundamental consolidation of the tangled situation soon proved to be a dangerous illusion. From the very first Nagy had only quite limited elbow room. Although the Soviet leadership had grudgingly accepted the line he was representing, Mikoyan made it clear at the Politburo meeting of the party that was in the throes of dissolution that this limit must not be exceeded: "If there are further concessions tomorrow, there will be no stopping things."[4] The discussions at the long session of the party Presidium in Moscow about the situation in Hungary on the day of the significant speech by Nagy reflected the growing apprehension, the deep split of that body, and, above all, Khrushchev's bewilderment: "There are two possibilities. The government acts, and we help it. That could end early. Or Nagy turns against us, demands the cease-fire and the withdrawal of the troops; then comes the capitulation. Or the establishment of a committee that takes power in its hands—that would be the worst variant."[5]

However, the next forty-eight hours showed that a consolidation on this basis was not possible. All of the insurgent groups, the proliferating workers' councils in the large concerns, the revolutionary organs of self-administration in the provinces, and the students and intellectuals demanded the end of the one-party system, the immediate dissolution of the State Security forces, and the full withdrawal of Soviet troops. The negotiations with the insurgents that had started in the meantime came to nothing. No one laid down his arms. On the contrary, the number of armed insurgents grew steadily. At the same time the inexorable disintegration of the demoralized party and state apparatus continued relentlessly. The exciting news from the capital mobilized people in the entire country. György Litván, the well-known historian of the revolution, has refuted a number of myths circulating about 1956,[6] among them the one about the "revolutionary town and the peaceful countryside." Impressive personalities with leadership qualities arose who before long headed the local movements in important municipal and industrial centers such as Győr, Miskolc, and Debrecen. Thus, for example, Rudolf Földvári, the Borsod County first secretary of the party, led a delegation to Budapest as early as 25 October to talk to Nagy in favor of radical measures. In Győr they even founded a supraregional amalgamation of the local revolutionary organs, the Trans-Danubian National Council, which exerted political pressure on the central leadership, and personally on Nagy.

Senseless and provocative endeavors to set up a kind of counter-government were thwarted by the prudence of the council's chairman, Attila Szigethy, and the workers' councils of Győr. His colleague, the theater director Gábor Földes, made every effort to prevent further bloodshed after the massacre on the twenty-sixth in front of the barracks at Mosonmagyaróvár. The high school teacher Árpád Brusznyai has to be mentioned here as one of the capable persons; as the chairman of the Veszprém County Revolutionary Council, he used his influence to keep the peace and prevent violence. In the provinces and in Budapest there were thus potential leaders who—had they but more time granted to them—could have played important roles in political life on the national level as well. At the same time one should not underrate the political pressure on the government of Nagy by the regional self-governing bodies legitimized by the revolution.

Like scenes from a screenplay, similar revolutionary incidents were played out in towns and villages all over the country.[7] They started with a mass rally by students and other young people. This usually took place before the local buildings of the State Security and the police, the party committee and the town council, as well as the jail. These were the symbols of the party state. The crowd demanded the disarmament and dissolution of the State Security Service, the removal of the symbols of authority (red star), and the release of political prisoners. The demonstrators then proceeded to the Soviet war memorials. Their removal was an expression of spiritual liberation and the aspiration for independence. The next goal was the army barracks, where they demanded that the soldiers change sides and supply them with weapons for self-defense. Finally the mass rally ended, mostly at the main square, often with a reading of the most important demands and sometimes with the improvised election of delegates, who were to negotiate with the incumbent representatives of state power. Even the fusillades of machine guns and submachine guns by the State Security and army units in forty-five localities between 26 and 29 October could not avert the collapse of the old order.

As far as the revolutionary committees, national committees, and other new organs of self-administration were concerned, it has been established that these were founded in 2,804 of the 3,419 administrative communal units. The dynamics of the revolution are demonstrated by the fact that 63 percent of the revolutionary institutions had been created before the twenty-eighth, and altogether 82 percent by 30 October. In some provincial towns and in the smaller communities, the change came about quickly and without violence. The following statistics show that the resentment against the officeholders of the old regime and against the Soviets was very strong: In 1,170 communities in 348 cases, employees of the local administrative councils were dismissed, in 315 cases the persons in charge were let go, and in 215 cases the files were burned. In 681 settlements the demonstrators damaged symbols of authority (red stars, Stalin or Lenin statues), 393 Soviet war memorials (and three Bulgarian) were destroyed or damaged, and in 122 communities books were burned.

Research shows therefore that there was no question of a "peaceful" countryside, even though in most cases there were either no bloody confrontations or they led immediately to the collapse of the old system. The chairmen or secretaries of local party organizations and the district or local councils either escaped or sought to adapt to the new situation. Within a few days a younger leading stratum emerged. Social scientists estimate that several thousand people participated countrywide in the various revolutionary organs.[8]

The rebels experienced and effected a historic change, particularly in the capital. Five days earlier who would have imagined that the "counter-revolutionaries," threatened with death under martial law, would negotiate not only with generals and ministers about laying down their arms but also in Parliament with the prime minister? As the reform Communist Ferenc Donáth observed in his recollections about the last session of the Central Committee: "During these five days the decisive bankruptcy of the party leadership, tarred with the same brush as Rákosi, became clear to everyone. It also became questionable whether the power of the working class could at all be maintained. The party fell utterly to pieces during these days. It had lost its influence not only over the masses but also over the working class."[9]

In the course of the following days it became obvious also to Nagy that the consolidation in the country depended in part on the attitude of the insurgents and in part on the government's control over the state apparatus and the armed forces. His biographer János M. Rainer justly criticizes him in that, at least at first, he was occupied more with the neutralization of the armed opponents than with creating a new armed force.[10]

This grave mistake soon had dire consequences. The army's leadership was disoriented, and Interior Minister Münnich caused utmost confusion at a conference in the ministry—whether unconsciously or in the light of later developments perhaps on purpose—by contradictory explanations about the future of the State Security apparatus. On the one hand he praised the State Security's militia for its "steadfastness in the fight against hostile elements," while on the other he announced the dissolution of the State Security Service (ÁVH); at the same time he told those present to remain at their posts. Yet over the radio the minister did not say a word about the generally desired disbanding of the ÁVH. Although Münnich spoke about the creation of a new police and militia, he did not do anything tangible in this regard.

The three Soviet representatives—Mikoyan, Suslov, and the KGB chief Serov—had portrayed the process of the party's and state structure's breakup so pessimistically in their last reports of 29 and 30 October to the Soviet party leadership that in retrospect it seems surprising that the decision on the second Soviet intervention was made only on 31 October and not sooner. While Nagy was spending the night at home and did not achieve any results regarding the disarming of the rebels, reported the Soviet politicians, two party committees and the offices and printing presses of the *Szabad Nép* were occupied by the insurgents. The Hungarian Army had so far exhibited a wait-and-see attitude; there existed a substantial risk that in the event of a deployment against the rebels, the units could change sides. For the time being no further Soviet units should be sent to Hungary as long as the Hungarian troops did not adopt a hostile attitude.

The last report to Moscow leaves it open as to how grave the Soviet politician deemed the deterioration of the situation. The fact that in the last sentence Mikoyan and Suslov recommended the immediate dispatch to Hungary of Marshal Konev, commander in chief of the Warsaw Pact forces, was an ominous warning sign.[11]

The decisive days between 30 October and 2 November were characterized by the almost permanent interplay between the efforts for political consolidation from above and the attempts at pressure from below for the fast realization of national demands. Contemporary witnesses who lived through these days and the researchers who hour by hour were able to follow events reflected in the radio broadcasts and the new independent newspapers are overwhelmingly of the opinion that what was happening was a revolutionary process and not a single symbolic act.

The unanimous demands for free elections and for the introduction of a multiparty system, expressed not only by the armed insurgent groups but also by all the revolutionary and workers' councils in the entire country, forced a breathtakingly rapid change, an actual breakthrough toward democracy. At 3:24 p.m. on Tuesday, 30 October, precisely a week after the start of the student demonstrations, the prime minister announced in a brief radio broadcast the abolition of the one-party system and the return to the government of the four coalition parties of 1945. It was now that Nagy spoke for the first time of a revolution and the recognition of all the democratic self-governing bodies that had arisen in the course of the revolution. He also informed the people that the national government would request the immediate withdrawal of Soviet troops from Budapest and would forthwith commence negotiations with the Soviet government for their further withdrawal from all of Hungary. The break with the one-party system was arranged with the Presidium of the party and the Soviet emissaries. Following Nagy, Tildy spoke in the name of the Small Landholders, Erdei for the Peasant Party, and Kádár for the Communists. The Social Democrats (who had been forced to merge with the Communists in 1948) resolved that day to reestablish their party, and a place was reserved for them in the seven-member cabinet.[1]

The enormous implications of the party dictatorship's capitulation became evident within the next few hours. In the past few days thousands of prisoners had already been released. During the revolution a total of 9,962 common criminals and 3,324 political prisoners had been let loose or released.[2] Directly after the speech by Nagy, the Revolutionary National Defense Committee was set up at the Ministry of Defense, a number of pro-Soviet generals were dismissed from command of the army, and a decision was made to have the armed units of the ÁVH disarmed by the army. At the same time Soviet tanks and troops began their withdrawal from Budapest. The focus now shifted to the reestablishment of order in the capital through the formation of new forces of law and order and the incorporation of the rebel groups into the planned National Guard. Cessation of the general political strike, recognition and integration of the workers' councils and other democratic organs into a new power structure, and the guarantee of freedom of the press—these were the most significant further factors of the desired consolidation. In his report published on 1 November, the correspondent of the *New York Times*, John MacCormac, drew the right conclusion: "Now that the Russians have left Budapest no one seems to know who rules Hungary. But everyone knows it is not the Communists. The Communist Party itself appears to be in a state of terror." Anna Kéthly, who two days earlier had been elected president of the refounded Social Democratic Party, expressed herself similarly at the Vienna meeting of the bureau of the Socialist International: "No one knows, not even Nagy or Tildy, how to create order in this situation, and actually one does not even know who holds power."[3]

It is well known from the history of revolutions that after a lightning-fast collapse of a lengthy (and on top of it foreign-controlled) despotism, a power vacuum is inevitable. Still, in a chaotic and fundamentally suspicious atmosphere, surprisingly the Nagy government managed speedily to reach seemingly sustainable agreements with the insurgents about the establishment of a national guard. Besides the already mentioned reform Communist police chief, Sándor Kopácsi, two exceptional professional officers played prominent roles in this process. They were General Béla Király and Colonel Pál Maléter, who, through a bizarre upheaval of history, overnight became historical figures. The careers of both men were as convoluted as a labyrinth. The flood of publicity surrounding them not only during the revolution but for decades after proves the significance of their roles.

Only in such incongruous times could the former general Béla Király, who had been released only recently after a five-year term in prison, become within one day chairman of the Revolutionary Special Forces Committee and the Revolutionary Home Defense Committee, commander in chief of the National Guard, and military commander of Budapest. The exceptionally talented Király (born in 1912) was a graduate of the Ludovika Military Academy and a general staff officer during the Horthy era.[4] Just before the end of the war, the highly decorated Király and his units changed to the Soviet side. After his escape from a prisoner-of-war camp, he joined the Hungarian Communist Party as early as 1945. Eventually he became commander of the infantry and in 1950 commander of the Army Academy, with the rank of major general. The marriage of the high-ranking officer to the niece and later foster daughter of the rightist prewar prime minister Gyula Gömbös most probably contributed to his arrest in 1951 (simultaneously with a number of other high-ranking prewar officers). He was sentenced to death on the usual trumped-up charges, but on appeal this was changed to life imprisonment.

After his release at the beginning of September 1956, his friend Márta Sárközi, daughter of the world-famous Hungarian dramatist Ferenc Molnár, who had excellent connections to numerous artists and intellectuals, found him a job as a gardener. Király immediately sought full rehabilitation by way of a retrial and wrote to the minister of defense. During the solemn reburial of the generals executed after the Rajk trial on 13 October, Király, who was escorting one of the widows, was greeted demonstratively by numerous high-ranking officers. He also had a brief conversation there with his former fellow officer Ferenc Jánosi, the son-in-law of Imre Nagy. As a result of a medical examination after his five years in prison, he had to undergo a minor surgical procedure, of all things on the eve of the uprising. He listened to Nagy's important radio speech in the army hospital and that same day, 28 October, wrote a letter to Jánosi, in which he offered "all his energy, enthusiasm and solidarity to Nagy and his program." Just two days later he was picked up from the hospital, given a change of clothing, and taken to Kopácsi at police headquarters. That happened not because of his letter, though, but as the result of a chain of peculiar coincidences, which characterized not only this particular instance during the chaotic and unforgettable days of the October revolution. The man who made the general's cometlike career possible was Vilmos Oláh, a young insurgent who was present everywhere during the first days of the uprising; he was there at the siege of the Radio Building and, brandishing a blood-soaked flag, at the head of the protest march of 25 October. Detained by the army, he was sent to the military hospital on 28 October, together with other arrested freedom fighters, to transport Soviet and Hungarian corpses. Here he met the slowly recuperating Király and conveyed to him that "the people" requested that he take over the post of chief of the general staff, to which Király consented.[5] Earlier, as leader of the students, Oláh is said to have kept the medical staff up-to-date on the state of affairs at the request of the hospital's head. On 30 October Oláh volunteered for the National Guard at police headquarters, where he informed Colonel Kopácsi about his "negotiations" with Király. He suggested that the general should be included in the guard. Kopácsi sent his liaison officer to the Defense Ministry to learn more about Király. Having received a positive assessment, Oláh was instructed with two other associates of Kopácsi to escort Király to police headquarters in an official car.

The appearance of the general was the watershed in the hitherto chaotic conference held by representatives of the insurgents, the police, and the army. He was immediately elected chairman of the conference by acclamation. Everybody acknowledged his personal charisma and leadership qualities, and he soon succeeded in working out a concept acceptable to all sides for the immediate measures that were required. The significance of the compromise that Király reached was that the insurgents were admitted to the newly established National Guard not singly but in groups under their own commanders, thus forming a decisive force in its units. The guard also accepted students and workers into its ranks. The new Revolutionary Special Forces Committee was to supervise all army and police units in charge of maintaining law and order. The elected commanders of the National Guard were to make up half of the membership of the new committee. At the same time only those persons who were registered members of the National Guard would be permitted to bear weapons. This political concept was endorsed in writing on 30 October by Imre Nagy after a discussion with a delegation led by Király, and late that evening the radio broadcast the creation of the Revolutionary Special Forces Committee. The new organs served as a recognition of the revolution's legitimacy as well as the underpinning of the government. According to a compilation, the committee issued some 18,500 guard identity cards up to 3 November.[6]

The seemingly complicated structure of the three new organs (Revolutionary Special Forces Committee, Revolutionary Home Defense Committee, and National Guard) was simplified by the fact that General Király virtually concentrated the management of all these institutions in his own hands. Prime Minister Nagy arranged for his full rehabilitation on 31 October, including the award of his old rank of major general, at the same time appointing him military commander of the capital. This cometlike ascendancy of the "gardener" to key military figure of the revolution would, of course, have been hardly likely without the fortuitous mediating role of the above-mentioned Vilmos Oláh.

Who in fact was this young man? Many freedom fighters remembered him because of his conspicuous looks. Oláh, with his gold-rimmed spectacles, pockmarked face, red beard, and limp, was at one stage an unskilled laborer who had to interrupt his theatrical studies because of a criminal record for embezzlement. At the time of the uprising, the twenty-nine-year-old was a freshman high school student doing an evening course in Budapest. During the turbulent final days of the revolution, Oláh was regarded by all as Király's closest confidant. He accompanied him to the Parliament in the delegation to see the prime minister, and it was he who had Nagy's declaration typed up. He became leader of one of the four subcommittees of the Revolutionary Special Forces Committee and liaised by special telephones and radio transmitting sets with the insurgents and police stations, the Ministry of Defense, the Parliament, and the radio station. With Kopácsi and Király, he negotiated as a "student leader," and at police headquarters he was a roving "police officer"; many believed he was a major of the police. Oláh was not a con man; he did not harm anybody and did not gain any financial advantage. The author László Gyurkó, who researched his case, is probably correct in his reasoning: Having at last found his dream role, Oláh played it with such talent and intelligence that everyone, from Király to a string of generals and politicians, believed him.[7]

Suddenly, practically at the same time as Király, a much younger professional officer stepped into the center of events and even more into the glaring limelight of the Hungarian and foreign media. The uncanny biographical and historical metamorphosis of the thirty-nine-year-old Colonel Pál Maléter from a lowly administrator to hero of the uprising, first as deputy minister of defense and finally as minister of defense, forms the core of the "Maléter legend." His unusual story, which has a tragic ending, is also the paradigm of a man tossed around by the vagaries of history.

As we have seen in the description of the Corvin Passage insurgents' successful actions, the massive stronghold of the Kilián Barracks at the intersection of Üllői Avenue and the boulevard opposite the Corvin Passage was in an extremely important strategic position along the usual route of the Soviet troops. The barracks came under periodic attacks by the insurgents, who aimed to capture weapons and to fortify the side wing at the crossing for attacks against Soviet tanks. Only the central section was occupied by three battalions of unarmed so-called auxiliary soldiers, who worked on building sites. There were twenty-four such battalions in the Hungarian Army at the time (altogether thirteen thousand men), whose service entailed working in mines and at construction jobs. Their commander was Colonel Pál Maléter. At the time of the telephone call for help by Lajos Csiba, the officer in command of the barracks, Maléter was on duty at the Ministry of Defense.[8] The chief of staff ordered Maléter, a trained tank officer, to relieve the siege of the Kilián Barracks with five tanks and a company of students of the Artillery Academy. He was to liquidate the armed insurgents at the boulevard side of the building and to secure the barracks. The colonel went to the Thirty-third Tank Regiment of Esztergom, which was stationed near the Danube at the Margaret Bridge, and ordered their commander to give him five tanks. Maléter dictated a very fast tempo in order to drive unhindered through the city to the barracks. For unknown reasons, two of the tanks dropped behind en route. The company of officer cadets was supposed to join the tanks at Üllői Avenue to act as escorts and in due course to occupy the barracks. However, in no time a huge crowd of protesters gathered around the tanks and the cadets. The latter refused, probably for fear of the insurgents' barrage of fire, to obey Maléter's orders to attack and returned with their commander to the academy. The three tanks with Maléter in the lead then drove to the barracks under heavy fire without an infantry escort. Here the insurgents attacked the three tanks from neighboring houses and tried to put them out of action with

Molotov cocktails and hand grenades. Two of the tanks caught fire and had to retreat spewing smoke.

To shield himself from the Molotov cocktails, Colonel Maléter ordered his driver to slow down in front of the barracks, swivel the tank, and reverse into the main gate. However, the entrance was too narrow, and the T-34 got stuck between the columns. The insurgents fired their machine and submachine guns at the paralyzed monster. It returned the fire, but Maléter could not leave the tank because of the shooting. He therefore asked an officer from the barracks, who had to crawl to the tank because of the heavy firing, to request help from the Ministry of Defense.

Maléter took over command of the Kilián Barracks in a particularly chaotic situation. By the time he arrived with his tanks, the massacre at Parliament Square had already begun, and when he got stuck in the gateway with his T-34, Gerő had just been deposed as first secretary. At 2 p.m. Maléter, still sitting in his tank, received news of a cease-fire ordered by the chief of staff and a new amnesty offer to the insurgents, as well as the instruction conspicuously to display a national flag without the Soviet star.

The colonel asked for such a flag, which he stuck out through the tank's trapdoor, waving it a few times. Shouts came from the barracks: "There's a cease-fire! Cease-fire!" The insurgents stopped the shooting. Maléter climbed slowly and carefully out of the tank and stepped out onto Üllői Avenue. There he stood now, almost six feet and six inches tall, a stately apparition in uniform in front of the main gate, next to the T-34 tank. Then, within a second, something happened that his biographer called "a miracle." From the side streets and the neighboring houses a large crowd gathered around the tank. Cheers rang out: "The army is with us! Hurrah! The army is ours!" And with that the armed civilians raised the surprised colonel, who towered above them, onto their shoulders. Maléter announced the cease-fire: If the barracks were not attacked, the soldiers would not use their weapons either. He ordered his escorts to immobilize the tank, take the ammunition with them, and aim their guns backward. He also ordered the Hungarian flag to be hoisted on the barracks and the tank, with the Soviet emblem cut out, of course.

Those minutes saw the start of a unique chain reaction of misunderstandings, accidents, conscious and unconscious assumptions, and finally misleading press reports that soon catapulted this hitherto unknown, cautious, and rather introverted officer into the center of general attention. Born into an intellectual family in what was to become Czechoslovakia, Maléter came to Budapest only at age twenty-one after an interrupted medical course at Prague University. However, he always wanted to be a soldier and eventually graduated from the Hungarian Ludovika Academy. As a lieutenant in an armored unit, he was taken prisoner by the Russians in May 1944. After a political retraining course, he was deployed in September as the commander of a Hungarian-Russian partisan unit parachuted into Transylvania, where he saw action just before the end of the war. Maléter always stressed—even during his interrogation after his arrest thirteen years later—that he had never switched sides to the Soviets, but wanted only to fight against the German occupiers. After the war he joined the Communist Party and remained a professional officer, now serving under the Red Star.

During the four or five days after his arrival at the barracks, suddenly two Maléters were born, as it were. The real Colonel Maléter endeavored, as far as was possible, to hold the barracks as ordered against the insurgents and to protect his subordinates and their families, many of them women and children, who had sought refuge from the Soviet tanks' grenade fire in the cellars of the central section. As an efficient officer, he also tried to clear the side wings at the intersection of the boulevard and Üllői Avenue and at the narrow Liliom Street, used as workers' hostels, of insurgents. The commander of the barracks, Csiba, later described the situation as "total pandemonium. One of our officers was shot by a Soviet soldier, another by the insurgents, while our barracks were under fire by Soviet tanks. Who could have known his way about in such a situation? It was more than tragic. Then on 28 October, at 1:00 p.m., the government ordered a cease-fire. The army was to remain in its emplacements and only to shoot in self-defense. They called the insurgents patriots. So we had been fighting against patriots. That created a totally new situation for us."[9] Maléter made direct contact with the commanders of the Corvinists—László Iván Kovács and Gergely Pongrátz—only after the turnaround on 28 October.

But there was another Maléter as well: the hero of the legend. At first he seemed suspect in the eyes of those officers who had observed from the distance of Üllői Avenue on 25 October how a large crowd of people had paid homage to the colonel in front of the barracks, while the units led by these officers—ordered to relieve the same barracks—were being fiercely attacked by the insurgents. It was the same company of cadets who earlier had refused to give Maléter's tanks protection; it had been deployed again and had lost one dead and seven wounded. Of the four Soviet tanks sent to support them, three were set on fire with their crews by the insurgents. The fact that the unit was shot at also from the barracks' Liliom Street wing reinforced the suspicion that Maléter had changed sides. After their withdrawal to the Artillery Academy, these officers reported all of this to the Ministry of Defense. There were yet other suspicious incidents. As it happened, the barracks' telephone number had been changed only a few days earlier and switched over to the district command office. During the following days Maléter was called on that number again and again. The district command instructed two of its officers to take these calls apparently in the name of Maléter. The insurgents gave information, requested advice and instructions. The officers who answered these calls reported everything to their superiors. This gave the impression, which the insurgents probably also spread around, that they had spoken with the leader of the uprising in the barracks, Colonel Maléter.

At the same time Maléter, who was unaware of these rumors, complained on several occasions to the Ministry of Defense that the barracks were being shelled by Soviet tanks, although he and his soldiers were doing everything to put a stop to attacks from the barracks. He did not know that thirty or more soldiers had secretly joined the insurgents and were taking over the rooms of the huge building complex one by one. Despite Maléter's passionate protests, the massive building was repeatedly shot at by passing Soviet tanks, which had been attacked by the freedom fighters from various improvised bases. Prior to the announcement of the cease-fire and Imre Nagy's speech, a message was broadcast by the radio station at 11 to the insurgents "also in the Kilián Barracks." Maléter and Csiba called the Ministry of Defense several times to protest against "this disgraceful canard."

But this is not the end of the legend. The revolution needed a hero, and the tall, dashing colonel decorated with a Soviet medal was perfectly suited for this role without any effort on his part. The superficiality and sensation-mongering of the newly established independent papers also played a significant part. Striking photos and TV pictures showed the barracks and its ravaged surroundings with a number of burned-out tanks and armored vehicles in front of the building. This gave the impression that the center of the uprising and the battles with the Soviets was the barracks and not the Corvin Passage.

Unfortunately, we cannot pass over the fact that the late Péter Gosztonyi, a well-known Hungarian military historian, residing in Bern since 1957, was perhaps the key architect of this legend. He had served in the barracks on 25 October as a lieutenant in the reserve. At that time he disseminated the Maléter myth in a few articles and then in several books. During that brief period of confusion, other journalists and a few foreign correspondents kept embroidering the Maléter myth in line with the well-worn model of tabloids, whose traces still exist in quite a few books on 1956. Only the émigré barracks commander Lajos Csiba's records published abroad in 1988 and the first Maléter biography of 1995 succeeded in replacing the fictitious Maléter with the real one.

After 28 October Maléter himself was, of course, also involved in the endeavors at cooperation between the insurgents and the Nagy government. Gergely Pongrátz, the leader of the Corvinists, turned against Maléter early on for reasons of distrust and envy; he even tried to torpedo his appointment as minister of defense. This was partly the reason for the dismissal of the first commander of the Corvinists, László Iván Kovács, who from the very first was sympathetic toward Maléter, was willing to cooperate, and even supplied him with bodyguards. During the 31 October founding conference of the Revolutionary Special Forces Committee at the Kilián Barracks, Gergely Pongrátz openly and viciously attacked the host, Maléter, for having ordered the Corvinists to be shot at and for other alleged misdeeds.[10] Maléter rejected the censure, referring to his duties as an officer. Nor did he have anything to do with the so-called advertising campaign concerning his person and the barracks, which Pongrátz so sharply criticized.

In the evening of 30 October Maléter was summoned to Prime Minister Nagy and State Minister Tildy. In 1948 he had been commander of the then president of the republic Zoltán Tildy's bodyguard. Having informed the two politicians about the defense of the barracks and his endeavors regarding a cease-fire, Maléter, who by then had become a popular figure and was considered loyal to the government, was appointed deputy minister of defense and on 3 November minister of defense. Not only Gergely Pongrátz but also General Béla Király opined in their memoirs that many freedom fighters were skeptical about Maléter because, unlike Kopácsi, he had not belonged to the early group of followers of Nagy and because he was supposed to have given the order to shoot at the insurgents.[11]

Yet others regarded General Király as an unreliable character. Shortly before the Soviet intervention, Colonel Szűcs, who was later arrested together with Maléter, even suggested that Király be discharged because he was too untrustworthy and allegedly attempted to smuggle Horthyist officers into the ministry.[12] The covert rivalry between the two most important officers with such different careers, in Nagy's close circle, was unpleasant for the prime minister, but it did not play a significant role in those last dramatic days. Maléter's appointment as minister of defense undoubtedly reflected his preference for the former partisan.

In conclusion, one more word about the Maléter myth. It was uncannily characteristic that after the defeat of the revolution the Kádár regime used the same legend in the death sentence pronounced on Maléter in 1958, namely that he had switched over to the insurgents' side long before the announcement of the cease-fire. None of this, however, changes the fact that—for whatever reason—the most popular man of the revolution did everything to foster consolidation after the turnaround, and that he had behaved courageously after he had been trapped by the Soviets. Part of the Maléter legend, spread by some of the freedom and resistance fighters, was the belief that he had been able to escape from captivity and was already organizing resistance in the mountains![13]

The decisive days between the revolution's ostensible victory and the second Soviet intervention were marked by a peculiar ambiguity. The Nagy government endeavored to gain the people's confidence by a number of gestures, at the same time pushing ahead to achieve consolidation. It reached agreements not only with the revolutionary and the grassroots democratic organizations but also with the newly reconstituted former coalition parties. Yet precisely these partners were the ones who speeded up the tempo by maximalist demands in order to exact more and more concessions from a basically powerless government.

The state party was by now merely a shadow of the old tightly organized cadre party, and it was soon decided to establish a new labor party. The other so-called coalition parties were still only shadow parties because they did not yet have organizations at their disposal. The State Security (ÁVH), the dreaded pillar of the dictatorship, was first demoralized and then virtually demolished. The National Guard existed only in a rudimentary form. The army was also largely paralyzed and was regarded with undisguised suspicion by both the insurgents and the Soviets. The police played only a marginal role all through the revolution.

Under these circumstances, for the time being Imre Nagy could offer only rhetorical solutions and try to convince the numerous delegations of workers' and revolutionary councils from the provinces and large firms, as well as the representatives of the insurgents, of the practical steps needed to achieve consolidation. In the evening of 30 October alone, Nagy, together with Kádár, Tildy, and Erdei, received no fewer than ten important delegations. Notwithstanding the announcement made just then about the introduction of the multiparty system, the delegates demanded almost everything straightaway: free elections, freely elected trade unions, secession from the Warsaw Pact, declaration of neutrality, withdrawal of Soviet troops from the country, and the removal from the government of the old discredited Rákosi-era ministers. A variety of organizations, among them the Trans-Danubian National Council (Győr), made similar demands. Nagy's personality, determination, and sincerity, coupled with his plea for "a little patience," made a deep impression on most of his interlocutors. The day after the 31 October meeting of the Trans-Danubian delegation led by Attila Szigethy with the head of the government the regional National Council gave its vote of confidence to the government and resolutely rejected any efforts at establishing a Trans-Danubian alternative government.[1]

Although the revolution defeated the Communist Party dictatorship, the final victory depended on the outcome of the national War of Independence. In its solemn declaration of 30 October, the Soviet government admitted the mistakes of its policy vis-à-vis its allies. At the same time it promised not only to withdraw its troops from Budapest but to commence negotiations with the Hungarian government and other member states of the Warsaw Pact about the presence of Soviet troops on Hungarian territory. This pronouncement elicited great joy in Hungary. Even the cautious Nagy, to whom Ambassador Andropov formally handed the text in Parliament, was so thrilled that in an improvised speech in the early afternoon of 31 October he announced to demonstrators on Parliament Square the "triumph" and the "victory of the revolutionary fight." "We shall not tolerate any interference into Hungary's interior matters.... We are experiencing the first day of the victory of our sovereignty and our independence.... Long live the independent, free, democratic Republic of Hungary! Long live the free Hungary!"[2]

Appearances were deceptive. The Soviet Presidium had unanimously decided in the morning hours of that day—in stark contrast to the spirit of just twenty-four hours earlier—to crush the Hungarian Revolution by the force of arms. Khrushchev was so preoccupied with the whole problem in Hungary that according to his memoirs, when he finally got to bed after the all-night session of 30 to 31 October where he had suggested a change in the earlier assessment of the situation and the adoption of a military solution, "it kept [him] from being able to sleep."[3] The real causes of this about-face in the Kremlin are still a bone of contention among historians and experts on Hungarian events. However, before we attempt to look into the details and consequences of this fateful decision, let us first examine the contradictory events in Hungary and above all in Budapest.

In the last days of October, Budapest was the scene of indescribable joy at the manifest breakthrough achieved by the revolution. When discussing the inconceivably rapid collapse of the Hungarian Workers' Party (what the Communist Party was called after 1948), one has to conjure up its incredibly central position in the system of government. The party, with its membership of 800,000 to 900,000 (the fluctuation was due to the various "vigilance campaigns"), had 6,225 full-time political party workers, 9,966 administrative staff, and 1,079 technical staff. There were a further 1,400 political employees of the Union of Working Youth alone, plus the apparatus of the trade unions and the women's and children's organizations. Incidentally, the number of people employed by the party-controlled state apparatus in 1955 amounted to 280,000—and that in a country of nine million inhabitants![4]

In his reminiscences Ferenc Donáth, the above-quoted reformer and farsighted thinker, posed the following question: "What does it imply if the working masses take up arms and fight with a weeklong general strike against a regime that has existed for eight years and where the power is applied in the name of the working class?"[5]

During those days many party activists from big concerns and offices were harassed, chased away, or mocked, while others tried, with or without success, to join the current victors. In his forced exile in the Romanian Sagov, Nagy was to write: "When I was placed at the head of the government, there was no longer a party behind me."[6] The party buildings in the capital's districts and in country towns were the political symbols of the party state, which until 28 October had called for a ruthless battle against the "counterrevolutionaries." That is why these institutions were consistently the targets of armed attacks.

In their articles for the two most influential Belgrade papers, two well-informed Yugoslav correspondents reported—as had their above-quoted American colleagues—the total disappearance of the state party. "Leftist groups are the least noticeable. First of all, the Hungarian Workers' Party seems not to exist," and "Disorder still prevails in the streets. In fact there is no real authority as yet, at least not a centralized one ... for the last two days no copies of the *Szabad Nép* appeared, the organ of the Hungarian Workers' Party. It is questionable whether it will be published at all any more."[7]

After lengthy discussions, the Politburo declared the old party dissolved on 31 October and founded a new one, the Hungarian Socialist Workers' Party. As far as its chances were concerned, no less a personality than the minister of culture since 27 October, the philosopher Georg Lukács, judged them with undisguised skepticism: "In free elections the Communists will obtain five percent of the vote, ten percent at the most. It is possible that they ... will go into opposition."[8]

Nonetheless, during these last October days, according to some of its functionaries, this disintegrating phantom party was supposed to organize armed "workers' guards" in the capital's districts—probably also with a view of integrating them into the future National Guard. Because of the chaos that already reigned at the time, the weapons and uniforms for the planned one-hundred- to-three-hundred-strong groups were either never delivered or looted en route by the insurgents. Eventually the party secretary of Budapest, Imre Mező, took over the organization of the armed workers' groups, and a military staff consisting of two army colonels became active in the premises of the party's Budapest Committee. Three Soviet tanks were stationed at first in front of the huge building, but at the request of the party secretary they were later ordered back to their base.[9]

After 23 October, a detachment of the Ministry of the Interior's State Security militia (ÁVH), consisting of forty-six recruits commanded by a lieutenant and a sublieutenant, had taken up positions to guard the building. Although Prime Minister Nagy had announced the disbanding of the State Security armed units and their entire hated apparatus on 28 October, this armed detachment remained in the building. Earlier the ÁVH soldiers and officers had sent out reconnaissance patrols to the neighborhood on several occasions and had taken several prisoners. On the morning of the thirtieth, an exchange of fire took place between insurgents, who wanted to check whether the State Security militia was still there, and the guard detail, some of whom had meanwhile changed into police uniforms. Rumor spread like wildfire that the building was the site of a secret State Security underground prison. At that all hell broke loose.

In no time at all several armed groups from farther away joined the attack on the building complex, which was situated on one side of the large, open, tree- and shrub-lined Republic Square; at the other side stood the Erkel Theater. Fighting became increasingly frenzied. The siege lasted three hours. Party Secretary Imre Mező—a prewar Communist and friend of János Kádár—and the officers telephoned everywhere in search of aid. The ÁVH soldiers even fired on Red Cross workers tending the wounded. Eventually several Hungarian tanks appeared in the square. They decided the battle, since they inadvertently fired at the party building instead of defending it. The defenders gave up the fight. Mező and two army colonels emerged from the badly damaged building carrying white flags of surrender. They were promptly shot.

The enraged crowd stormed into the shattered building and embarked on a carnage unparalleled in the history of the revolution. Militia soldiers in uniform were executed without further ado or brutally manhandled; one was strung by his feet from a tree, and an army officer had his heart cut out while he was still alive. Twenty insurgents lost their lives that day, most of them at Republic Square. Of the defenders, twenty-five fell during the siege, most of them victims of mob justice. Photos of this horrible massacre, especially of the execution of the guards and the mutilation of their corpses, appeared in the illustrated magazines *Life* and *Paris-Match* and soon after were reprinted worldwide. For decades after, Communist propaganda capitalized on these photos in order to conjure up the ghost of an extensive "counterrevolutionary" rightist terror.

An exceptionally bizarre footnote to this last bloody excess during the revolution was the daily atrocity stories in the press about the secret underground prisons in the party building, where hundreds of political prisoners were supposed to have been tortured by the ÁVH security forces or starved to death. An unimaginable wave of hysteria broke out. Thousands, perhaps tens of thousands, of people drifted to Republic Square to watch the search for the casemates with drills, dredging machines, and precision instruments. Among all the fictitious stories that were circulating, the report of the well-known British Hungarian humorist George Mikes achieved the greatest success in the world press; it was an eerie story that he had made up out of thin air.[10]

It has been proven that many escaped common-law criminals took part in the particularly abhorrent and bestial acts of revenge before the party building. Up until the time that the situation became consolidated at the beginning of November, altogether thirty-seven ÁVH officers and soldiers, policemen, and regular army soldiers were lynched. Some three hundred members of the State Security Service placed themselves under the protection of the National Guard or were captured by the insurgents; others went underground. Whole groups or units joined the Soviet troops or fled to neighboring Communist countries.[11]

The State Security Authority was from the very beginning a state within the state, the party dictatorship's most important instrument of terror, and via the Soviet agents and advisers also an obedient instrument of Soviet control. At first it was called State Security Department. The abbreviation of the Hungarian name (ÁVO) was linguistically so catchy that even though the dreaded institution was renamed in 1948 State Security Office (ÁVH), the abbreviation ÁVO remains the label attached to members of the secret police to this day, just as Stasi is the trademark of the East German Ministry of State Security.

During these chaotic days all identifiable members of the special armed force units were regarded as "ÁVO men." Because of this, innocents or uninvolved persons, such as ordinary soldiers of the militia (with blue caps and uniforms) and the border guard (with green caps and uniforms) who were only performing their compulsory military service in these units, were in danger of capture or even death. Apart from the reenlisted noncommissioned officers, the so-called Internal Special Forces (7,338 strong) and the border guard (15,233) were composed predominantly not of volunteers but of (politically carefully chosen) conscripts. The difference between these armed units that were under the aegis of the Interior Ministry and those that belonged to the army was a much stricter control by the party and more rigorous basic training. Naturally the secret police's monitoring of the militia soldiers was more thorough than that of the ordinary soldiers. I experienced this myself from November 1951 to the end of 1952, since at the time the recruiting board, probably as a prelude to my later arrest, assigned me to this branch of the service. Our task, for instance, after three months of training, was to guard a munitions depot in the picturesque Bakony Forest. During my time in the service I was arrested as a former functionary of the Social Democratic Youth Movement and interned as a "Trotskyite," without ever having read a single book by Trotsky. In the remand prison and during the later years of my battle for rehabilitation, I had the opportunity to get to know at firsthand the officers of the dreaded and hated State Security, the real "ÁVO men," not as a bystander but as a victim.[12]

The nucleus of the State Security Service consisted, of course, of 5,885 political detectives, the officers of State Security, who were in charge of interrogations in Budapest and in the more important towns and who—especially between 1949 and 1953—not infrequently tortured suspects.[13] Documentation and reports about suspect persons were provided by 30,885 agents (as of 1 July 1956).

As early as 23 October, the paradoxical situation arose whereby the Interior Ministry's and the General Staff's emergency plans proved to be totally useless, and nobody dared to deploy the troops of the hated State Security—except for the purpose of guarding property. Incidentally, it was subsequently ascertained that of those sixty-one cases of fusillades directed against unarmed civilians between 23 and 29 October where twenty-four people died and several hundred were wounded, State Security was involved in only fifteen cases.[14] Even more revealing is the case discovered by the military historian Miklós Horváth of a rebellion by militia recruits at the siege of the Radio Building. A group of soldiers had initially refused to use weapons on the as-yet-unarmed demonstrators. Thereupon the commander of the militia, a certain Major Fehér, ordered his noncommissioned officers to shoot at the rebellious soldiers. The next day, once the insurgents had occupied the house, the commander was beaten to death by embittered militia soldiers and the insurgents.

There is evidence that some of the recruits joined the insurgents and fought with them against the Soviet troops. In the battalions at Debrecen and Miskolc, there were also rifts within the Security Service militia units.[15] The operational political detectives, as well as the counter-espionage and intelligence officers, whose number was estimated by the KGB general Serov at some two thousand, were primarily the ones who returned with the Soviet troops as their accomplices after the second intervention.[16]

One must not gloss over the fact that during the latter part of the revolution there was isolated looting here and there, as well as more or less aggressive harassment of prominent Communists, such as house searches, short-term arrests, and interrogations by insurgent groups. Still, all in all one can agree with the British historian of the Hungarian Revolution Bill Lomax, who wrote: "The Hungarian Revolution was one of the least bloody revolutions of all times."[17] Although the acts of revenge were promptly and sharply condemned by several of the insurgent leaders, the free press, the Writers' Association, and a whole series of revolutionary and grassroots organizations, Communist propaganda organs from Moscow to Paris and Peking used the gruesome pictures of the victims of the lynchings to accuse the revolution across-the-board of "counterrevolutionary terror" and "Communist hunting."

The Condottiere, the "Uncle," and the Romantics

Prior to 23 October hardly anybody had heard of him, and even today only very few people recall his name: József Dudás. Yet at the time of the revolution, he generally counted, in the eyes of hostile, friendly, and indifferent observers at home and abroad, as by far the most interesting, colorful, and unpredictable personality of the revolution. He was the first revolutionary leader whom Imre Nagy summoned for talks. After his arrest, *Pravda* portrayed him as the "key figure of the counterrevolutionary putsch." The French author Nicolas Baudy noted that "Dudás brought with him that tiny grain of madness, which germinates in every revolution."[1]

Who was Dudás? Where did he come from, and what did he want to achieve?[2] The son of working-class parents, he was born in 1912 in Maros-Vásárhely, in the heart of Hungarian Transylvania. After graduating from high school and the Bucharest Polytechnic, the young locksmith was arrested in 1933 as a leading functionary of the illegal Communist youth movement in Romania and sentenced to nine years in prison. He was freed in 1939, and after the Second Vienna Award (which transferred northern Transylvania, including Maros-Vásárhely, to Hungary) he moved to Budapest. In addition to studying at the Technical University, he worked as a liaison between groups within the anti-Fascist movement. As a member of the resistance movement, he met several leading politicians, such as Rajk, Tildy, and Kállay, and was even sent by Regent Horthy to Moscow in September 1944 as part of the first, unofficial cease-fire delegation. He was also a founding member of the Liberation Committee of the Hungarian National Uprising. After 1945 the Communist Party broke with him because of his contacts with a fractional group. Dudás then joined the Independent Smallholders' Party and in 1946 was elected as a Smallholder candidate to the Budapest local government. As the Communist attacks on the Smallholders' Party mounted, Dudás was interned at the South Buda Camp. Although freed in 1948, he was soon arrested again and held at Kistarcsa and then at Recsk. In 1951 he was extradited to Romania, where the Communist State Security Service investigated his alleged activities as a police informer. Dudás was released for lack of evidence in 1954 and returned to Hungary. There he worked as an engineer in a factory and was not active politically. His cometlike rise to veritable "mediastardom" began on only 27 October. Two great orations before a huge crowd at Széna Square in Buda, the site of one of the freedom fighters' most important future bases, established Dudás's reputation as a people's tribune. He called on the enthusiastic crowd to appoint a hundred delegates. These and other representatives then established the Second District National Committee on 29 October and elected him as its president. At their meeting in the district council building, Dudás read out his twenty-five-point program, which became famous for appearing radical at that time. Its main demands were a coalition government made up of freedom fighters, elected revolutionary representatives, as well as Béla Kovács (the former secretary-general of the Smallholders, imprisoned for years by the Soviets), Imre Nagy, and János Kádár; a multiparty system; secession from the Warsaw Pact; neutrality based on the Austrian pattern; the immediate withdrawal of Soviet troops; the release of Cardinal Mindszenty; the disbanding of the ÁVH; and the formation of a national guard.

That evening Dudás, with more than a hundred armed followers, occupied the editorial offices and printing press of the central party daily, *Szabad Nép*. With the cooperation of several former prison mates, who used to be well-known journalists, the swashbuckler started a newspaper, *Függetlenség* (Independence), later renamed *Magyar Függetlenség* (Hungarian Independence). The first issue, published on 30 October, was a political bombshell. In a five-column banner headline, a national committee—which did not even exist yet!—announced, "We do not recognize the present government!" Then followed Dudás's twenty-five points.[3] Next to it was a call, signed by him as chairman of the Hungarian National Revolutionary Committee, to convene a countrywide congress of revolutionary delegates on 1 November in the Budapest Sportshall. (It never actually took place.)

All that duly gave the impression to the entourage of the prime minister that Dudás had appreciable armed forces and even a political center with its own communications mouthpiece and program behind him. Many intellectuals from the revolutionary organizations, as well as Communist and non-Communist politicians, had known Dudás during his adventurous life. That is why several members of the Revolutionary Committee of the Hungarian Intelligentsia accompanied him to the meeting in Parliament with the prime minister in the late-afternoon hours of 30 October.[4]

The encounter took place in a tense atmosphere, but ultimately Dudás accepted Imre Nagy. However, the prime minister rejected the suggestion of Dudás's attendants that the (self-appointed) president of the Revolutionary Committee should take up the post of interior minister. Nonetheless the meeting was the actual acme of Dudás's revolutionary career. After all, the noncommittal official communiqué had tagged him as the spokesperson of the revolutionary freedom fighters and as president of the Revolutionary National Committee, and had made him famous in these capacities at home and abroad.[5]

Posterity owes perhaps the most succinct portrayal of this unusual personality to Wiktor Woroszylski, the correspondent of a Polish cultural magazine: "Tall, colorful, black-haired, a large expressive but repulsive face, with mildly prominent cheek bones. A Tyrolean hat, a coat thrown around his shoulders like a fantasy cape, a gun at the belt, black trousers. He enters the room, surrounded by his following."[6] When asked to define the movement he represented, Dudás gave four adjectives: "national—revolutionary—democratic—socialist." During the conversation Woroszylski could distinctly sense "an uncommon personal ambition" and concluded his article with these questions:

> But who is this chief of the National Revolutionary Committee, who publishes his own paper, surrounds himself with an entourage worthy of an ataman, who boasts of a "contact with Moscow" and who, in an interview accorded Polish journalists, proclaims his desire to enter the Hungarian government? Is this really "a Fascist"? What does it all add up to? Is he simply the leader of a gang, an adventurer, a "strong man" pushing for personal popularity and power? And if this is the case—how important is the danger of Dudás threatening the popular revolution? How many more Dudáses may there be in the country?

These questions also preoccupied most leaders of the army and the insurgents, who regarded him as a loudmouth and the principal enemy of consolidation. His paper, with a circulation of 50,000 to 100,000 copies, criticized the indecisiveness and the composition of the government but at the same time warned against vigilante justice and looting and pleaded for the resumption of work. He permitted the printing of other papers too in the press building that he controlled, such as that of the future party organ *Népszabadság*. His newspaper was an instrument of power, yet Dudás ultimately discredited himself by his missionary zeal and boundless ambition. Because of misinterpreted directives, a group from Széna Square attacked the Foreign Ministry on the banks of the Danube. Dudás was unjustly blamed for the incident and temporarily arrested. After his release he had a disagreement with representatives of the National Guard, which was in the process of being formed, and then—once again wrongly—was accused of being the éminence grise behind an alleged looting of the National Bank, and once again arrested for a short while.

Although the Széna Square group, in a strategically significant location in Buda, was the second (after the Corvinists) most important unit of the freedom fighters and was formally under the supervision of the Second District National Committee, whose president was Dudás, he had absolutely nothing to do with the group's activities. At first 140 and by the end some 800 to 900 insurgents belonged to this detachment.[7] However, Dudás never took part in any of their actions. On the day of the Soviet attack he was wounded and taken to the hospital. Despite repeated warnings, he did not leave the country. On 21 November he was lured by Kádár into entering the Parliament Building, where he was immediately arrested by KGB officers. The Soviet Presidium had made the political decision at the end of November that some of the well-known revolutionary leaders, among them Dudás and the commander of Széna Square, János Szabó ("Uncle Szabó"), should be sentenced to death as soon as possible as a deterrent. The Special Council of the Military College of the Supreme Court sentenced Dudás and Szabó to death without a possibility to appeal, and they were executed on 19 January 1957.[8]

"Uncle Szabó" did not become as well known abroad as Dudás or Maléter, but as commander of the Széna Square group he won legendary fame within the ranks of the freedom fighters who had fought against the Soviets and the State Security forces on the Buda side of the capital. Szabó, like as the Corvinist Pongrátz brothers and Dudás, was born and bred in Transylvania in straitened circumstances.[9] He settled in Budapest only at the age of forty-five. Imprisoned and tortured several times for illegal attempts to cross the border and on suspicion of espionage, Szabó had to eke out a living as a casual laborer and later as a truck driver.

"I saw that government policy had not changed even after the Twentieth Congress. I worked day and night, earned very little and was dissatisfied," he said and added the following about the outbreak of the revolution:

> The people and the students marched, and they fired into the crowd. That is how it started. If that is so, one has to find those who fired the shots—the ÁVO people. If so, who gave the order to shoot, because the unarmed people overran the shooters. If that is true, then I do not see a preplanned armed organization, because it was leaderless and no other armed unit supported it. A few guns and gasoline-filled bottles in the age of modern weapons: virtual suicide. Who is culpable, who is responsible for it? Where are those certain politicians? Because they are holed up now, they are collecting the little people and are shifting the blame on them, or if they have fled, get them extradited, transport them home, so that *they* should have to answer for their actions in court.

Within twenty-four hours of his appearance at Széna Square, the young fighters unreservedly accepted the fifty-nine-year-old truck driver and highly decorated First World War corporal as their commander. All of them admired "Uncle Szabó" for his modesty, integrity, and unselfishness. "Szabó made speeches on several occasions, stressing that we were not bandits, and that who ever steals or loots or starts a personal action that sullies the purity of the revolution belongs on a lamppost," commented one of his company commanders. "Uncle Szabó symbolized for our unit the purity of the revolution." It was thanks to him in the first place that the 150 or so ÁVH officers and high-ranking functionaries, whom the unit had imprisoned in a former barracks, managed to survive the revolution unscathed. He fought until the very end, after which his wife hid him in the cellar of a children's home she ran. The janitor betrayed his hiding place: that is how they could arrest "Uncle Szabó" a fortnight after the Soviet invasion. He was the first of fourteen Széna Square fighters to be executed; subsequently another seventy-six of them were sentenced to lengthy jail terms.[10]

One of the members of the Széna Square group sentenced to death was the then fifteen-year-old apprentice Péter Mansfeld, whom "Uncle Szabó" had initially sent away because of his youth. Later the intelligent and courageous boy acted as a motorized courier, transporting everything from medicines to ammunition and hand grenades for the insurgents. After the Soviet intervention, he was given a suspended sentence for theft, but what he heard from his fellow prisoners while in remand changed him into an unforgiving enemy of the Communist regime. After his release he founded a "gangster band" with some of his friends as revenge for the execution of "Uncle Szabó" and the incarceration of his brother-in-law and to free imprisoned friends. As a first step the boys disarmed a policeman guarding the Austrian Embassy. They were unable to undertake any further actions, as they were arrested in no time. His imperturbability raised the hackles of his judges to such an extent that the Supreme Court changed his life sentence in the first instance to a death sentence. He was executed on 21 March 1959, eleven days after his eighteenth birthday.[11] He was the youngest among the victims of reprisal.

Any further account of the other significant insurgent groups and of the heroes soon to become victims and martyrs would go beyond the scope of my treatment of the subject. Still, for several reasons, I have to make an exception for István Angyal, the legendary commander of the Tőzoltó Street group (a small side street behind the Kilián Barracks) and his deputies, Olaf Per Csongovai and Otto Szirmai.[12]

Angyal, a Holocaust survivor, lost his mother and sister in Auschwitz; as a sixteen-year-old, he was forced to watch the public hanging of his sister because of her aborted escape attempt. His deputy, Otto Szirmai, who worked in radio drama, was also a Jew, as, incidentally, were many other prominent personalities during the revolution—such as the commander of the large insurgent group from Baross Square, László Nickelsburg, and the trailblazing thinker and journalist Miklós Gimes. All of them were executed. This aspect has to be emphasized, because in the propaganda writings of the Kádár regime, the few anti-Semitic manifestations during the revolution were vastly exaggerated. In view of the fact that Rákosi and the three other members of the "quadriga" (Gerő, Farkas, and Révai) were Jews, as was about half of the membership of the illegal Communist Party and numerous officers of the State Security, the absence of anti-Semitic incidents was regarded almost as a "miracle."

Admittedly the time was very short, and had the revolution lasted longer, one could not rule out the possibility of such a future tendency.[13]

Angyal was an exceptional phenomenon, a convinced Communist who had never been a party member. In the words of the chronicler László Gyurkó, he was the revolution's "knight without fear and without reproach"[14] without ever carrying a weapon. Initially he organized the provisioning of the fighters with the help of cars borrowed from a neighboring garage and the defense of his "quarters." Some 310 fighters from Tőzoltó Street joined the National Guard. Together with Olaf Per Csongovai, a student at the Film Academy, Angyal took part in the bloody banners protest march on the boulevard after the massacre at Parliament Square. His unit arrested suspicious persons and saved the lives of the recruits of an ÁVH detachment, who later fought with the insurgents against the Russians. Angyal duplicated and distributed poems and leaflets, took up personal contact with outstanding intellectuals, and, together with Csongovai, participated in a meeting and negotiations with Imre Nagy and János Kádár. After the uprising had been crushed, Angyal fought on in the resistance. Everyone admired him for his personal integrity, his extraordinary courage, and his determination.[15]

Angyal, Csongovai, and Szirmai were extreme left-wingers and by disposition and for family reasons represented a reform Communist position. "We felt that the party should put itself at the helm of the revolution ... so that all could see that the people were fighting for socialism. Socialism wanted to be fought for. ... Had it occurred thus, we could have fought with united effort for the basic achievements of socialism, the nationalization of banks, businesses and factories and the land," noted Angyal in prison.[16] These views were, of course, not shared by most of the insurgents, nor by most Hungarians active in the revolution. Both his deputies, Csongovai and Szirmai, were also leftist rebels. Csongovai, who was born in Ankara, Turkey, started to speak Hungarian only as a nine-year-old. His father, an army officer, fled to Turkey after the collapse of the Hungarian Soviet Republic of 1919, where as manager of a nightclub he met his wife, a Swedish German dancer. That is how their son came to be called Per Olaf. When on 29 October a delegation of insurgents negotiated with Imre Nagy in Parliament, an interesting exchange took place. During the heated discussion, Nagy posed the rhetorical question to his visitors: "Boys, do you think I am not as good a

Hungarian as you are?" The quick-witted twenty-six-year-old Csongovai retorted: "That's possible, but there is a revolution going on outside, and what matters now is who the greater revolutionary is, not who is what sort of a Hungarian."[17] The following day the rebels met for three hours with Kádár; five of the ten participants had their party books with them and showed them to the mistrustful Kádár to prove they were not counterrevolutionaries. The discussion took place after the massacre in front of the party building in Republic Square. The revolution could be saved only if, after accepting the revolutionary demands, the party were also to take over leadership of the revolution, said Csongovai. Kádár considered the suggestion very interesting but said that first the young fighters should provide a symbolic guard for party headquarters. Csongovai's repartee was prompt: "My suggestion was not that the revolution should join the party, but that the party should join the revolution!"[18]

The other deputy commander of the Tőzoltó Street group, Otto Szirmai, also represented the political Left. He came from a poor Jewish working-class family that had been involved in the Socialist movement for several generations. Szirmai joined the Communist Party in 1945 and worked in radio drama. As his right hand was paralyzed since birth, he did not bear arms, but even after the second Soviet intervention he remained extremely active, producing and distributing flyers, kept up contact with the workers' councils, and took part in organizing a women's demonstration. István Angyal and Otto Szirmai were sentenced to death and executed on 1 December 1958 and 22 January 1959 respectively.[19]

Csongovai managed to escape to France via Austria. When he heard in Paris that troops commanded by General Király were carrying on the fight in the Bakony Forest in Transdanubia, he and his wife returned to Budapest after three weeks. Only then did Csongovai realize that they had been taken in by a legend. The number of such rumors, about Maléter as well, was legion. Numerous escapees became victims of the Kádár regime's retaliation campaign after their return.

Legends, rumors, and lies also surround the tragic fate of three women who took part in the revolution, and who imprudently returned to Hungary after their escape to the West. The freedom fighters' successful battle against a superior force would hardly have been possible without the help of women, who cooked for them, tended their wounds, and supplied their provisions. However, some of them, with weapons in their hands, replenished ammunition supplies or transported the wounded to the hospital. Quite a few of them were photographed by friends or photojournalists. So too were two young working girls, both of whom had grown up in foster homes, had joined the Corvinists, and had their photo taken with machine pistols in their hands. Mrs. Béla Havrila, then twenty-four, and Mária Wittner, who had just turned nineteen, managed to flee to Switzerland and Austria respectively. Both went back to Budapest soon after.[20] Havrila spoke on the telephone with her boyfriend, who asked her to return. Wittner believed in the amnesty. Both were identified by a photo in July 1957 and arrested; Havrila was executed at the beginning of 1959, although the court could not establish any proof of a serious crime. Wittner also received a death sentence in the first instance, but probably because of her age this was altered on appeal to a life sentence. Despite a general amnesty decreed in 1963, she remained behind bars for another seven years until 1970 because she did not mince her words, even in front of the political education officers. Today—in failing health—she is active in right-wing politics and, at close to seventy, was elected to Parliament on the Fidesz list in the spring of 2006.

Last, a third example is the story of Erzsébet Márton, a nineteen-year-old tram conductor who joined "Uncle Szabó's" group. Although she did not actively participate in the fighting, with a few other insurgents she took György Marosán, a top Communist functionary and later minister, in custody on behalf of the group. He was released a few hours later. Following her successful escape to the West, Márton returned to Budapest in the spring of 1957. She too believed the news about an amnesty. Arrested in August, she was badly beaten in prison and sentenced to death. Her hair turned gray overnight after the sentence was pronounced. In the course of the four months she spent on death row, somebody was hanged almost every day. Her death sentence was eventually commuted to life imprisonment; seriously ill, she was released in 1963. Her health deteriorated so badly that before her untimely death in 1999 she had twenty-three stays in the hospital.

Three feminine fates singled out from the chaotic days of the revolution, which tragically confirm Paul Valéry's words: "This young person is faced with the *unpredictable*, which is entirely different from what used to be the *unexpected*."[21]

It was always known that the fate of Hungary in October–November 1956 was ultimately decided neither on the Pest streets nor in the Parliament on the banks of the Danube, but in the Kremlin. The handwritten notes of the sessions of the CPSU Presidium during the days of the Hungarian crisis prove that behind the seemingly monolithic façade were imponderable human factors and argumentative "toings and froings" whose role in the chain of events should not be underestimated. The head of the General Department of the Central Committee, Vladimir Nikiforovich Malin, the only outsider admitted to the discussions, recorded who was present and made sketchy notes of what was being said as a kind of aid to the formulation of decisions.[1] In the fall of 1956, the Presidium consisted of eleven members; apart from these, six candidate members without voting rights and three Central Committee secretaries took part in the sessions of the forum. They met two to three times a week, and even during the most critical days of the empire there were items on the agenda such as, for example, the sending of a Komsomol delegation to Britain, the amount of the subsidy for the French-Soviet Friendship Society, and the question whether the Soviet consumer cooperatives should be permitted to barter fifty vehicles for North Korean apples and peanuts.

The Russian historian Vyacheslav Sereda, publisher of a book containing these seventeen records and relevant documents,[2] points out in his introduction that, for instance, the fateful decision about the first military intervention in Budapest on 23 October is not even mentioned in the minutes, probably because Mikoyan raised objections to it. Only unanimous decisions were minuted, or else the meeting was simply adjourned to a later date. Besides, the full members of the Presidium frequently met before the sessions or during intermissions in the "walnut room," close to the meeting room. This was situated on the second floor of the Council of Ministers' old office building, above Stalin's former office. It is entirely possible, therefore, that the agenda was already set in an interim consultation prior to the decisive meeting of 31 October. According to Sereda, not all discussions were recorded in those days because many of them took place not in the Kremlin and party headquarters but in the Presidium's rest home at Lipky or sometimes even in the government lounge of Vnukovo Airport. Malin, who kept the minutes, could not even write shorthand: he only tried to adhere to the speakers' ideas, style, and sometimes indirectly their emotions.

These fragmentary notes nevertheless give us a fascinating and rare insight into the at times pointed discussions in the course of the decision-making process in the Kremlin. The previous day's declaration—as referred to earlier—about the relationship to the other Socialist countries and to the situation in Hungary with reference to the possible partial or complete withdrawal of Soviet troops served as a background to the Presidium's resolution. The hesitation, the fluctuation, and the differences of opinion were the outcome of the enduring power struggle within a Soviet leadership faltering in the wake of the dynamics of the de-Stalinization process.

The publication of the Soviet secret documents in 1993 and 1996 gave a renewed impetus to the arguments about the putative missed chance of a possible peaceful alternative to the solution of the Hungarian crisis.[3] However, when assessing the theoretically feasible alternatives, one should not, of course, disregard one basic fact: even those who on 30 October expressed self-criticism about the Soviets' relationship with the other Eastern Bloc countries, such as the CC secretary Shepilov or Marshal Zhukov, by no means intended to give completely free rein to Hungary. Shepilov emphatically drew the line for the concessions: "The fundamentals [of the system] must remain unchanged." And: "An ongoing struggle must be fought against national communism." Even the flexible and farsighted Anastas Mikoyan made it clear on 1 November that his proposal of a ten to fifteen days' waiting period would not imply a change in the status quo. "We simply cannot allow Hungary to be removed from our camp." We have retrospectively to note therefore that the Communist power system and Hungary's attachment to the Soviet Bloc were never really negotiable items. According to all available information, no member of the Soviet leadership would have been willing to give up these two columns of the Soviet empire.[4] The issue all along was only what further concessions should be made to the Nagy government to enable it miraculously to consolidate the situation without jeopardizing the Communist regime and the integrity of the Soviet Bloc. Yet during the last day of October it became obvious that even the chances for a "Polish solution" had been gambled away by the Soviets themselves by their catastrophic decision of the night of 23–24 October in favor of a military intervention. In the light of later events, we are fully justified in doubting that this divided Soviet leadership—under pressure also from such antithetical forces as Mao Zedong and Tito—would have been prepared to withdraw its troops for the sake of saving the substance and unity of the system, and thereby granting Hungary relative domestic freedom and relative elbow room in external affairs.

How then did the decisive session proceed on that Wednesday, 31 October? According to Khrushchev's somewhat tendentious memoirs, the preceding day's meeting was not concluded even by nightfall. "I don't know how many times we changed our minds back and forth. . . . We finally finished this all-night session with a decision not to apply military force in Hungary." However, he was soon assailed by doubts on whether he had acted correctly. "When I climbed into bed that morning, I found I was still too preoccupied with the whole problem to rest. It was like a nail in my head and it kept me from being able to sleep."[5]

We are informed from the notes about the proceedings at the session on 31 October.[6] Khrushchev unexpectedly declared: "The previous day's assessment has to be reviewed, we should not withdraw the troops from Hungary and Budapest; we should take the initiative for the purpose of restoring order. If we withdrew from Hungary, it would encourage the American, English, and French imperialists." With these allusions to the Israeli, British, and French actions in the Suez situation, he continued: "They would attribute it to our weakness and would swing into attack. We would demonstrate our weakness [with the withdrawal]. In that case our Party would not understand us. Besides Egypt, we would give them [that is, the Western powers] Hungary as well."

After Zhukov, Bulganin, Molotov, Kaganovich, Voroshilov, and Saburov pronounced their agreement, Khrushchev stressed the power vacuum in Hungary. "We have no other choice. It has to be said that we accommodated them [that is, Imre Nagy and his government], but now there is no government." And he posed the question: "What sort of line should we follow now? A Provisional Revolutionary Government has to be constituted." At that point, however, Khrushchev was still undecided as to who should become the new head of government. At first he mentioned János Kádár. He then added: "It would, after all, be best if he were only the deputy. Münnich should be Prime Minister, Minister for Defense and Interior Minister." That the former Spanish Civil War veteran, Soviet officer, and trusted member of the Soviet Military Secret Service was his first choice became clear from the next sentence, when Khrushchev announced point-blank: "Münnich is asking us for help, we provide help and we straighten matters out." Then there followed an ambiguous, but to the initiates well-coded, sentence: "We shall invite this government [that of Nagy], let us say for negotiations about the pull-out of troops, and we solve the problem. If Nagy agrees, we shall include him as deputy Prime Minister." We can interpret this sentence as a hint of what was to happen later when the Soviets actually set a trap for a Hungarian delegation. In the end Khrushchev explained his plans. He and Malenkov would discuss the situation with Tito on the island of Brioni, but first he would fly to Brest with Molotov and Malenkov to meet Gomułka and the Polish leadership. The Chinese, the Czechs, the Romanians, and the Bulgarians would duly be informed. The Presidium entrusted top functionaries with the military and propaganda groundwork, as well as with the formulation of the future (Hungarian!) government's manifesto to the people. All that was played out behind the back of the directly involved government of Imre Nagy and the Hungarian people. Nor did the Western governments and their intelligence services and the international media have the faintest inkling of the preparations for the assault against Hungary.

The international context was not auspicious for the revolution either before or after the ultimate Soviet decision. And here we want to consider only those factors that would have influenced Khrushchev when weighing the risks. An essential factor was the pressure—caused by different motives, but on the whole acting in the same direction—by the Communist parties of China and Yugoslavia. Today we know from Chinese publications how persistently Mao and the Beijing leadership were occupied with developments in Poland and Hungary.[7] In the case of Poland, the Chinese leadership took an extremely firm stand against a Soviet intervention. In reference to Hungary, Beijing at first adopted a similar position and warned the Soviet leaders against big-power chauvinism. However,

Mao's attitude to the situation was gradually changing in view of the increasingly obvious breakup of the regime and as a result of alarming intelligence reports and diplomatic cables from the Chinese Embassy in Budapest. On 30 October two emissaries, Liu Shaoqi and Deng Xiaoping, who had been staying in Moscow since 23 October, received instructions to extend their visit by a day in order to dissuade Khrushchev from pulling out the Soviet troops from Hungary. In Beijing's view what was happening there was no longer an anti-Soviet emotional outburst elicited by Soviet domination but an "anti-Communist reactionary restoration." At the time, the Chinese leadership was still critical only of Soviet big-power chauvinism in the privacy of internal consultations; they expressed disapproval of Soviets, out-of-control, far-too-rapid de-Stalinization, as well as their flawed tactic vis-à-vis Poland, where the Soviets wanted to interfere at first, and vis-à-vis Hungary, whence for a while they were willing to withdraw their troops, which would have destabilized the situation even further.

When Liu Shaoqi and Deng Xiaoping left Moscow on 31 November, the entire CPSU Presidium traveled to Vnukovo Airport to bid farewell to the departing Chinese officials and smooth over any ruffled feathers. On the way to the airport, Khrushchev, who sat in the car with Liu, informed him that the Presidium had come down on the side of military intervention to put down the "reactionary rebellion" in Budapest and would assist "the Hungarian party and the people to defend socialism in Hungary." According to Liu, before their departure the Soviet leaders expressed their sincere thanks for the help of the Chinese party in both the Polish and the Hungarian questions.

In view of Poland's special significance in the Eastern Bloc, Khrushchev, Malenkov, and Molotov hurried to the border town of Brest in order to be able to inform the Polish leadership on 1 November of the Presidium's final decision. The deputation led by Gomułka did not agree with the intervention. Although the Poles recognized the serious danger of a counterrevolution and realized that in free elections the Hungarian Communists would at best receive 8 to 10 percent of the votes, they insisted on a wait-and-see policy. The gist of the telephoned information sent by the Russian delegation to the rest of the Presidium was that although no full consensus had been reached, the Poles acknowledged the decision. Incidentally, in his conversation with the Chinese prime minister

Zhou Enlai in Warsaw two and a half months later, Gomułka claimed that the Soviet comrades had mentioned nothing about their intentions, but that they, the Poles, had asked them about the situation in Hungary. Gomułka had always held the opinion that the presence of Soviet troops was the precondition of most of the Communist systems.[8]

Following the trip to Brest, Khrushchev and Malenkov traveled first to Bucharest and Sofia, where they informed the top Romanian (as well as the Czechoslovak party chief, Novotny, who was there) and Bulgarian officials of the impending invasion. By far the most important meeting took place in full secrecy with Marshal Tito in Yugoslavia. It was only twenty-one years later that one of the six participants, the then Yugoslav ambassador to Moscow and later member of the Yugoslav Presidium, Veljko Mićunović, divulged in his explosive memoirs the secret of Tito's complicity in the preparations for crushing the revolution in Hungary.[9]

Khrushchev and Malenkov flew in a small two-engine plane in very bad weather to Pula, whence they were taken by a tiny motorboat in rough seas to the little harbor near Tito's villa on the island of Brioni. Both of them were visibly exhausted when they arrived at 7 p.m. They talked until 5 in the morning with Tito and his then closest associates, Edvard Kardelj and Alexander Ranković, about the happenings in Hungary. All this was played out during the night from 2 to 3 November. Mićunović, who was present at the discussions, not only confirmed that the Yugoslavs were in agreement with the necessity of the Soviet intervention but also revealed that Khrushchev and Tito were already discussing in detail the program of the future government to be installed by the Russians, even about its composition and the identity of the future prime minister. Paradoxically, it was the Yugoslav side that suggested Kádár for the post, whereas Khrushchev argued for the choice of Ferenc Münnich, who was well known to him. He even told the story that in the thirties they had been officers together on maneuvers in Russia, when they had shared the same tent. The Yugoslavs eventually more or less convinced their interlocutors that Kádár, who had been in prison, would have less trouble in gaining the people's confidence than Münnich, who had been ambassador in Moscow. The discussions during that fateful night at Brioni were so secret that the six participants did not take any notes. Nor were there any interpreters or secretaries present. Still, Mićunović's reconstructions from memory reveal that the Yugoslav leadership was far more involved in the preparations for the violent overthrow of Imre Nagy's government than even Khrushchev has implied in his memoirs.

A whole series of other factors undoubtedly facilitated the option for a hard-line solution. Mao Zedong and Tito were not the only ones arguing for an invasion. The Communist leaderships of all the Eastern Bloc countries, in particular the Romanians and Czechoslovaks with their large Hungarian minorities, were on the alert. Secretary-general of the Italian Communist Party, Palmiro Togliatti, long acclaimed as the father of the Communist world movement, warned in a letter written to the Soviet party leadership on 30 October that "the Hungarian Government is going irreversibly in a reactionary direction."[10] The leaders of the Italian party were worried that Polish and Hungarian events could damage the unity of Moscow's collective leadership. As soon as the following day the Soviet Presidium expressed agreement with Togliatti's assessment of the situation, but stated that "for the time being we are not acting against [Nagy], but we do not accept the reactionary turn of events." Besides, the collective leadership was united and would unanimously reach the necessary decision.[11]

As far as the West was concerned, the U.S. government under President Eisenhower sent a public signal on 27 October by way of a speech made by Secretary of State John Foster Dulles that in case of their becoming independent, the United States had no interest in gaining the satellite states as potential military allies. On 29 October, during the decisive period of the Hungarian Revolution, while the U.S. broadcast station Radio Free Europe was still agitating against the Nagy government and for continuing the armed struggle, the U.S. ambassador in Moscow, Charles Bohlen, was assigned by Secretary of State Dulles urgently to transmit this message to the Soviet leaders. Great Britain and France were totally caught up in their preparations for the war in Suez, and their governments publicly demonstrated prior to the Soviet intervention that they were neither interested nor moved by the fate of the Hungarian people.[12]

In retrospect, the picture before the inevitable catastrophe is spine-chilling. While in Moscow plans were being made for the decisive strike after Khrushchev had personally ensured the support of the most important Communist parties from China to Yugoslavia, most Hungarians were still deluding themselves with the false hope that the turbulent times of gunfire would soon be a thing of the past. At the beginning of November, the situation seemingly entered a qualitatively new phase of stabilization. During the last week in October workers' councils sprang up all over the country like mushrooms after a spring rain. To be exact, there were 2,100, with 28,000 members. At their combined conference held in the evening of 1 November, the workers' councils of Budapest decided to suspend the strike and resume work on Monday, 5 November. Delegates of the more important workers' and revolutionary councils turned up in the Parliament and assured the Nagy government—which had been reshuffled for the third time by 3 November—of their support. Indeed, work resumed in several places on Saturday, the third, so that production could begin on Monday at full capacity, and in some parts of the capital trams and buses were running again.

Even the Soviet military command's ploys, such as the initiation of official negotiations about the technical circumstances of the pullout, added to the deceptive feeling of security despite press reports of an influx of Soviet troops. To bolster the plausibility of these feigned negotiations, the Soviet emissaries from General Malinin to Ambassador Andropov had no compunctions in lying through their teeth during the conferences.

When reading the collections of the revolution's radio broadcasts and press reports today—fifty years after the event—one has the predominant impression of an almost unbelievable dichotomy: hectic activity in domestic politics and a flight into the future, throwing caution to the winds as far as foreign policy was concerned. In the course of barely 150 days, the mendacious party dictatorship's gray nothingness had been transformed into a vibrant political life with a free press and a diversity of grassroots organizations. As a result of appeals by the insurgent groups and the revolutionary committees, virtually all acts of violence were prevented. The establishment of the National Guard and the incorporation of the insurgents into its framework were meant to restore public order despite the release or escape of thousands of common criminals. There was general agreement after the withdrawal of the Soviet tanks from the inner city and the announcement of bilateral military negotiations that the Soviets were not to be given any cause or pretext for a renewed intervention.

In our cellar we had hardly any idea of the embittered tug-of-war going on within the stressed and split party leadership. We started to be hopeful again only on 28 October. Imre Nagy announced the cease-fire and acknowledged the uprising as a "national-democratic movement." We found out about the fast demolition of the party's monopoly of power. Although on 29 October sporadic fighting still continued around the Kilián Barracks and the Corvin Passage, and in the capital a further twenty people fell victim to the clashes, there were signs that the situation was slowly returning to normal even in our neighborhood. Despite my parents' entreaties, I could no longer idly await further political developments. I left our building next to the Kilián Barracks. Amid the general feeling of optimism I too—as so many others—at first believed in a peaceful outcome. During those hectic days I met a number of acquaintances in the partly destroyed newspaper building and in the Journalists' Association, all of whom were forging bold plans as future publishers and editors in chief. Although the paper *Esti Budapest* no longer appeared, I was able to pick up my monthly salary, or at least an advance—fair sum for the first time in five years—at a side entrance of the building, which had been badly damaged by enraged demonstrators.

As we had been cut off in the ninth district from the main events, I luckily did not experience any excesses or cases of lynch justice personally. I shall, of course, never be able to wipe out the memory of dead bodies, young insurgents as well as Soviet tank crews who had lost their lives in Üllői Avenue or in the side streets around the Corvin Passage or in the Kilián Barracks.

While the party Presidium in Moscow conferred about the person of the future Hungarian prime minister and Khrushchev vacillated between the candidature of Münnich or Kádár, the former still held the office of interior minister and the latter was still chairman of the newly formed Hungarian Socialist Workers' Party's seven-member executive committee. Lengthy discussions in the Presidium of the old party preceded this reorganization.[1] Kádár, whose checkered career, including his arrest in 1951, was at all times overshadowed by the controversies about his culpability for the dissolution of the Hungarian Communist Party in June 1943, voted at first with the majority of the party Presidium (five to one) against the restructuring suggested by Zoltán Szántó. However, in a revolution twenty-four hours suffice to change events and opinions. Just two days later Kádár himself said in Moscow: "The party has already ceased to exist; in one-third of the county committees the leaders take part in the revolutionary committees (on a district, county level). The lower-level organizations have been destroyed."[2] These words recall Rubashov's in Arthur Koestler's classic *Darkness at Noon*: "The Party remained dead, it could neither move nor breathe, but its hair and nails continued to grow."[3] Nothing was easier than to dissolve the old party; it crumbled of its own accord.

On this 31 October, the composition of the Hungarian Socialist Workers' Party caucus reflected a determined symbolic break with the past. Besides Kádár and Nagy, the executive committee included two of the prime minister's closest followers, Losonczy (now minister of state) and Donáth, both of whom had been instrumental in Imre Nagy's volte-face; in addition, there were the courageous police chief of Budapest, Sándor Kopácsi, the philosopher Georg Lukács, and Zoltán Szántó, a reformist Muscovite and at one time leader of the illegal party. The idea to publish the announcement of the new party's founding signed by thirty or so well-known writers, artists, and personalities of the workers' movement had to be abandoned because the best-known literati and pioneers of the change, such as Tibor Déry, Gyula Háy, and others, immediately declined to join the party.[4]

The inaugural meeting in a cinema at party headquarters, with some hundred to a hundred and fifty hastily convened participants, took place in an atmosphere of determination and distrust, and not least probably also of worry and uncertainty. Some of those present had already counted on going into illegality. Kádár's speech was short. According to oral reminiscences, he summed up the necessity of total renewal, outlined the tasks

of the party and its members, and stressed the importance of their participation in the new institutions and the National Guard.[5]

Apart from the later analyses of the various probable or possible principal political trends, the diagnosis of Zoltán Ripp was the most appropriate. According to him, neither a workers' self-management based on the
Yugoslav pattern nor the so-called national Communist Polish Gomułka-
model could have formed the basis for consolidation.[6] Both systems, or
rather experiments (in the case of Poland), had been feasible only through
the hegemony of a single party. However, in Hungary the state party was
by then irrevocably in ruins. Historians of the revolution aptly indicated
that many party members and functionaries—and not only members of
the armed forces—were scared and apprehensive, especially after the massacre at Republic Square but also because of other cases of popular justice.
Numerous members hid or burned their party books. The great majority
of the population and the masses of demonstrators of 23 October not
only did not take part in the excesses but condemned them, among other
places, in the columns of the literary and youth magazines.[7]

Many of my Jewish friends and acquaintances were worried that now,
when everything was out of control and there was no functioning central
authority, there could be an explosion of pent-up anti-Jewish sentiment.
In fact, nothing of the sort occurred. By the way, during the revolution
people of Jewish origin stood on both sides of the barricades. In other
words, the origin of the politicians and intellectuals had nothing to do
with their political attitude. In any case, indiscriminate labeling—here the
nasty Communists, there the dashing freedom fighters—is far too superficial. Admittedly, the people showed an admirable unity against foreign
rule; at the same time, though, they consisted of a coalition of divergent
forces, spanning the gamut from Communist reformers or democratic
Socialists to elements of the extreme Right. One must not forget that
within only a very few days Hungary underwent a 180-degree turn from
a disintegrating terror system to a restored multiparty system. Constella-
tions, attitudes, and behaviors changed abruptly.

At that time a number of prominent personalities who had been
imprisoned or persecuted by the Communists stood up unequivocally
against a return to the Horthy era and against Right extremist tendencies. Thus, for example, Béla Kovács, the former secretary-general of the
Smallholders' Party, who had recently returned from the Gulag, declared

before he joined the Nagy government as minister of state: "No one must dream of going back to the world of counts, bankers and capitalists: that world is over once and for all. A true member of the Smallholders' Party cannot think along the lines of 1939 or 1945." Anna Kéthly, who had just been elected head of the revived Social Democratic Party after a long stretch in prison, argued for a radical new beginning, but at the same time against the danger of counterrevolution. Finally, the populist-nationalist novelist and playwright László Németh, who had been gagged by the Rákosi regime, warned in two (later much-quoted) articles against a backslide: "We must be vigilant, while the people in arms are focused on the withdrawal of Soviet forces, to assure that the new opportunists do not make a counterrevolution out of the Revolution and set the Hungarian struggle for freedom on the course of 1920." In his opinion the "histori-cally significant" political system for which the revolution fought was "a multi-party system of shared overall principles, which would fuse the determination of social systems based on ideological unity with the flex-ibility of the parliamentary system."[8]

The double danger of a counterrevolution and an intervention from outside also formed one of the recurrent motives in the most important speech that János Kádár made during the revolution. This was recorded in the morning of 1 November, but broadcast only directly before 10 p.m., at a time when Kádár was already en route to Moscow to found another party. The fact, incidentally, that this programmatic pronouncement in the name of the new party was put on the air expressly at his wish sub-stantiates the assumption of his biographer Tibor Huszár that Kádár's "disappearance," of which I shall speak in the next chapter, had not been prepared beforehand.[9]

After mentioning that the popular uprising had reached a cross-roads, there followed a warning of dangers threatening from within and without. However, the most significant statements concerned Kádár's unambiguous distancing from the Stalinist clique around Rákosi and the patent commitment to "the glorious uprising [by which] our people have shaken off the Rákosi regime. They have achieved freedom for the people and independence for the country, without which there can be no Socialism." He then paid unqualified tribute to the insurgents: "We can safely say that those who prepared this uprising were recruited from your ranks. The Hungarian Communist writers, journalists, university students, the youth of the Petőfi Circle, thousands and thousands of workers and peasants and veteran fighters who were imprisoned on false charges fought in the front lines against Rákosi's despotism and political hooliganism. We are proud that you have honestly stood your ground in the armed uprising and in leading it. You were permeated by true patriotism and loyalty to Socialism." After stating his commitment to Marxism-Leninism and to scientific socialism, whose teachings would be applied in accordance with Hungarian traditions, Kádár concluded his speech with a fiery call: "Our people have proven with blood their intention to support unflinchingly the Government's efforts aimed at the complete withdrawal of Soviet forces. We do not want to be dependent any longer; we do not want our country to become a battlefield."[10]

It is therefore more than understandable that for thirty-three years it was forbidden to quote this speech, since it was the most convincing evidence of the crown witness's own complicity. It would be idle to speculate whether this new party would have had any chance at all to cooperate in the consolidation of the Nagy government.

The time left for free and independent Hungary was, of course, far too short to evaluate the prospects of the reestablished former coalition parties and the rash of fringe parties that had broken out over the past few days.[11] There were more than thirty registered party formations, but I shall confine myself briefly to mentioning only the most important ones. The Smallholders' Party, which had won an absolute majority in 1945, was formally reestablished on 30 October and represented in the last Nagy government by three ministers of state: Zoltán Tildy, Béla Kovács, and István B. Szabó. Apart from the above-quoted warning by Kovács regarding a restoration of the prewar political system, the party had no program; it lacked the time to work one out. The statement printed in their republished newspaper demanded the dissolution of the forced collectives in agriculture and in general the promotion of the small and medium agrarian and industrial enterprises. Like all parties, the Smallholders championed Hungary's independence, secession from the Warsaw Pact, and early parliamentary elections. As the secretary-general of the reborn Peasant Party recalled, after the announcement of its reconstitution, a large crowd assembled in front of the old party headquarters. "Everyone wanted to become something." Tension between the Communists' fellow travelers and the persecuted, as well as the politicians who had fled to the West, were, of course, already palpable by then. In consideration of international complications, ex–prime minister Ferenc Nagy (1946 to 1947), who had returned from his American exile to Vienna, left the country at the request of the Austrian authorities.

For the Communists the politically most explosive concession was the reestablishment of the Social Democratic Party (SDP), and it is extremely likely that in the prevailing atmosphere the Social Democrats would have come out the winners in free elections.[12] Anna Kéthly (1889–1976) was indisputably its leading personality, who after eight years of house arrest and prison regarded all Communist functionaries, including Imre Nagy and his reforming entourage, with the deepest distrust. That was the reason why on 2 November Kéthly and her associates were willing to take up only the three ministerial posts reserved for them in the coalition cabinet. The allegations in the propaganda writings ("White Books") published after the defeat of the revolution and the counterrevolutionary horror stories promulgated by the chief propagandist János Berecz—about the so-called secret negotiations between Nagy and Kéthly, as early as the summer of 1956, on the creation of a multiparty system—were, of course, pure fabrications. Kéthly was also worried about the Right extremist danger and wrote in the first edition of the SDP paper *Népszava*: "Freed from one prison, we will not tolerate that the country should be made into a prison of another color."

Even after their release from prison and internment camp, the differences between the former leftists, who championed the merger with the Communists, and the confessed Right Social Democrats, remained irreconcilable. Eventually, after 1949–1950, almost all of them were arrested with few exceptions, but even in jail they did not communicate with each other. On 1 November Kéthly left for an extraordinary meeting of the Socialist International in Vienna and could no longer return to Hungary. She became the most reputable advocate of the 1956 emigration abroad. György Marosán, the crypto-Communist renegade, released after six years in prison, promptly made a deal with the same Rákosi who had had him arrested at the time and became a high-ranking party functionary before and after the revolution.

The fourth former and new coalition party, the National Peasant Party, was deeply split between known collaborators such as Ferenc Erdei and József Darvas—secret CP members since 1945, both of them were important ministers during the Rákosi era—and the intellectual and literary followers of the "Third Road." At the inaugural meeting they therefore changed their name to Petőfi Party and delegated their newly appointed secretary-general Ferenc Farkas and the respected political thinker István Bibó as minister of state to the coalition cabinet.[13]

However, the political landscape was far more vividly colorful, even during these chaotic days, than what the picture of a reborn four-party coalition is able to convey. The freeing of Cardinal József Mindszenty on 30 October by a military detachment after eight years' imprisonment and his arrival the following day in Budapest evoked great interest both at home and abroad. The prime minister dispatched Tildy and Maléter to the primate in order to encourage him to take a positive stance toward the resumption of work and support for the coalition government. Mindszenty did not promise them anything, and in the end he made an anxiously awaited speech on the radio on the evening of 3 November. It was relatively long-winded and somewhat contradictory, and as far as "successors of the fallen regime" were concerned, to whom evidently Nagy and his government belonged, rather belligerent. Even for many Catholics his laconic observation that "everyone in the country should know that this fight was no revolution but a fight for freedom" was rather confusing. His sociopolitical notions were rather vague as well: "We want to live in a constitutional state, in a society without classes, and develop our democratic achievements. We are for private ownership rightly and justly limited by social interests." He also spoke in favor of the immediate resumption of work and against acts of personal revenge. It was less the content than the unaccustomed style that elicited bewilderment in some people.[14] Communist propaganda, of course, later made the most of the vagueness of some of his pronouncements in order to distort them into a blanket demand for a restoration of the pre-1945 political and social order.

However, his mere presence served as an encouragement for the conservative, predominantly Catholic politicians who gathered around him. During these days several such groupings emerged. Although because of the lack of meaningful surveys it is difficult to assess their electoral strength, it is certain that the Democratic People's Party (whose predecessor in 1947 received 800,000 votes), the Catholic People's Party, the Christian Democratic People's Party, and other Christian right-conservative parties would have received many votes in free elections. Already leaflets and posters, as well as some commentators at Radio Free Europe, demanded that Mindszenty be appointed head of the government or head of state. The primate, however, declined any political role but stressed: "I am and remain independent of any party and—because of my office—also above it."

As far as the general political scene was concerned, according to the historian György Litván[15] there were four main strains of thought: reform socialist, national democratic, national conservative, and extreme right-wing. In 1986 the former oppositional historian Miklós Szabó distinguished four political trends and factors behind the façade of the oft-invoked "revolutionary national unity": the groups of the former inner-party opposionists led by Imre Nagy, the non-Communist parties of the coalition, the armed insurgents and workers' councils, and finally political Catholicism.[16]

In recapitulating, one can see that the contours of a multiparty system became visible after a few days. It is a moot question whether in a free and secret election the coalition parties would have received a sufficient majority of votes, and whether their cooperation would have survived the tensions of a transitional period. We should not forget, though, that in 1947, when the elections were already manipulated and were held under overt political pressure, the Catholic and bourgeois parties nonetheless received 40 percent of the votes.

The apparent relaxation and the process of political consolidation in the country were the direct outcome of those weighty foreign policy decisions which the Nagy government made on 1 November and which it announced at 7:15 p.m.[17] This illustrates the inherent and irresolvable contradiction of the Hungarian Revolution's triumph and tragedy. The only way in which Nagy could surmount the problem of his government's being constantly out of step with the revolutionary masses was by resorting to action. After the Soviet Presidium's crucial secret decision of 31 October, massive Soviet troop movements signaled to the government and the people that the Kremlin had reached the end of its tether.

This predicament left only two options for preventing an invasion: capitulation or flight forward. Nagy chose the latter alternative. The cabinet, including János Kádár, unanimously decided to renounce the Warsaw Pact and declare Hungary's neutrality, calling upon the four permanent members of the UN Security Council to guarantee this. Nagy, who had also taken over the foreign affairs portfolio in the early morning of 1 November, informed Ambassador Andropov of this decision, asking for the immediate withdrawal of the new Soviet units that had entered Hungary. All accredited ambassadors in Budapest were informed as well, and the secretary-general of the United Nations requested that the Hungarian question be put on the agenda of the forthcoming UN General Assembly.

For three and a half decades politicians, diplomats, and historians in the West and the East have regarded these decisions as an imprudent provocation and as the actual cause for the second Soviet intervention, laying the blame for their tragic consequences at the door of the Nagy government.[18] Today we know from the afore-quoted secret documents that the actual decision had already been reached in the Kremlin, and all that the Nagy government could do was merely to give the optimal answer to it. However, we also know that the international conditions for the open repudiation of the status quo laid down at Yalta were extremely poor, even hopeless; that the United States and the other Western powers neither could nor wanted to pick up the gauntlet of the unilateral announcement of neutrality; and that the putative allies, such as China, Yugoslavia, and Poland, acted either as Moscow's accomplices or as mute but clued-up witnesses to the crushing of the revolution. The assumption that the announcement of neutrality before the international public could be a trump card against the Soviets and that this would restrain them from attacking the country also turned out to be illusory.

This package of ominous choices was doubtless a leap in the dark. Was Nagy aware that, as a statesman of a nation and as a Hungarian patriot, he was acting for the first time in his life in tune with the will of the people? And did this knowledge overshadow everything from the indoctrinated Communist Party discipline to the circumspection of an experienced real-politician?[19] Was he aware that the country he was leading was totally isolated? Was his confidence in the United Nations or the Western powers more than just the proverbial clutching at straws? Until the very last, Nagy also attempted to use all the remaining possibilities to influence the Kremlin. He spent the valuable last hours with the Romanian deputy foreign minister, Aurel Malnaseanu, to try to recruit the Romanian party chief, Gheorghiu-Dej, as an intermediary. What a naive notion! Gheorghiu-Dej had the Hungarian announcement of neutrality publicly condemned and took extraordinary precautionary measures, especially in Transylvania. What is more, he even offered Khrushchev the participation of Romanian troops in crushing the Hungarian Revolution.[20]

On this fateful evening, even before Nagy's radio speech, János Kádár and Ferenc Münnich disappeared.[21] The flight to Moscow for Minister of State Kádár, chairman of the Hungarian Socialist Workers' Party, was an adventure with a dubious outcome. In a more profound sense, it was on this day that the agenda was set for the future of Hungary. It was actually a double dive into darkness: for Nagy by his uncompromising choice in favor of the nation and against "the Fatherland of the Proletariat," and for János Kádár by desertion to the opposing side and the mark of Cain for all the world to see. On this day the seal was set on the personal destinies of these two men and of the country.

The scenario for crushing the revolution was finalized along general lines on 31 October, prepared militarily during the following days, and, after Khrushchev's discussions with the Chinese, Polish, Romanian, Czechoslovak, and Yugoslav party leaderships, politically secured. What had not been decided yet, though, was the identity of the male protagonist. Who should become the prime minister of the government forced on Hungary by the colonial power? The debates in Moscow at a session of the Presidium and then during the night-long negotiations with Tito at Brioni concerned the choice between János Kádár and Ferenc Münnich.

The then seventy-year-old Münnich, barely known abroad, was without doubt one of the most interesting personalities, with an unusual career in the Communist movement of Hungary.[1] A doctor of law and a lieutenant during World War I, he was captured by the Russians as early as October 1915 and soon joined the Russian Communist (Bolshevik) Party. He then fought in the Russian Civil War as commander of an international unit. After his return to Hungary, he became a founding member of the Hungarian Communist Party. After the fall of the short-lived Hungarian Soviet Republic, where he had been a political commissar in the army, and a brief sojourn in Austria and Germany, Münnich emigrated to the Soviet Union in 1922. From 1936 on he fought in the Spanish Civil War as a divisional chief of staff in the International Brigade. After the defeat of the Republicans, he was interned in France and returned to Moscow in 1941. During World War II he fought at the front and later became head of the Hungarian Department of Radio Moscow. From 1946 to 1949, he was chief of police in Budapest, and following that he held diplomatic posts as envoy in Helsinki and Sofia and from 1954 to 1956 in Moscow. Prior to the uprising in 1956, he had filled the post of ambassador to Belgrade for a mere three months. As early as 24 October he was co-opted into the Hungarian Working People's Party's Central Committee and served on its Military

Committee and the Presidium, concurrently holding office in the capacity of interior minister.

During the Stalin era the so-called Spaniards, that is, those who had served in the civil war, belonged to a politically suspect category. That is why, despite his merits, Münnich was given politically insignificant if personally pleasant posts. He could attribute his survival during the time of the purges and also the important ambassadorship to Moscow to his contacts with Soviet military intelligence (GRU). He stepped into the limelight at home during the posthumous Rajk funeral, when in his speech he condemned the "sadistic criminals crawling into the light out of the bog of the personality cult" for the murder of Rajk. The corpulent Münnich was a hard drinker, a fun-loving womanizer, and a convivial man who had married his secretary, who was thirty-five years younger, just before the revolution. None of that, however, influenced his decades-long absolute loyalty to the Soviet leadership. He spoke several languages, foremost among them, of course, Russian, as he had spent some twenty years in the Soviet Union—albeit with some interruptions.

Münnich's key role in the Soviet decision-making process had already become manifest when Khrushchev mentioned his cry for help at the decisive Presidium session on 31 October. He had most probably kept in close contact with the Soviet military prior to their withdrawal from the inner city, as well as afterward with the Soviet Embassy. On 1 November, after the sound recording of his above-mentioned fiery commitment to freedom and independence, Kádár had voted also for the secession from the Warsaw Pact and for neutrality at the session of the coalition government. In the course of that evening he also took part at a discussion with the Chinese ambassador at the prime minister's office. Then came a call from Münnich from the Interior Ministry that the Soviet ambassador, Andropov, wanted to speak to him and Kádár.[2] As there are no documents available about the events, one can build only on the various reminiscences. All of them confirm that Andropov spoke to Münnich on the phone and that subsequently Münnich and Kádár drove to the Soviet Embassy in a service car. The entrance gate, however, was locked. Several minutes later, a car appeared with two Soviet representatives, who asked them to get in. After a brief consultation the two Hungarians sent their own car away. From that moment on, the two of them disappeared without a trace. It was only the following morning that Kádár's disappearance was noticed. Most of the ministers were in the habit of spending the night in the Parliament, as was Kádár. His wife was staying with a friend. When she was informed of his disappearance and escorted to the Parliament, she broke into tears. She was convinced that her husband had been abducted. When Andropov later appeared in Parliament to receive yet another protest against the Soviet troop concentrations, Nagy irritably asked him to give some information about Kádár's and Münnich's disappearances as well. The embassy was dealing "with nasty matters" that could "make a bad impression," and Andropov should find out where the two of them were. According to his telegram to Moscow, Andropov "categorically rejected" this suspicion. His hypocritical behavior only reinforced Nagy's conviction: "Kádár and Münnich, but in the first place Kádár, have been lured into a trap by the Russians and abducted. (It is possible that Münnich helped them!)"

On the other hand, the official version, promulgated for decades, affirmed that Kádár and Münnich had decided "to leave the government and to find a solution that would bring to an end the looming tragic process and the approaching catastrophe." In reality Kádár had no intention of leaving Budapest. He wore only a suit jacket when he left the Parliament Building; it is most unlikely that he would have wanted to betake himself to Moscow on a cold November night without an overcoat. At the Tököl Soviet military air base on Csepel Island near Budapest, Andropov advised him that the highest Soviet leadership wished to confer with him at soon as possible and in the greatest secrecy about the situation in Hungary. Whether Kádár protested against this unusual form of "invitation" or whether he got into the plane without any protest is just as little known as the reason for the fact that, after a stopover at Munkács (Mukacheve) in Carpatho-Ukraine, Münnich and Kádár were separated and transported in two different military airplanes to Moscow. According to the notes of an interpreter written up thirty-four (!) years after the events, Kádár was picked up by him and a colleague at daybreak at Vnukovo Airport. Kádár was wearing a gray jacket and dark pants, and later that day he was provided with an additional pair of socks and an overcoat.[3] Not exactly the established method of protocol for welcoming a high-ranking guest in the Soviet Union! There is another indirect piece of evidence for the remarkable circumstances of this flight. At the time Leonid Brezhnev, then still in the Soviet leadership's second echelon as CC secretary, received the two Hungarians in the party headquarters of Munkács during their stopover. Sixteen years later, during a break in a delicate one-on-one negotiation in a hunting lodge about the "overly liberal" Hungarian course, Brezhnev suddenly turned to the worried Kádár: "The two of us have already been in a difficult situation. Do you remember our flight at dawn on 2 November 1956? You were sitting there, sunk into yourself, alone, not knowing what kind of fate awaited you. But I wasn't in a better situation either, because Khrushchev had told me: 'You are risking your head if this operation misfires.' But it succeeded," said Brezhnev emotionally, almost with tears in his eyes, and embraced the old man, who was also touched. This is the story told to Kádár's biographer by the erstwhile interpreter and later Russian ambassador to Budapest Valeri Musatov.[4]

At any rate, all these conditions show that on that morning Kádár was not—or not yet—received in Moscow as the party chief of a fraternal country. Hungarian historians are hardly wide of the mark in their assumption that he was taken to Moscow as a potential or halfway prisoner, if not by physical force then at least under strong political pressure. So far there is nothing, either in Budapest or in Moscow, that approximates an exact or reliable picture of these fateful events. The only thing that is certain is that Kádár was neither physically nor politically prepared for this trip to Moscow.[5] We therefore have to pose the fundamental question: Why was he party to events in Budapest and then in Moscow?

The unprovable, yet most likely, answer can be only fear.[6] The then forty-four-year-old Kádár, born out of wedlock to a housemaid, was active all his adult life in the Communist movement. He spent three and a half years behind bars in the interwar years and almost as much time during the Rákosi era. If Kádár was in fact abducted that night, he would have been fully aware that he was completely in the hands of the Soviet leaders. Were he to refuse the role intended for him, his next appearance could be only as the second defendant in the Nagy trial, or he could simply disappear for a very long time in a cellar of the Ljubljanka or somewhere in Siberia. Kádár never spoke about those days, not even with his closest party comrades. Only once, when his mind was already clouded, on the eve of his complete mental derangement when he made an obscure and dramatic speech to the Central Committee in April 1989, did he speak in erratic, barely comprehensible sentences about his trip to Moscow: "It wasn't just my responsibility that was on the line; my life and many other people's lives depended on [it] ... and it's not just your life that's at stake but the lives of God knows how many other people.... My most important objective by far at that time was to get to Szolnok in safety. Whichever way I could!" And then came the most important, the telltale, sentence: "When I was again free to move about (in Szolnok). . . ." He repeated over and over, almost manically in this last homily before his death: "I was not a Soviet agent."[7]

We shall return to his harrowing statements in connection with the trial of Imre Nagy. The point at issue now is the background of the historically significant decisions in Moscow and the key role played by Kádár. This is how the Hungarian contemporary historian Miklós Szabó describes Kádár's personality:

> In every important phase he behaved in a cowardly manner. In the illegal movement he gave evidence against others and was expelled for this. Reactivated in 1942, by 1943 he became secretary of the practically nonexistent party. In prison during the German occupation, Kádár escaped after a bombing attack on the building, but did not join the resistance movement. According to his own statement, Kádár was willing in 1951 in Rákosi's prison to accept every false accusation to avoid being tortured. In 1945–55 he did not take part in the intraparty opposition for fear of Rákosi, and he had the same motive in November 1956, as Rákosi's return could have cost him his head.[8]

Kádár was always a typical Bolshevik Party soldier. Neither a leopard nor a tiger, but not a field mouse either: This was the gist of what he said about himself in what was, for him, an upfront speech on the occasion of a dinner in honor of his sixtieth birthday. One cannot even speculate about what he must have thought during the flight to Moscow. Probably something similar to what the four Communist agitators did in Brecht's parable *The Measures Taken* while standing in front of a party tribunal represented by a chorus of controllers.[9] They had been in China on a propaganda mission, in the course of which they had to shoot their youngest comrade. The aim of the didactic play therefore is to demonstrate politically wrong behavior, thereby to teach what is right: "Who fights for Communism must be able to fight and not to fight, to say the truth and not to say the truth, to render and to deny a service, to keep a promise and to break a promise, to go into danger and to avoid danger, to be known and to be unknown. Who fights for Communism has of all the virtues only one: that he fights for Communism."

According to corresponding Russian sources, the experiment with Kádár and Münnich's assignment to lure him into the trap were due to a large degree to the Soviet ambassador Yuri Andropov's scheme. The best Russian experts on the revolution and on Kádár's role, among them Vladimir Kryuchkov, the former secretary of the Soviet Embassy in Hungary and later KGB chairman, and the Soviet leadership's Hungarologist and later Russian ambassador to Budapest Valeri Musatov, confirmed to me in Budapest and Moscow that Andropov had played a very significant role in the choice of Kádár as head of the Soviet puppet government.[10] He was ambassador to Budapest from 1954 to 1957, incidentally cotemporaneously with Kryuchkov. Andropov became increasingly suspicious of Imre Nagy. In contrast to Mikoyan, the ambassador put all his money on Kádár, and it was he who played the principal part in deceiving the Nagy government. According to Georgi Arbatov, Brezhnev's adviser and Andropov's colleague, the telegrams that the latter had sent to Moscow in the fall of 1956 were unusually candid and even unusually sharp.

> Perhaps these reports saved his political career after the invasion of Hungary when, in his own words, all communications sent home were scrutinized with microscopic accuracy ... he was a forty-two-year-old provincial party functionary, brought up during the Stalin era, who had not yet accumulated any international experience and had been trained entirely in the spirit of the ideological dogmas. I always had the impression that the idiosyncrasies of Andropov's intellectual preconceptions and the historic events in whose center he happened to find himself produced in him what people who got to know him later called his "Hungarian syndrome." They defined it as an extremely oversuspicious attitude vis-à-vis the domestic difficulties in the Socialist countries.

At the same time Andropov was also more farsighted than many other Soviet politicians, and that is why he supported Kádár "as much as possible." According to Arbatov, a number of politicians in Moscow did not understand Andropov's recommendation and, because of his arrest by Rákosi with Moscow's approval, regarded Kádár as a potentially unreliable ally. "In the meantime Andropov succeeded in convincing Moscow that Kádár should become head of the party. Kádár's assumption of power helped to bring Hungary out of her deep crisis and allowed society to recover to a certain extent," Arbatov concluded in his reflections.[11] Kryuchkov and the young diplomats serving in Budapest had greatly admired Andropov's courage, tenacity, and composure in the midst of the gun battles in October–November 1956.[12]

Most observers and contemporaries rightly emphasize that apart from the particular case of Republic Square, there were very few instances of lynch law in Hungary during the revolution. Still, one must not overlook these either, and especially not as far as their influence on the Soviet, but also the Chinese and Yugoslav, diplomats and observers was concerned. Only then can one understand the change in the Chinese and Yugoslav attitudes based on the reports received from their representatives in Budapest. Even today, fifty years later, Kryuchkov, who speaks fluent Hungarian, recalled the "terrible events" in his conversation with me. Andropov's attitude, too, according to Arbatov, was determined by his personal and profoundly emotional impressions; allegedly he too had been in danger several times. Well-timed toughness and, afterward, flexibility was Andropov's motto after his Hungarian experiences. It is not generally known that not only did Andropov and Kryuchkov play key roles in Hungary, but that conversely the trauma of their experiences in 1956 had a formative effect for years, perhaps even decades, on both men, who later became heads of the KGB. According to Oleg Gordievsky, the top Soviet intelligence defector in London, in his first address to the KGB directorate, Andropov explained that "only by flexibility can we avoid a repetition of 1956."[13] Alexei Adzhubei, Khrushchev's son-in-law, wrote after the change of regime that "the Hungarian Revolution brutally shaped Andropov's view of Eastern Europe."[14]

In contrast to the overwhelming majority of the leadership and the line represented by Andropov and the KGB chief Serov, Mikoyan, who had just returned from Budapest, appealed for a revision of the invasion plans reached in his absence. At the Presidium meeting on 1 November he insisted that the use of force would not help anything, and that they should support the current government. He argued that it was still possible to wait ten to fifteen days to see how the situation would unfold, although he agreed that "we cannot let Hungary escape from our camp."[15]

Mikoyan had already protested against the decision to invade at a meeting with Khrushchev, and had asked that another meeting of the CPSU Presidium be called, a demand Khrushchev refused on the grounds of a unanimous resolution. At this meeting all the members, and in particular Marshals Zhukov and Konev, argued for the occupation of Hungary. During the continuation of the meeting, Mikoyan repeated his earlier comments, albeit in a more moderate form, about at least maintaining contact with the Nagy government. However, he too regarded it as a tactical move: "If Hungary becomes a base for imperialism, then there is no more place for discussion." As far as the immediate future was concerned, Suslov's suggestion that "the honest ones should be separated"[16] was significant. That was a hint that the members of the "Provisional Revolutionary Government," that is, in particular Kádár and Münnich, should be brought to Moscow.

Kádár gave a very long and nuanced presentation before that august body, eight of whose members attended on 2 November.[17] His comments on two possible alternatives clearly indicate that he had not known anything definite—even if he might have had a vague inkling—about the earlier decision and its confirmation the previous day, nor that preparations had already been made for a military intervention. While stressing the danger of a counterrevolution, he argued that the promised withdrawal of Soviet troops would give a much better chance for the Communists than the use of military force, which would be destructive and lead to bloodshed. He did not doubt that Hungary could be held by military means. But what would happen afterward? asked Kádár; he drew the devastating and profoundly true conclusion: "The moral position of the Communists would be equal to nil." According to Malin's notes, Münnich spoke much more briefly and pessimistically. His conclusion was that events could not be successfully resolved merely by political means. István Bata, the dismissed minister of defense, who was also present for unknown reasons, insisted that order must be restored through a military dictatorship.

The die was cast on 3 November at the next session of the Presidium, when Khrushchev and Malenkov, back from Yugoslavia, joined in as well. After the leadership unanimously approved the scenario of Operation Whirlwind (the code name of the invasion), the topic on the agenda was the composition of the "Provisional Revolutionary Government."

Khrushchev tells us in his memoirs that prior to the appearance of Kádár and Münnich, Molotov had argued strongly against Kádár and in favor of Münnich. However, when the session was continued in the presence of the two Hungarians, Mikoyan at the very start suggested Kádár as the head of government. Before the session, Khrushchev had spoken to Kádár, informing him of the Presidium's decisions. Kádár had agreed. In his speech Khrushchev at first struck a self-critical tone about the earlier mistakes of Soviet policy in Hungary and—contrary to some current legends in Hungary—made it crystal clear that the time of Rákosi and Gerő was irrevocably gone, although he described both men as "honest and loyal Communists." In contrast, he reviled Imre Nagy as a traitor—if he did not resign, then he was in the enemy's pay.[18]

In his speech Kádár did not play down the negative influence of Soviet policy either, but as far as Nagy was concerned, he limited himself to saying that as prime minister he was liable for the murders committed by the counterrevolutionaries, and that the government was not strong enough to rout them. And then came his agreement: "What is to be done? You cannot surrender a Socialist country to counterrevolution. The correct course of action is to form a revolutionary government."

This, however, was followed by some interesting statements, which in this situation must have come as a surprise to the Soviet leaders. Kádár stressed that "the entire nation took part in the movement, and it did not want to destroy the system of the people's democracy. The withdrawal of Soviet troops from Hungary will be of great significance. If we strengthen the military ties, we will become politically weaker." Finally, he talked openly about the injuries to the national sentiment, referring to uniforms, coats of arms, street names, Transylvania, and Upper Hungary. Then he uttered perhaps the most remarkable sentence, condidering his appointment and the impending assault on the legal government whose minister of state he still was: "This government must not be puppetlike; there must be a [popular] base for its activities and support among workers." The next to talk was Münnich, who expressed his agreement with Kádár's assessment and conclusions.

As a result of the party Presidium's resolution, the so-called Provisional Workers' and Peasants' Government was formed in the Kremlin on 3 November; it was led by János Kádár, with Münnich as his deputy as well as defense and interior minister. Khrushchev read out the names of four other ministers, who were, of course, unaware of their luck, as at the time they were in Budapest. They would be brought to Szolnok in eastern Hungary only on 5 November in Soviet armored cars, there to meet Kádár, who had arrived in the meantime from Ungvár (Uzhgorod) in Carpatho-Ukraine. The proclamation of this government was first composed in Russian, so that the party Presidium in Moscow would be able to read and approve it. There are some amendments in the draft in Kádár's handwriting. The fabrication of this Moscow-contrived and compiled government was further fictionalized by the concocted place and date on the document: "Budapest, 4 November. 1956."[19]

What was to take place during the following days and weeks in Budapest and Hungary would far exceed the worst fears of János Kádár, the head of a Soviet colony's phantom government, placed in power with the help of Soviet tanks, and closely supervised for a long time to come.

Operation Whirlwind and Kádár's Phantom Government

At 4:15 a.m. on a foggy, cold, and damp Sunday—it was the fourth of November—the people of Budapest were startled out of their sleep by the sound of tank cannons and gunfire. With the password "Grom-444"(Thunder-444), Marshal Konev, commander in chief of the Warsaw Pact forces, gave the final signal for Operation Vikhr (Whirlwind, the code name of the invasion for crushing the Hungarian Revolution) to commence. Throughout the country some sixty thousand Soviet soldiers were deployed. Hundreds of tanks moved toward the center of the city. The Soviet military acted far more brutally than during the first intervention. If anyone shot at them, they responded by shelling whole blocks, loosing off streams of gunfire indiscriminately into the houses to force the insurgents to capitulate and to terrify the people. The divisions of the Special Corps were now supported by tanks, artillery, and airborne troops.

To Khrushchev's question how much time would be needed for the Soviet troops to restore order in Hungary, Defense Minister Marshal Zhukov replied: "Three days." Even though the attack had taken them by surprise, the insurgents did not surrender to the numerical superiority of the enemy without resistance. On the Danube island of Csepel and in the industrial center Stalintown (today's Dunaújváros), fighting continued until 11 November. It was characteristic of the enormous force, which the Soviet High Command had decided to employ this time, that, for instance, 170 cannons and grenade launchers shot at the positions of the insurgents at the Corvin Passage for two full hours before an entire division could storm the fortress of the Corvinists.[1]

When the general attack by the Soviet troops commenced, and the fighters at the Kilián Barracks opened fire on the Soviet tanks, which once again tried to penetrate the inner city via Üllői Avenue, the barracks and with it our building on the corner automatically became targets of the grenade launchers, heavy artillery, and the tank cannons. For five whole days we could barely leave the cellar. Eleven and a half years after the end of the war, the inhabitants in the vicinity of the core of the resistance found themselves in an even worse and more dangerous situation than in the last days of World War II. When our building came under direct fire by the tanks, we escaped through the underground connecting cellars and backyards, sometimes on all fours, in order to reach a building at the far end of the block. When after a few days the thunder of cannons fell silent, we went back, and I cautiously approached our apartment. A horrible sight opened before my eyes. The two rooms facing Üllői Avenue were burned and lay in ruins. My entire library had fallen victim to the shelling and cannon fire, as had the lovely furniture, together with the filing cabinets in my father's chambers. Due to an irony of fate, only the collected works of Marx and Lenin survived unscathed in an old laundry basket that we had stored away in the bathroom. We had needed the valuable space on the bookshelves for more interesting books, yet we were not game enough simply to throw out the "classics." I still own a few singed dictionaries and novels that remind me of those November days. We had lost practically all our clothing, and we were homeless, as were many other people in the hard-fought-for nest of resistance of the József- and Ferencváros.

The military-political significance of the fighting can be assessed by the unusual fact that Marshal Zhukov personally sent reports on the military situation to the members of the CPSU Presidium between 4 and 9 November (three times on the fourth, twice on the fifth and sixth, then daily). These reports described the disintegration of the Hungarian Army and the ease of disarming twelve divisions, two armored regiments, and other military units, as well as the entire air force.[2] Even so, there were strong clashes between Hungarian soldiers and the occupation forces in various places in Budapest, but also in the vicinity of Pécs in the Mecsek Mountains in western Hungary, as well as in the former Stalintown. One of the most audacious attacks was carried out by army and National Guard units in the twentieth district against a Soviet convoy of armored vehicles on their way from Soviet headquarters in Tököl to a military air base. These panzers and their escorts were carrying Defense Minister General Pál Maléter, Chief of the General Staff István Kovács, and other high-ranking Hungarian officers. They were members of the delegation of negotiators whom General Ivan Serov, the head of the KGB, had arrested in the evening of 3 November in the building of the Soviet headquarters. Hungarian ÁVH officers had also taken part in that action. There are no documents available concerning this unprecedented act of violence against the authorized delegates of the legal Hungarian government. Several Soviet vehicles were destroyed, and seven Soviet soldiers and four Hungarian State Security officers were killed in the attack. Eventually, Maléter and his associates were taken in the afternoon by helicopter to the military air base.[3]

General Béla Király, commander in chief of the National Guard, withdrew with his unit to the Buda Hills. On 10 November it came to a clash between them and the Soviets at Nagykovácsi (Pest County). After resisting for a short time, General Király and the surviving guardsmen retreated westward. In Budapest the freedom fighters, estimated at most at ten to fifteen thousand, put up a desperate resistance against the oppressive and brutal superior strength of the enemy. The struggle was concentrated above all in the working-class stronghold of Csepel, where on 10 November, according to Marshal Zhukov, three Soviet tanks were blown up, and in the Castle District of Buda. The Soviets paid dearly for the "normalization" of the situation. It was only thirty-five years later that Valeri Musatov, the Soviet expert on Hungary and later Russian ambassador in Budapest, revealed that the Soviet casualties amounted to 699 dead, 1,450 wounded, and 51 men unaccounted for. Hungarian military historians estimate that close to 80 percent of Soviet losses were sustained in skirmishes with the insurgents of the eighth and ninth districts in Budapest.[4]

Much young blood was shed during the fighting. Statistics prove that this was an uprising of the workers and of the young. Casualties amounted to a total of 2,500 dead and some 20,000 wounded. In Budapest 1,569 civilians lost their lives. Half of them were under thirty, and every fifth was under nineteen. Every second wounded person was younger than twenty-five. In Budapest 53 percent of the dead were workers, and of those, 70 percent were industrial laborers and miners. In the armed forces—Army and Interior Ministry forces (secret service special forces, border guards, and police)—423 were listed dead, but the military historian Miklós Horváth estimates that 105 soldiers fell on the side of the insurgents and the National Guard. One cannot even speculate how many of the 200,000 refugees were actual insurgents. The historian of the insurgent groups, László Eörsi, is of the opinion that perhaps one-third of the civilian insurgents left Hungary.

During these clashes the Nagy government did not make an appearance. Strange though this may seem in retrospect, the invasion at the crack of dawn on 4 November came out of the blue not only for average Hungarians. They went to sleep the night before in the belief that at last work would resume and life would go back to normal on Monday. I too was optimistic, and therefore on Saturday I left the apartment of my childhood friend, the actor Pál Elekes, where I had spent a few days during the apparent phase of normalization. The government was also totally surprised. Why? With hindsight and in view of numerous available documents it would, of course, be obvious to accuse Imre Nagy and his advisers of gullibility, even of negligence. However, today we know that at the time there were indications of a compromise, or at least the possibility of gaining time. Let us just think of Mikoyan's attitude during his stay in Budapest and afterward in Moscow, the famous Soviet declaration of 30 October, and the negotiations held on the afternoon of 3 November with a high-ranking Soviet military delegation on the terms and technical details of Soviet troop withdrawals from Hungary that were very positively rated by the Hungarian participants. All these gave cause for a glimmer of hope that there was no imminent danger of an aggressive solution. The short-lived government's press chief, Miklós Vásárhelyi, sentenced to five years' imprisonment in the Nagy trial, tellingly recalled the prevailing atmosphere even four decades later.[5] Matters were different, of course, with regard to the Hungarian government's first (and last) public reaction to the Soviet invasion, which even Vásárhelyi considered questionable.

At 5:20 a.m. Nagy read the following declaration from the broadcasting station in the Parliament Building: "This is Prime Minister Imre Nagy speaking. Today at daybreak Soviet forces attacked our capital with the obvious intention of overthrowing the lawful democratic Hungarian Government. Our troops are in combat. The Government is in its post. I notify the people of our country and the entire world of this fact."

Half an hour later (at 5:56 a.m.) an appeal was broadcast in the name of Nagy for Defense Minister Pál Maléter and Chief of the General Staff István Kovács, who had gone to Soviet headquarters at 10 p.m., to return without further delay in order to take up their respective offices. When Nagy, who had spent the night in the Parliament Building, was woken with news of the Soviet attack, he called Ambassador Andropov between

3:30 and 4. He asked him to get in touch with the Soviet High Command. Andropov called back sometime later, advising that unfortunately he had not been able to establish any contact. He would keep on trying and would let Nagy know. Since Andropov failed, Nagy called the embassy again. The telephone operator advised him that the ambassador had gone to bed.[6]

In the morning, when General Király notified the prime minister of the attack by telephone, Nagy did not give the order for armed resistance but closed the brief conversation with the words: "Thank you, I do not require any further reports." Shaken to the core, the cardiac sufferer was utterly exhausted after a long night's fruitless negotiation with a Romanian delegation, sent to Budapest purely as a diversionary tactic. The text of the five sentences and forty-five words (in the Hungarian original) had been composed jointly by Nagy; the minister of state of the Smallholders, Zoltán Tildy; and Ferenc Donáth, member of the executive committee of the Hungarian Socialist Workers' party, founded a few days earlier. The details of the authorship of the individual sentences were discussed at length in the course of the interrogations prior to the Nagy trial. It was impossible, even during the manipulated trial, to impute to Nagy the intention of calling on the West for an armed intervention. In the brief address repeated, until 8:07 a.m., several times in various languages from the parliamentary radio station, Nagy did not ask for military assistance either from the Western powers or from the United Nations. Nor did he call for armed resistance.

Unfortunately the speech was poorly formulated and basically represented a declaration of political bankruptcy. That a high-ranking Communist functionary and former Soviet citizen should accuse the Soviet Union of naked aggression against a small country for all the world to hear was an unprecedented provocation. After this verbal barrage in the first sentence, the prime minister failed to say anything about what was to be done. During those fateful hours when the country's future was at stake, the people were left to their own devices. The next sentence—"Our troops are in combat"—was incomplete, ambiguous, and misleading. Inundated by a flood of telephoned questions, Nagy passed on the same advice: no resistance, no provocation, no shooting at Soviet troops. The phrasing could, however, be interpreted by insurgents as a call to arms. Many spirited officers and men could have misunderstood the sentence in this way, even if Nagy, according to his own explanation at the questioning, intended it otherwise.[7]

Be that as it may, the following sentence—"The Government is in its post"—was later justly criticized, since after the declaration the government remained "in its post" for only a very short time. While the prime minister, accompanied by Zoltán Szántó and Ferenc Donáth (still guarded by two policemen with submachine guns), fled to the Yugoslav Embassy in a staff car, the radio broadcast a last desperate appeal by the Hungarian Writers' Union: "To every writer in the world, to all scientists, to all writers' federations, to all scientific academies and associations, to the intelligentsia of the world! We ask all of you for help and support; there is but little time! You know the facts, there is no need to give you a special report! Help Hungary! Help the Hungarian writers, scientists, workers, peasants, and our intelligentsia! ... Help! Help! Help!"[8] This appeal, written by the dramatist Gyula Háy and read out by him and his wife also in English, German, and Russian, was repeatedly broadcast until 8:07 a.m. Then Radio Free Kossuth went off the air with a repeated SOS signal.

Imre Nagy's hasty decisions, made under chaotic circumstances and enormous time pressure, have been the subject of endless debates over the decades. Why did the government not stay "in its post," that is in the Parliament, as indicated in the declaration? Or why did not Nagy and his friends, like the three ministers of the Smallholders' Party, simply go home? The asylum offered by the Yugoslav Embassy was then only one of the alternatives. As his biographer János M. Rainer conjectures, it was evidently his "biological and political instinct for life" that caused Nagy to take that course in order to avoid immediate arrest by the Soviets. The impression, however, was politically and morally shattering. The prime minister and his comrades did not inform the close-at-hand minister of state Zoltán Tildy of their flight, nor did they offer the same option for escape to him and the two other ministers of state, István B. Szabó and István Bibó, who had arrived in the meantime after the telephoned summons from Nagy's secretariat.

What happened to the other ministers? The government fell apart within a few hours. Cardinal Mindszenty too went to the Parliament after a telephone conversation with Tildy and fled in the early morning hours to the American embassy. On the other hand, the Americans denied asylum to Minister of State Béla Kovács, as did the British to Szabó. Under these circumstances, the only Hungarian politician who showed any determination and vision was Bibó, a jurist and political scientist who had been sworn in on 3 November, that is, only one day before the attack. He remained in the Parliament Building until 6 November. Under the impression that Nagy was being held at the Soviet Embassy, Bibó, as the only representative of the legal Hungarian government, framed a declaration, which he telephoned through that same morning to the U.S. Embassy, and on 6 November, with the help of the French cultural attaché, passed on to the British and French diplomatic representatives. In this last official act of the legal Hungarian government, Bibó, among others, pointed out the following:

> Hungary has no intention of pursuing an anti-Soviet policy.... I reject before the entire world the slanderous claim that the glorious Hungarian Revolution was stained by fascist or anti-Semitic excesses.... The Hungarian people only opposed the alien army of the conqueror and its own units of executioners. The rough and ready justice that we experienced for a few days in the streets was brought under control just as the new government brought to a halt the unarmed reappearance of old conservative forces. The assertion that this need justified calling or, better, recalling a large alien army into the country is cynical and irresponsible. On the contrary, the presence of the army on our soil is a principal cause of unrest and disruption. I call upon the Hungarian people to regard neither the occupation force nor the puppet government it may install as a legal authority but rather to employ every means of passive resistance against it, excepting only the interruption of public services and water supply in Budapest. I am not in a position to order armed resistance. I joined the government only one day ago and it would be irresponsible for me to decide about shedding the blood of Hungary's youth. The Hungarian people have sacrificed enough blood to demonstrate to the world their commitment to freedom and justice. It is now the turn of the powers of the world to demonstrate the force of the founding principles of the United Nations and the power of the peaceloving peoples. I beseech the Great Powers

and the United Nations to intervene wisely and courageously
for the freedom of my subjugated people. I declare that the only
authorized representative of Hungary abroad and the legal head
of the diplomatic service is Minister of State Anna Kéthly.[9]

While this declaration, dated 4 November and signed by Bibó as
minister of state, had no practical significance, its political and symbolic meaning was all the more important, just as his *Draft Proposal for a
Compromise Solution of the Hungarian Question*, which was formulated two
days later and conveyed to the Indian and three Western embassies.[10] In
this document Bibó, once again in his capacity as the only lawful representative of the last legal Hungarian government, detailed the manner
in which the security interests of the Soviet Union could be protected
(for example, by substituting a bilateral Hungarian-Soviet treaty for
the Warsaw Pact) and in what way the anxieties of the Communists
could be placated (for instance, by an amnesty for all political transgressions). Finally he suggested a schedule for the withdrawal of Soviet
troops within a month and a half. Only if the withdrawal of Soviet forces
could not be managed smoothly would the intervention of UN forces
become necessary. In the domestic sphere Bibó proposed the conven-
ing of a revolutionary national constitutional assembly. It should consist
of delegates from workers' councils and revolutionary committees who
would decide about the nature of the new state structure on the basis
of a republican constitution and a parliamentary democracy. He envis-
aged the retention of the land reform of 1945, and the nationalization
of mines, banks, and heavy industry, as well as cooperatively organized
enterprises through workers' self-management, public shares, or profit
sharing. Private property would also be guaranteed with the proviso of
prohibition of exploitation.

Notwithstanding the difficult conditions of the occupation, this
measured approach of arguably the most significant Hungarian thinker
of the twentieth century was discussed and approved of in wide circles
of intellectuals, organized labor, and the political parties. Bibó eventually
handed the document in early December to K.P.S. Menon, India's ambassador in Moscow, also accredited in Budapest, with the request to forward
it to Soviet prime minister N. A. Bulganin. The ambassador complied;
however, Bulganin's reaction was "noncommittal."[11] Incidentally, that day

Bibó gathered impressions in Parliament, which he described only more than twenty years later in an interview.[12] To get a picture of events one has to realize that the Parliament Building, planned by Imre Steindl, completed in 1902, and built, after the model of Westminster, on the banks of the Danube, was at the time the largest structure in the world housing a legislative body. This huge edifice, built in an eclectic mixture of styles embracing Westminster gothic, Hungarian medieval, and French Renaissance, boasted no fewer than twenty-seven gates. It was also, from its inception, the seat of the Council of Ministers and other associated institutions. In view of the endless corridors and innumerable offices, as well as a number of apartments and reception halls for the deputy prime ministers and ministers, it was quite possible that on two different floors the remainders of two phantom governments would be waiting independently from each other for decisions from the outside.

The Nagy government's three ministers of state believed—as already mentioned—that Imre Nagy was in the Soviet Embassy. The officer on duty of the parliamentary guard had heard only the words "to the embassy" when Nagy and his escorts fled in the car. He had presumed that on this occasion too, as during the past few days, this could only mean the Soviet Embassy, and he informed Minister of State Tildy. When Bibó arrived back at the Parliament from his lightning visit to the American embassy, he saw a large gathering in the room adjoining the radio studio, where Tildy, his wife, and István B. Szabó were sitting. Present also was the nominal head of state of the Rákosi era, the former Smallholder politician and crypto-Communist István Dobi. Next to him sat his former party colleague, the fellow traveler József Bognár, who had served in the governments of Rákosi and Hegedüs, as well as in the first cabinet of Nagy. Finally there appeared the long-standing president of the assembly, Sándor Rónai, a former Social Democrat who had been a secret CP member from the outset.

Meanwhile there were already rumors about a radio broadcast in which it was said that János Kádár had formed a countergovernment in Szolnok and that Sándor Rónai was also mentioned as its member. Consequently, Tildy asked Rónai whether it was true that he was a member of that government. Rónai replied, "I know only as much about it as you do, since I am sitting here, I too have only heard about it now." To this Tildy retorted: "Well, and would you be its member if they asked you to?" "You know I have always been a supporter of the coalition and I am for taking part in every good Hungarian cause," replied Rónai. Whereupon Bibó remarked with a certain edge that he could see only one good Hungarian cause in this situation, which led to Dobi's somber interjection that this Hungarian cause could be viewed through a number of various glasses. Bibó countered: "Through a number of various glasses, yes, but when one takes the glasses off, there is only one way."

However, it was not merely a harmless exchange of bons mots, but an accidental, yet profoundly symbolic, encounter between victors and vanquished, ensnared weaklings and innocent sinners—with the sinister presentiment of soon-to-be settled scores. The parliamentary guard put down their arms at 8 a.m., and soon after Major General K. Grebennik, the deputy of KGB chief Serov, entered the building. The ministers of the Rákosi-Hegedüs government, holding out on another floor, particularly Dobi and Rónai, welcomed the general as their savior. Some time later, Dobi, more or less constantly under the influence, fabricated the story that in the night of 4 November, shortly before the arrival of the Soviet "liberators," he and Rónai had been led into the cellar by "a former Horthy major in the old uniform and four soldiers." He then presented this horror story during the first sitting of the reconvened Parliament in May 1957.[13] Incidentally, Dobi held the office of head of state until 1967 (since 1952!) and Rónai as president of the assembly until 1962.

The rumor about Rónai squared with the facts. After 5 a.m. on 4 November, a Soviet radio station broadcast an "Open Letter to the Working People of Hungary," read out by Ferenc Münnich, in which he advised that he, Kádár, Antal Apró, and István Kossa had broken with the Nagy government on 1 November and founded the Hungarian Revolutionary Workers' and Peasants' Party. "As members of the government we could no longer watch idly ... while, under the cover of democracy, counterrevolutionary terrorists and bandits were bestially murdering our worker and peasant brothers and terrorizing our peaceful citizens, dragging our country into anarchy, and putting our entire nation under the yoke of counterrevolution for a long time to come." In a subsequent, lengthier manifesto read out by Kádár, among others Rónai was named minister of commerce, György Marosán minister of state, and Antal Apró minister of industry. In reality both Apró and Marosán found out about their appointments in Budapest, or rather at Soviet headquarters in Tököl.

They had decamped from the Parliament in the evening of 2 November with the help of Soviet troops in order to await developments there. Only on 5 November did they fly in a Soviet military plane to Szolnok. There they met Marshal Konev and Kádár. That evening the minister of finance designate, István Kossa, joined the group; he had fled with his wife from Budapest to Czechoslovakia, whence he was brought to Szolnok by the Soviets. Kádár, Marosán, and Kossa were then transported to Budapest in Soviet military vehicles on the night of 6 and 7 November. In the sleet and snow, the convoy avoided the main roads, lost its way several times, and required almost nine hours for the ninety-seven-kilometer drive.[14] At 7 a.m. Marshal Zhukov informed Khrushchev in his "top secret" report that the "the government of the Hungarian People's Republic has left Szolnok and has arrived in Budapest at 4:10 a.m."

The three or four members of Kádár's phantom government, who had been personally appointed by Khrushchev in Moscow, were brought to Budapest by the Soviet Army under the strictest security precautions. They met their eagerly waiting hangers-on, Dobi and Rónai, in the deserted Parliament, which was totally blocked off by the Soviet military. Five days earlier they had not dared to go to the Soviet headquarters at Tököl with Marosán and the others. On 7 November, at 2 p.m., three days after their proclamation on the radio, the ministers took the oath of office before "President" István Dobi and the phantom government's secretary of the Presidential Council; that is, they signed a piece of paper without any further ado.[15] The *Hungarian Gazette* appeared only on 12 November, so that the Kádár government's swearing in was backdated to 4 November, the day when Kádár and Münnich were still sitting in a Soviet plane on their way to Carpatho-Ukraine. Kádár's "revolutionary government" was born on 4 November by way of a constitutional fiction and became viable only much later. In the course of all the later considerable concessions, the regime had to uphold the fiction of its questionable birth during its thirty-three years of existence.

The phantom government at first had neither an army nor a police force; it did not even have a staff of administrative employees. It was totally dependent on Soviet protection. In his first order of the day of 6 November, Major General Grebennik, who had been appointed military commander of the city, ordered a curfew between 7 p.m. and 7 a.m. When Andropov visited Kádár in the Parliament at noon on 8 November, he was surprised to note that at the time, apart from the six ministers and the Soviet soldiers, there was not another solitary soul in the enormous building. In his, as usual, top-secret report to members of the Presidium, the Central Committee secretaries, and the leading officials of the Foreign Ministry, Andropov drew the correct conclusion that "our friends still have no contact with party workers, and for the time being still operate in isolation." During their conversation, Kádár himself admitted that he had hardly any contact with the provinces, nor with the Budapest factories.[16] What happened was exactly what Kádár had warned about in his earlier-cited remarkable speech in Moscow on 2 November, namely that the use of military force would cause the morale of the Communists to be reduced to zero—and it was.

Since his arrival in the shadow of Soviet tanks, János Kádár was *the* traitor personified in the eyes of the Hungarian and foreign public, the agent of a hated regime in the service of a foreign power. Only after the publication of many, though by no means all, Soviet secret documents can one appreciate in hindsight the extent of the close and complete control exerted over Kádár. The Soviet Army, as the occupying power, governed the rebellious colony. In all of Budapest's districts and in the larger towns, Soviet command posts were established. Under the personal leadership of the KGB chief, who had remained in Budapest, officers of the Soviet State Security, together with the reinstated Hungarian ÁVH men, made numerous arrests. According to a report by General Serov, in the course of a fortnight Soviet troops arrested a total of 4,700 persons, 860 of those having been deported to Uzhgorod and Strij in Soviet Carpatho-Ukraine.[17] In view of the extent of the deportations, promptly reported by the Hungarian railwaymen, and the people's indignation, Kádár and Münnich had to persuade Serov and Andropov to halt the transports to Soviet territories.

Kádár was not permitted to leave the Parliament; he was not only guarded but also supervised by Soviet soldiers. The Soviet tanks entering Budapest, which transported Kádár and some members of his government to the Parliament, also carried Kádár's personal adviser, V. S. Baikov, the Hungarian-speaking Soviet functionary (later embassy councillor in Budapest). He remained in his close proximity and did not let him out of his sight even during the night. Several times a day he gave Khrushchev status reports via a direct telephone line.[18] The most important decision, however, had been to send the CPSU Presidium members Suslov and Malenkov, as well as the Central Committee secretary Aristov to Budapest. Their task was to guide the impotent and isolated puppet government by "hand controls." The top three Soviet functionaries remained in the Hungarian capital for over a month in the strictest secrecy. The crucial decisions—from the deportation of the Imre Nagy group to the imposition of summary jurisdiction and the first executions—took place during their clandestine meetings with Kádár. The Russian historians of the period, Vyacheslav Sereda and Alexander Stikalin, aptly observed in this context: "It is hardly an exaggeration to assert that in a not exactly uncomplicated period of her history, Hungary was governed by Malenkov and Suslov."[19]

In the cliff-hanger days following the Soviet intervention, many people in Hungary and abroad wondered what would happen to Imre Nagy and his colleagues. Some observers were surprised that he had sought asylum in the Yugoslav Embassy, of all places. The reinstatement of the Nagy government was the principal demand of those workers and students, writers and artists, who were determined to resist. That is why the mere existence of the legitimate head of government, recognized by the people, constituted a lethal threat in the long run to János Kádár's phantom government, which was relying on Russian bayonets—irrespective of the fact that the group around Nagy in the embassy, that is, in extraterritorial territory, was totally isolated from the world.

There were not only two heads of government without power after 1 November, but also two party leaderships without parties. Of the seven members of the temporary executive committee of the Hungarian Socialist Workers' Party founded on 31 October, five were in the Yugoslav Embassy, and the sixth member, Sándor Kopácsi, was arrested in Budapest by the KGB on 5 November. At the same time, the president of that body, János Kádár, acted against his own comrades in the name of a phantom party. Against this background the appeal of the nonexistent temporary Central Committee of the nonexistent Hungarian Socialist Workers' Party—hailed as newly founded (dated 7 November)—must have appeared strange even to members of the Soviet Presidium.

Kádár had conveyed the draft from Szolnok to Moscow for approval. At the sitting of the party Presidium in the Kremlin,[1] Molotov and Kaganovich objected to giving a new name to the revived Hungarian Communist Party and to the term "Rákosi-Gerő clique" in the draft. Moreover, Molotov questioned the meaningfulness and legitimacy of the new party. He complained: "In whose name is this document being suggested? The composition of the new Central Committee is just as unknown as the principles from which it is supposed to originate." When he went even further in his second critical statement by saying that "we are responsible for Hungary—even without Stalin," Khrushchev, supported by his followers, flew into a rage. They vehemently rejected Molotov and Kaganovich's criticism and their attempts to exculpate the group around Rákosi. At any rate, it was resolved that the Hungarian friends should "tactfully" be informed of the Presidium's wish that the Nagy-Losonczy-Donáth group should be sharply condemned. Kádár incorporated these changes, though he dropped the mention of Ferenc Donáth. These episodes about the first steps of the Kádár government and the party invented by him distinctly demonstrate how minimal his elbow room was at that stage as head of the puppet government.

The Soviet-Yugoslav scenario for handling the political implications of the military intervention assigned a special role to Tito's regime, whose prestige at the time was at its peak in the eyes of the Hungarian reform Communist circles around Imre Nagy. The Yugoslav leadership was supposed to persuade Nagy and his followers officially to step down after—or even before—the Soviet attack on Budapest and to recognize the Kádár government. With the benefit of hindsight, this was one of the main topics, possibly by far the most important arrangement, in the course of Khrushchev's and Malenkov's ten-hour secret discussion on the island of Brioni with Tito, Ranković, and Kardelj during the night of 2–3 November.

In the course of the implementation, a request by Minister of State Géza Losonczy and Zoltán Szántó, member of the Executive Committee, on 1 November might have played an unforeseen role. In a conversation with the Yugoslav ambassador, Dalibor Soldatić, the two Hungarians asked whether in view of the unstable public safety conditions it would be possible temporarily to move some women and children to the embassy. This informal and personal request was then used two days later as a transparent pretext for selling the Nagy government down the river.

At around 1 a.m. on 4 November, Zoltán Szántó was roused from his sleep. The Yugoslav ambassador wanted to talk to him urgently. A few minutes later he was picked up by a Yugoslav diplomat in an embassy car. The ambassador informed him that he had passed on to Belgrade his request for accommodating the women and children, and that a few hours earlier he had received the following reply: "The situation is grave, there may be a fresh attack by Soviet troops at any moment, therefore the government has decided to extend asylum to Imre Nagy, to the members of his executive and anybody the executive considers worthy of it." Szántó had replied that he had no intention of fleeing, nor did he have any knowledge of Nagy or any of the other leading personalities wanting to flee. The ambassador retorted that after he had received the telegram he had phoned Belgrade. The advice was that the comrades should make up their minds quickly to avoid exposing themselves to further adversities.

The ambassador left it to Szántó whether to pass the information on immediately or to wait until the morning. Szántó answered that the comrades had broken up only a little while ago, and that Comrade Nagy was very tired and had already turned in. That is why he would prefer to postpone notifying them until the morning. Szántó then went back home. He was woken around 3:30 a.m. with the news of the Soviet invasion and was immediately summoned to the prime minister's office.[2] After Imre Nagy had read his dramatic appeal over the radio, Szántó informed him about the Yugoslav offer of asylum.[3] The confused, shocked, and over-tired prime minister fell into the trap laid not by Szántó, of course, but by the Yugoslavs.

By deciding to go home that night and—for whatever reason—not informing Nagy immediately, Szántó unwittingly foiled the Yugoslav-Soviet plans.[4] Nagy had spoken out against the intervention for all the world to hear. However, according to the rules of the collusive game between Khrushchev and Tito, he should not have been allowed to take sides against the intervention, nor against the Kádár government. During the night Yugoslav diplomats had been ferrying all of Nagy's closest collaborators and their families, a total of 48 people, including 14 women and 16 children, to the embassy.[5] It was too late, however, to put into practice the "Brioni plan." Meanwhile a fatal error had slipped into the stage directions: Nagy had created a new situation with his radio declaration. Once more the trap snapped shut, but this time Khrushchev, Tito, and Kádár were also caught in it. The Yugoslavs (Tito, Kardelj, and Ranković) at first tried to put Nagy under pressure and—even if belatedly—to persuade him to resign and preferably to withdraw his declaration referring to "reactionary pressure." All this would have been too late for the Soviets anyhow; the only thing they wanted now was for the Yugoslavs to hand Nagy and his group over to them.[6]

The "Brioni conspiracy," woven with the intention of eliminating the Nagy government and thereby legalizing the intervention and the puppet government, turned out to be a total fiasco. The Yugoslavs found themselves in an extremely embarrassing position. They could not afford to extradite the burdensome prime minister, his two ministers, the five members of the executive of the Hungarian Socialist Workers' Party, the widow of the executed László Rajk, and the world-renowned philosopher Georg Lukács. Such palpable treachery would have ruined the international prestige of Titoism in one fell swoop. At the same time the permanent presence of the group (including sixteen children) in the embassy building, surrounded by Soviet tanks and sentries and hermetically sealed off from the world (apart from the diplomats and embassy personnel), was in the long run untenable for everyone concerned.[7]

Discussions about a way out of the impasse were carried on between the Nagy group and various Yugoslav representatives from 4 to 22 November. Concurrently the Soviet and Yugoslav leaderships and Kádár negotiated about the fate of Nagy. Khrushchev and Tito, as well as the diplomatic representations of the two countries, inundated each other with angry reproaches. Nagy's initial wish to depart for Yugoslavia was categorically refused. Eventually negotiations focused on the formulation of Kádár's assurances of safety, according to which Nagy and his aides could return to their homes without fear of reprisals.[8] Once (probably on 9 November), Nagy was on the verge of caving in to Belgrade's urgings. In a small notebook, he formulated a predated declaration of resignation and a few sentences about his willingness to compromise and to distance himself from counterrevolutionary tendencies. His draft was turned down by the entire Hungarian Executive Committee present in the Yugoslav Embassy. On 11 November they drew up the following resolution: "The Nagy government is lawful; it must not resign, because that would vindicate the treachery of Kádár.... We will not negotiate with the Kádár government; we negotiate with the Soviet comrades ... but the resolution of the situation can only be effected on the basis of the principles represented by us."[9]

On that 11 November, coincidentally the same day, Marshal Tito gave a highly controversial policy speech before the party faithful in Pula.[10] He condemned the first Soviet intervention and described the second as a "lesser evil," because Nagy had only "bellyached" and done nothing against the "white terror." And then on 4 November Nagy had hightailed it and requested Western help. In contrast, Tito praised the Kádár government, as it represented everything that was "the most decent" in Hungary. The Soviet leadership was outraged by the speech, which elicited sharp controversies between Belgrade and Moscow. At the same time Nagy and his comrades, deeply offended, protested against the untruth about their "flight."[11] It was the Yugoslav ambassador who, on Belgrade's orders, had "urgently and emphatically called on us to accept the asylum offer." Referring to the speech by Tito, the journalist Éva Bozóky, widow of Ferenc Donáth, posed the question in her memoirs: "Was the invitation a provocation? The ambassador's telephone calls to all of us? To gather all those present here, so that they should not go underground and organize a partisan war? ... And now the host, who has so kindheartedly invited us, stabs us in the back? Has he only lured us here in order to extradite us?"[12]

In fact it was not a provocation, but rather a trap. But those who had set it, namely Tito and his comrades, were now also stuck in it. They wanted to get rid of the uncomfortable guests as soon as possible, but without completely losing face. Although they knew full well that the Nagy group's fate was sealed, the Yugoslav diplomats asked Kádár for a written safe conduct for Nagy and his companions. In an official letter to Kardelj, Kádár assured him (as incidentally did Münnich in a separate letter in his capacity as interior and defense minister) that "the government would guarantee the safety of the persons involved, and that it would not call them to justice for their past actions, and that they could leave the Yugoslav Embassy and proceed freely to their respective homes."

Kádár reiterated these promises as late as 22 November to the Yugoslav deputy foreign minister Dobrivoje Vidić and Ambassador Soldatić. Yet that day he arranged with the Romanian prime minister, Gheorghe Gheorghiu-Dej, who had arrived in Budapest that morning, for the Nagy group to be interned in Romania after their arrest.[13] Furthermore, there are now written pieces of evidence from Soviet archives that Kádár had been informed of the Soviet plan at a secret meeting with Malenkov, Suslov, and Aristov on 16 November, according to which, after leaving the embassy, Nagy and his followers would immediately be arrested and deported to Romania. The Soviet report specifically mentions that "we have advised Kádár of our scheme, with which he was in total agreement."[14]

Imre Nagy and his associates left the embassy on 22 November at 6:30 p.m. after Vidić conveyed to them Kádár's written guarantee for their safety. To the question about Moscow's attitude, Vidić declared that he was fully convinced the Soviets concurred, otherwise the agreement could never have been reached. The bus provided for transporting them to their homes first drove to the nearby Soviet headquarters. There Soviet officers unceremoniously forced the two Yugoslav diplomats, who were escorting the group to monitor the implementation of the agreement, off the bus. From there the bus, escorted by armored and military vehicles, took them to KGB headquarters in an outlying Budapest suburb. That same evening Ferenc Münnich called on them in one-on-one conversations to support the Kádár government in a declaration and to give a written confirmation that they were going to Romania of their own free will. This overture was rejected by all concerned. Walter Roman, head of the Romanian Security Service, who knew Nagy well from the Moscow Comintern times, asked him on behalf of Kádár and Gheorghiu-Dej to declare himself in favor of Kádár, and to travel to Romania voluntarily for three to four months. Nagy protested sharply against what was happening. Kádár and Gheorghiu-Dej should know that he would never leave Hungary voluntarily; they could at most abduct him. He had no intention of giving any declarations and would speak out about his political attitude only as a free and independent person.[15]

The families spent the night, separated from each other, in the offices and storerooms of the former military school, now used by the KGB. In the afternoon of 23 November they were transported, in two windowless military buses, once again with an armored military escort, to the military airport and flown to Bucharest in two Soviet aircrafts. That same evening the Romanian State Security took the Hungarians to Snagov, about forty kilometers from Bucharest. There, on the shores of the eponymous lake, the Nagy, Losonczy, and Donáth families were held in custody in separate villas, while the rest of the group was kept completely isolated in Prince Nicholas's former holiday residence. Some thirty, in part Hungarian-speaking, secret policemen watched over the abducted Hungarians practically around-the-clock. Moreover, the villa accommodating Nagy and his wife was constantly guarded by twelve soldiers.[16]

Meanwhile the startling news of the abduction and deportation of Imre Nagy and his adherents spread like wildfire among the

Hungarian public. On 23 November, at 8 p.m., the radio broadcast a brief communiqué: "Over two weeks ago, Imre Nagy and his associates requested permission from the Hungarian government to leave the Hungarian People's Republic for another Socialist country. On the basis of the agreement from the government of the Romanian People's Republic, Imre Nagy and his associates have moved to the territory of the Romanian People's Republic."[17] The aggressive solution had, of course, not been foreseen in the agreement reached between Khrushchev and Tito at Brioni. After his public condemnation of Nagy and in view of his paeans of praise for Kádár's puppet government, the conceited marshal now felt embarrassed and affronted by worldwide public opinion. The consequence was a lasting disaffection and later open political and ideological conflict between Belgrade and Moscow. At any rate, the Yugoslav government sent a sharply worded protest to the Hungarian government for "breaching the agreement arrived at on 21 November."[18]

The great rebel of Titoism, Milovan Djilas, promptly rubbed salt into the wound and revealed the Yugoslav Communists' hypocrisy. He wrote the following in the left-oriented New York periodical *The New Leader* (19 November 1956):

> The experience of Yugoslavia appears to testify that national Communism is incapable of transcending the boundaries of Communism as such, that is, to institute the kind of reforms that would gradually transform and lead Communism to freedom. That experience seems to indicate that national Communism can merely break from Moscow and, in its own national tempo and way, construct essentially the identical Communist system. . . . Yugoslavia supported this discontent (in the countries of Eastern Europe) as long as it was conducted by the Communist leaders, but turned against it—as in Hungary—as soon as it went further. Therefore, Yugoslavia abstained in the United Nations Security Council on the question of Soviet intervention in Hungary. This revealed that Yugoslav national Communism was unable in its foreign policy to depart from its narrow ideological and bureaucratic class interests, and that, furthermore, it was ready to yield even those principles of equality and noninterference in internal affairs on which all its

successes in the struggle with Moscow had been based.... And just as Yugoslav Communism, separating itself from Moscow, initiated the crisis of Soviet imperialism, that is, the inevitable birth of national Communism, in the same way the revolution in Hungary means the beginning of the end of Communism generally.[19]

This significant article had grave consequences for its author. Djilas was sentenced to three years' imprisonment, and later, for further publications, sent behind bars for a total of nine years. At the same time, the controversy about Yugoslavia's role in the Hungarian Revolution, which flared up time after time, subjected the Belgrade-Moscow-Budapest relationship to repeated crucial tests.[20] The tightrope walk between Yugoslavia's Kádár-friendly stance, which at the same time was critical of Moscow, led to an unprecedented intraparty scandal. In a rather pro-Yugoslav article, the journalists of the party organ *Népszabadság* wanted to criticize the strident Soviet invectives against the speech Tito had made at Pula. Meanwhile Kádár was fully occupied with the mendacious and misleading negotiations about the Nagy group's secretly decided fate. In a four-hour nighttime altercation with leading party journalists, he behaved in an extremely irritable manner and banned the completed article. Consequently, the newspaper's staff held a twenty-four-hour strike against the spiking of the article on 24 November, the first (and the last) time in the party's history, refusing to print and deliver the typeset issue. Kádár immediately relieved the editor in chief of his post, some of the editors left the paper, and others were punished by the party.[21]

All this happened in the midst of the general excitement over the deportation of the Nagy group. Apart from Münnich, who himself was involved with Serov in the execution of the kidnapping, Kádár had not informed the members of the provisional executive committee of the deportation. He did not divulge the truth to the party leadership, nor to the twenty-three-member provisional executive committee about the role of the Soviet troika in the decision making or about his own promises. Only a short while earlier, ten members of the Central Committee had suggested further negotiations with Nagy. Furtiveness was coupled with cynicism as Kádár declared to the seven members of the leadership: "They did not return to their homes—that much I can tell you in confidence—and it is nobody's business where they went. Not of the Yugoslavs, nor of any other government in the world." To Gyula Kállai's question whether Nagy had handed in his resignation, Kádár nonchalantly replied: "There is no more need for a resignation; that is already redundant."[22]

Khrushchev reacted even more cynically and arrogantly in the Soviet Presidium during the discussion about the most expedient reaction to the Yugoslav protests over the abduction: "We don't need to enter into correspondence with Tito about Imre Nagy; that is a matter for Hungary to handle. It was a mistake for our officer to get into the bus."[23] That is how the Soviet leadership from the start shifted the blame on Kádár's puppet government for the broken promises and the abduction of the Nagy group, which evoked worldwide censure.

On 26 November the Greater Budapest Central Workers' Council passed a resolution demanding that the Kádár government make a statement on the fate of Imre Nagy and his associates. Kádár, who with Apró and Münnich had taken part in the meeting, dealt at length with "topical political questions" in a radio address of the same day. In a lengthy passage on the question of Nagy, he plainly stated: "We have promised that we will not institute criminal proceedings against them despite their grave wrongdoings in the past, which they themselves have admitted to in retrospect. We shall keep to this, and we do not regard their departure as lasting forever." These were the last words given on the matter until the communiqué about the verdicts on 17 June 1958.[24]

Young demonstrators in front of Parliament House, 23 October 1956. MTI Photo

Demonstrators on Russian tanks on their way to Parliament House, 25 October 1956. Hungarian National Museum

Victims of the massacre in front of Parliament House, 25 October 1956.
Hungarian National Museum

Budapest: sites of the uprising. © János Csicsely

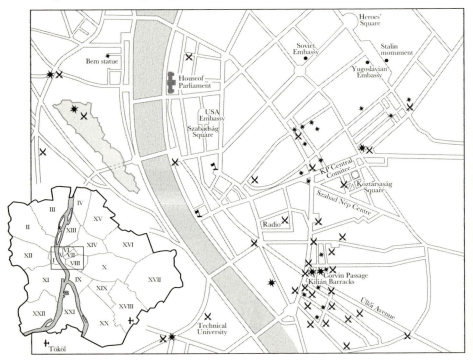

A speech being given on top of a destroyed Soviet tank, 29 October 1956.
Hungarian National Museum

Map of Hungary. Hungarian National Museum

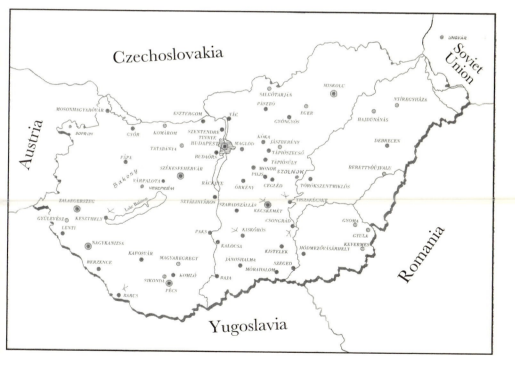

Two views of Corvin Passage, Budapest, 28–29 October 1956.
Hungarian National Museum

Minister of State
Zoltán Tildy, Prime
Minister Imre Nagy,
and Minister of
Defense Pál Maléter
(from left to right),
29 October 1956.
Hungarian National
Museum

A revolutionary
on the boulevard,
30 October 1956.
Hungarian National
Museum

Lynched State Security soldier in Republic Square, 30 October 1956.
Hungarian National Museum

Onlookers at the boulevard, 30 October 1956. Hungarian National Museum

Distribution of Austrian gift packages, 30 October to 4 November 1956. MTI Photo

Voting for the Central Workers' Council at the United Incandescent Lamp Factory, 14 November 1956

János Kádár (center) welcomes Khrushchev (on the right, Minister of the Interior Ferenc Münnich), 2 April 1958. MTI Photo

Hungarian refugees reach safety in Austria, 1956-1962. UNHCR

Although the massive Soviet military power broke the armed resistance within a few days, it could by no means destroy the revolution's autonomous organs of administration, especially the workers' councils and the local revolutionary committees. In particular the organizations of the local workers' councils soon became the strongest and most effective centers of national resistance against foreign rule and against the puppet government. In a spirit of rare unanimity, both the Soviet Presidium members sent to Budapest and Western journalists and diplomats acknowledged the remarkable power of the workers' councils. Though they had been established only during the revolution, in the course of the "rear-guard struggles" they developed into veritable bastions of organized resistance.

In a long and unsparing status report to the CPSU Central Committee dated 22 November, the three Soviet controllers—Malenkov, Suslov, and Aristov—were forced to admit the weakness of the regime set up by them and the unbroken strength of the workers' councils.

> In some locations and mainly in Budapest, the openly hostile
> attitudes toward the Kádár government are still quite strong....
> The "workers' councils" created under the Nagy government
> still play a big role in the political life of the country.... The
> reactionary forces try to undermine the work in various ways by
> inspiring the workers to go on strike until the government satisfies
> their demands for the withdrawal of Soviet troops, for bringing
> Imre Nagy back into the government, and for allowing a multi-
> party system. These demands were presented everywhere, and we
> tend to believe that they were disseminated from one center. Jour-
> nalists, writers, and a segment of students play the most active
> role in the dissemination of the above-mentioned demands.[1]

In spite of their sober analysis, the Soviet functionaries could not imagine that the constantly reiterated demands for independence and freedom as well as for the reinstatement of Imre Nagy came from the overwhelming majority of the Hungarian people and not "a center" of resistance. Brought up in the atmosphere of Stalinist conspiracy paranoia, it was natural for them to seek agents of homegrown or foreign centers of class enemies behind any spontaneous mass action. It is well known that the accusations and sentences in the Stalin era's "classic" show trials in the Soviet Union and after 1948 in Hungary (against László Rajk), in Bulgaria (against Traicho Kostov), and in Czechoslovakia (against Rudolf Slánsky), as well as in the secret trial against Imre Nagy and his associates, were prepared and executed on the basis of this reasoning.

At the same time Malenkov, Suslov, and Aristov were worried about "the process of party reunification … moving slowly and in a disorganized fashion.… So far, the district committees possess quite an insignificant number of activists (20–30 people) and have almost no political base in the enterprises and in the organizations.… The pro-Yugoslav mood and the negative feelings toward the CPSU are quite strong among members of the Provisional Central Committee of the Hungarian Socialist Workers' Party."[2] As a matter of fact, the Kádár group had to start from scratch. Reorganizing the party was indeed an extraordinarily difficult enterprise. The number of members reflects the true power relations. Those who joined in the first weeks and months were overwhelmingly individual members of the former ÁVH, a few senior officers of the Hungarian Army, and a small segment of former Communist Party officials, who had been dismissed during the uprising. On 1 December a mere 4.3 percent of the former members of the Hungarian Workers' Party were registered in the newly formed Socialist Workers' Party.[3]

The Kádár government of the time essentially and overtly embodied the paradox of contemporary communism: a "people's government" in flagrant opposition to the people and a "workers' state" in bitter class conflict with the workers. In line with their principles announced during the revolution, the workers' councils—which were entitled to direct the enterprises in accordance with a government decree of 13 November— did not tolerate any party to function in the factories, offices, and cooperatives under their control. As late as the beginning of February, the state party was forced to operate in a political desert. This is vividly illustrated in the Communist youth magazine by the account about a schoolteacher in Budapest who was boycotted by all her colleagues since she had joined the party: "If I enter the teachers' common room, everyone stops talking. There is an ice-cold, impenetrable wall between us. I am the only Communist teacher in our school.... I move among my colleagues as if I were branded."[4]

The puppet government had tried, in its first appeal and then by way of a series of measures, to win over the population. A general wage raise of 8 to 15 percent was announced; compulsory deliveries of farm produce were abolished; 7 November, the anniversary of the Russian Revolution, was made a normal working day, instead of which the fifteenth of March, the anniversary of the 1848 Hungarian Revolution, was reinstated as a national holiday. Moreover, in the first uncertain weeks of his regime, Kádár made all kinds of promises in his speeches. The Soviet troops? Negotiations for withdrawal of Soviet troops were to be initiated, but only following the restoration of order. Imre Nagy? It was entirely up to him whether to return to Hungary and take part in political life. Workers' councils were to be given a large amount of control in the factories and mines, and the democratic election of revolutionary councils would also be recognized. Many of the expressions he used were ambiguous. On 14 November Kádár explicitly declared to delegates of the workers' councils: "We want a multi-party system, we want clean, honest elections."[5]

Kádár himself was a "worker politician" (in the words of György Litván), a classical "centrist," later a cautious reformer, but only as long as his position of power was not endangered. Gyula Háy once wrote the following about him: "His personality *had* a certain fascination.... The fascination of weary compromise."[6] This observation might have applied to the Kádár of the sixties and seventies. However, in November and December 1956, the unremitting conflict with the Hungarian workers must have caused him, the authentic worker, grave moral, political, and personal embarrassment. Within the framework of the resistance of all classes, it was the working class that was the most hostile toward the so-called Revolutionary Workers' and Peasants' Government operating in the shadow of Soviet tanks.

After becoming acquainted with all the minutes of the meetings of the Hungarian party leadership and a number of Soviet secret files from this period, it seems justified to describe the general resistance—in the words of the historian Miklós Molnár—as the "Second Revolution."[7] It was a resistance movement of hopelessness, without any expectations of victory, but with the knowledge of the justice of their cause and the support of the entire nation. For two full months the Kádár regime was impotent in the face of the people's will. In spite of the arrest of 7,293 people by the Soviet occupiers and their Hungarian accomplices, the Kádár government could not get a grip on the administration and the economy. Ten weeks after the Soviet invasion, the government still consisted of only six ministers of state, although on paper it had twenty-two specialist ministries. In a conversation with Ambassador Andropov in late December, Kádár admitted that new ministers were not appointed because order had not yet been restored in the country. It was also totally impossible to hold the planned parliamentary elections in May.[8]

Until mid-December, the workers' councils exercised their considerable and decisive influence on political and social conditions not only within the individual establishments but also, through their regional organizations in the metropolitan and country districts and in the counties. In some industrial areas their influence continued until mid-January. According to the Interior Ministry's 1960 figures (cited earlier), there were 2,100 workers' councils during the revolution with a total of 28,000 members. In November the workers' councils were newly elected in most places and even reinforced by prorevolutionary workers and leading employees. It has been estimated that participation figures became even higher than in October. In their resolutions and appeals, the freely elected representatives of the workers continued to press for the withdrawal of Soviet troops, free elections, a free press, the reinstatement of the Nagy government, immunity from prosecution for participants in the revolution, and the return of all deportees from the Soviet Union.

Their clout was further strengthened and extended through the cooperation of the workers' councils on the district and county levels. The establishment on 14 November of the Greater Budapest Central Workers' Council (KMT) at a rally of five hundred delegates at the United Incandescent Lamp Factory (Egyesült Izzó) signaled a watershed.[9] Several writers also took part in the inaugural meeting. There was also occasional cooperation with the Revolutionary Council of Hungarian Intellectuals, founded on 21 November under the chairmanship of the world-famous composer Zoltán Kodály. In view of the persisting strike movement and the impressive organization of the workers' councils, the government was obliged to parley with them. During the nightly negotiations, when the workers frequently had to wait several hours for Kádár, the government's principal aim was the resumption of work, but also to gain time and to try to split the workers' councils. Kádár rejected the establishment of a national Central Workers' Council as well as the legalization of the right to strike. As already mentioned, he made the negotiations for withdrawal of Soviet troops dependent on the restoration of order. Despite the fruitless discussions, on 16 November the overwhelming majority in the Central Workers' Council called for a return to work, in view of the economic crisis facing the country and the weariness of the public.

Although in their appeal to the workers the spokespersons of the Central Workers' Council had confirmed that they had not yielded an inch on the popular uprising's basic demands, the following day they were replaced by two radical labor leaders: Sándor Rácz, a twenty-three-year-old toolmaker, and a steelworker, the thirty-three-year-old Sándor Bali. However, Soviet tanks and troops prevented the establishment of a nationwide workers' council that had been slated to take place on 21 November in the Budapest National Sports Stadium. The workers' response was to call a forty-eight-hour general strike, which was widely observed in the entire country.

The most impressive demonstration of the Budapest population's unbroken resistance took place on 23 November to mark the first month since the outbreak of the revolution. On the initiative of the Revolutionary Council of Hungarian Intellectuals, joined by the Central Workers' Council, traffic stopped and the streets emptied; all life seemed to be at a standstill. The writer István Örkény wrote about his impressions of that day in his diary (which was found and published only after his death): "Wonderful effect of the leaflets. At noon the offices emptied. Oppressive silence spread over everything. Slowly the snow was falling. No one in the streets; only the Russian armored cars are cruising around. It would be good to know what those sitting in those cars are thinking. I don't know whether there has ever been such a demonstration in the world. I can see the silent protest from the window, the nothingness, the silence, the emptiness, the immobility.... The last weapon of the vanquished is silence."[10]

The abduction of the Nagy group, which coincided with the nighttime negotiations between the government and the representatives of the Budapest Workers' Council, certainly did not lead to a softening of the workers' belligerent attitude. The Greater Budapest Central Workers' Council protested against the government's ban on publishing a press organ of their own. At the same time the councils refused to recognize the regime's discredited trade unions, and former shop stewards were often locked out altogether from factories, as were members of party organizations. Representatives of both sides met five or six times in Parliament. In spite of the intimidation attempts and waves of arrests, the leaders of the workers displayed admirable determination.

Sándor Bali denied that the workers' councils wanted to assume governmental powers. The independence of the working class in its relationship with the state was, in his view, the most important of the gains achieved by the October revolution: "We know that the workers' councils will become organs directing the country's economy. That is exactly what we want them to be. We do not want to commit the same mistake as the Party did in the past, namely, when it was at the same time master both of the country and of the factories and also the organization which represented the interest of the workers." Then Bali posed the urgent question:

> Why doesn't the government help us to restore the morale of the workers? Why didn't a single member of the government come to talk to us? If he was afraid he should have come under the protection of armed guards. Why did they expect the members of the Budapest Workers' Council to sit here until midnight and even 2.00 in the morning waiting for the various members of the government? We know you are very busy, and are engaged in international discussions. But, in our opinion, Hungarian home affairs, the affairs of our workers and peasants, are the most sacred things today. Everything should have been put aside in order to face these. I think that the duty of the Workers' Councils in connection with striking and working is quite clear to you.[11]

The only effective political weapon still left in the hands of the workers' councils was the political strike. Of course, Kádár and the other representatives of the borrowed power were fully aware of that too.

At the same time Kádár had to maneuver between two forces in a political vacuum. On one side were the revenge-hungry Stalinists in their Moscow exile, but also in Budapest, while on the other, the hostile, mistrustful, or at best indifferent but numerically stronger group of reformers. In a series of letters to Khrushchev and the Soviet leadership, Rákosi, but also Gerő, Hegedüs, and (the former Budapest party chief) István Kovács, denounced practically everything that Kádár did or—in their opinion— failed to do. In one of these letters, dated 18 November, they advised the Soviet party Presidium that "the workers' councils represent practically a second power against the government."[12]

As already mentioned, at the Central Committee meeting, which was so vital for future developments, Kádár dealt not only with the Nagy question but also with the evaluation of the past and not least with the policy vis-à-vis the workers' councils. This is what he had to say on this crucial topic: "These workers' councils represent a very significant political force.... If we compare them with the influence of the leaders of state organs or the managers or with the influence of the party organization and the trade unions, then we have to state that today the workers' council represents the greatest political force." Kádár then made it quite clear: "The workers' council, which is under a certain anarchic, Fascist-counterrevolutionary pressure or influence, is also against the party of the working class, is hostile to the Soviets, persecutes the state and party functionaries, throws out even the remainder, but also the simple party members on the pretext that the councils are fighting against Rákosi, Gerő and Stalin."[13]

It was evident that neither the Soviet leaders residing in the capital nor their puppets, Kádár and his comrades, were willing to come to terms with the existence of this dual power. After the period of ostensible concessions, intrigues, and attempts at splitting the councils, they were once again preparing to employ naked force to break the back of the resistance. Meanwhile, in view of the fruitless negotiations and the new wave of arrests, the Greater Budapest Central Workers' Council came under increasing pressure from below. That is why, in a last desperate call to the government, the council warned against hounding the members of the councils. That would only lead once more to a general strike, bloodshed, and another national tragedy. The next day the negotiations broke down.

The last and almost certainly most dramatic meeting of the council took place on 8 December. Behind closed doors, the 150 to 200 delegates, among them representatives of the more important mining and industrial centers from the provinces, passionately and desperately debated the hopeless future and whether, despite a resolution to strike, it would be useful to suggest another round of negotiations with the Soviets and the government. In the tense atmosphere, it took a while before they became aware of the loud hammering on the door. It was the telephone operator, who wanted to inform Chairman Rácz of the news of the bloodbath in the northern Hungarian Nógrád County town of Salgótarján, whereupon the delegates, with one dissenting voice, called for a general strike on 11–12 December.[14]

What happened in Salgótarján belongs to the most horrendous crimes of the Soviet occupiers and their Hungarian henchmen. Some three thousand workers demonstrated in the industrial town in front of police headquarters, calling for the release of two miners, members of the workers' council, who had been arrested. Following a provocation by Hungarian special forces, two Soviet tanks stationed in front of the building, Soviet soldiers, and the men of the Hungarian special forces opened fire on the unarmed miners. The carnage claimed the lives of 131 miners, and some 150 people were wounded. A few hours later leaflets were handed out, blaming the workers' council of the county for the tragedy.[15]

Following the resolution to strike, the government put its machinery of repression into full gear. Two hundred labor leaders and intellectuals were arrested, on 9 December the Greater Budapest Central Workers' Council and the district and regional councils were outlawed, martial law was introduced, and summary courts were established with jurisdiction to pronounce verdicts with immediate effect and in some cases for death sentences to become enforceable with immediate effect. Rácz and Bali were lured to Parliament on the pretext of new negotiations and arrested. In spite of the arrest of the Greater Budapest Central Workers' Council's leadership, the call for a general strike was observed in the entire country.[16] The Belgrade paper *Borba* published the following dispatch: "Anyone who this morning went out in the streets of Budapest could see that the underground was not running, and that there were no buses. In the afternoon, only one trolley-bus, the 75 line, passed crowded with passengers across the Square of the Heroes. Later, that trolley-bus also disappeared from the streets. We were told that somebody had fired at it. On the line to Kispest, a street-car was running under the protection of military escort. In Budapest, I saw one train running on a local line; it departed, but did not return. It was alleged that the line had been blown up in one place."[17]

The arrest of the popular labor leaders Rácz and Bali promptly led to a new wave of strikes. The strikes began in the Beloiannis Telecommunications Factory, where the two men were employed. Tools were downed in several other plants as well. Some factories were occupied by Soviet units on the behest of the government. Protest demonstrations were held in many provincial towns. Massive demonstrations took place at Eger for three days running. The crowd demanded the withdrawal of foreign troops and the release of arrested freedom fighters. They occupied a printing shop and printed leaflets calling for a strike. On 11 December a unit of special forces dispatched from Budapest and commanded by the notorious Lajos Gyurkó fired on the demonstrating crowd, causing 2 fatalities and wounding 14. Another huge crowd gathered the following day. The special forces, supported by Soviet tanks, let off a salvo. This time the tally was 8 dead and 27 wounded.[18]

There were spontaneous acts of resistance not only in Budapest but all over the country. The Yugoslav deputy prime minister and Tito's principal ideologist, Edvard Kardelj, spoke sarcastically about the "paradox of a Workers Government that is afraid of Workers Councils."[19] Eventually the government issued a decree on 7 January 1957, which made strikes and "the incitement to strike" punishable by death. This, in effect, sounded the death knell for the workers' councils. Under these circumstances the workers' council of the largest industrial enterprise in the capital, the Csepel Iron and Metal Works, dissolved in protest. Two days later, the entire Central Works Committee of Csepel followed suit. There were protest strikes and a mighty demonstration of fifteen thousand workers, which the regime was able to disperse only with the help of Soviet tanks. The deployment of troops once more claimed several dead and wounded. That same day Elek Nagy, the chairman, and several members of the workers' council were arrested.

The "fall of the fortress Csepel" signified the end of the workers' councils.[20] Kádár, satisfied and cynical, announced at the end of February 1957 before the party's Central Committee: "The future prospect for the workers' councils is clear. We have nothing to say about them in the resolution. We have nicely and quietly let the workers' councils turn gray, and that is how it should be."[21] By the end of the year they once again reinstated the trade unions as the party's transmission belts in the factories and liquidated the workers' councils by a decree.

Although the workers were the heroes of this nowadays frequently forgotten—because relatively peaceful—"Second Revolution," one should not underrate the activities of the intellectual resistance. One of the most poignant and internationally noted demonstrations was the memorial march on 4 December, a month after the Soviet intervention. It was organized by the underground paper *Élünk!* (We Live!) and the Revolutionary Council of Hungarian Intellectuals. Several thousand women and girls marched in the streets, all clad in black: all of them, without exception, had flowers in their hands. The marchers reached Heroes' Square in midmorning, where they wanted to lay the flowers at the Tomb of the Unknown Soldier, but the demonstration was broken up by Soviet soldiers with armored cars in the background. Several hundred women assembled in the afternoon in front of the American legation and held a silent demonstration. The Indian ambassador, K.P.S. Menon, appeared on both occasions, accompanied by Indian diplomats and Árpád Göncz (the later president of the democratic Hungarian Republic). Menon, to whom István Bibó's memorandum was also handed during those days, reported with strong emotion on this silent expression of grief and solidarity.[22]

After 15 November, another underground paper appeared alongside *Élünk!* The hectographed *Október Huszonharmadika* (Twenty-third of October) was edited by the daredevil resistance fighter and journalist Miklós Gimes. He and his brave colleagues managed to put together and circulate seven issues. Together with other courageous intellectuals, Gimes, who was personally attacked by Kádár for his activities, founded the Hungarian Democratic Independence Movement. There were also several resistance groups that distributed posters and leaflets. The Revolutionary Council of Intellectuals was banned as early as 11 December.

Among the many photocopied pamphlets, the most noteworthy ones were those containing a two-part study under the pseudonym Hungaricus. The booklet was soon smuggled out of Hungary and circulated in the West—partly in excerpts—in various foreign languages. In a brilliant analysis, the author Sándor Fekete, a former editor of the central party daily *Szabad Nép*, dealt with the history of the Hungarian Communist movement and with the perspectives of a "new Socialist path." Fekete and the coauthors, among them Ferenc Mérei and György Litván, were later sentenced to lengthy prison terms.[23]

The writers—both individually and in the framework of the Writers' Union—played an important part before, during, and after the revolution. The executive committee of the Writers' Union published an appeal on 12 November, calling for the withdrawal of Soviet troops and against arbitrary official measures. On 28 December, at a momentous full-membership meeting, the assembly expressly committed itself to the goals of the revolution and condemned the Soviet intervention as a "historic mistake." Tibor Déry, who had played a prominent role during the prerevolutionary state of flux, spoke at the meeting about "the greatest, purest and most unified revolution" in Hungarian history and the Hungarian workers' movement that had been "put down because of an abysmal shortage of statesmanlike wisdom." By way of response, the government banned the Writers' Union (as well as the Journalists' Union) on 17 January. Déry and Háy soon received the reckoning for their courageous actions—nine and six years in jail respectively.[24]

For the sake of the chronology of events, now would be the time to talk about the dreadful period of reprisals. Yet if we want to comprehend the Hungarians' attitude at that time and the Kádár regime's later record of success, we first have to examine the stance of the West, and in particular of the United States, before, during, and after the revolution.

When the general attack by the Soviet troops commenced in the early morning of 4 November, and the fighters at the Kilián Barracks opened fire on the Soviet tanks trying to penetrate the inner city via Üllői Avenue, the barracks and with it our building on the corner automatically became targets of the grenade launchers, heavy artillery, and the tank cannons. For five whole days we could barely leave the cellar. Many young Hungarians put up a desperate resistance. I shall never forget that during a lull in the shooting, a young freedom fighter in Üllői Avenue sanguinely told me that UN troops were already on their way to the Austrian-Hungarian border.

He was not alone. There were more than a few among the officially registered 2,700 dead and 19,000 wounded who had entered the hopeless fray against the superior forces in the naive expectation of Western assistance. Pollsters of the Washington-controlled Radio Free Europe (RFE) in Munich subsequently interviewed some eight hundred refugees, asking them whether they had expected help after the second Soviet intervention. Almost all of them answered in the affirmative. Twenty percent expected the United States to intervene, 48 percent expected the United Nations to intervene, and the rest expected help from the "free world." According to another survey conducted among Hungarian refugees in Austria, 96 percent of those questioned had expected some form of American assistance in Hungary, and 77 percent believed it would come in the form of military support.[1]

These expectations were the direct consequence of the radical psychological warfare that the Eisenhower-Dulles administration had for years conducted against world communism in general and Soviet domination in Eastern Europe in particular. The principal tools for these promises of a "liberation policy" and the corresponding doctrine of "rollback" were the RFE, which began broadcasting in 1951, and after 1953 Radio Liberty, both set up in Munich. RFE broadcast in Czech and Slovak

(20.5 hours daily), in Polish and Hungarian (19 hours), in Romanian (13 hours), and in Bulgarian (8 hours), while Radio Liberty (RL) transmitted programs in Russian and fourteen other languages for the Soviet Union. From the RFE's very inception, the U.S. government had carefully nurtured its image as a "privately financed radio," although covert state-approved support for both radio stations was channeled through the CIA until 1971.[2]

According to William E. Griffith, the then chief American political adviser to Radio Free Europe, and the Hungarian-born George R. Urban, the later director of RFE, many of the 140 or so staff of the Hungarian service were more or less strongly influenced by sympathy for the Horthy regime—not only anti-Communists, therefore, but with a right-wing tendency. The Hungarian-language weekly programs consisting of 115 hours were strongly news oriented. Cultural and religious broadcasts, sports reports, and music programs complemented the daily program. Only decades later—after the general relaxation and the limited freedom to travel in Hungary—could the public opinion research institutes establish reliable assessments about the number of listeners of foreign radio broadcasts. According to these data, during the 1970s three out of four Hungarians listened at least once a week to Western radio stations, and every second Hungarian turned the dial to RFE. One should not, of course, disregard the fact that until 1964 foreign broadcasts were regularly jammed. Nonetheless, very many Hungarians listened to RFE programs, and the influence of the news and commentaries was augmented—as well as frequently distorted—by word-of-mouth propaganda.

There were also other important Western radio stations, which regularly broadcast programs for the Soviet Bloc, thus also for Hungary: the Voice of America, the official U.S. government mouthpiece; the BBC from London; and the Deutsche Welle from Cologne. However, as only RFE broadcast news and commentaries around-the-clock to Hungary and the neighboring countries with large Hungarian minorities, only the Munich station functioned as a surrogate for the domestic radio. RFE thus became an authentic source for listeners, who would otherwise have been completely dependent on information controlled by the Communist state.

Incidentally, during the Truman era, RFE and the staff of the station were also involved in other forms of psychological warfare against the Soviet Bloc. To intensify the liberation propaganda, leaflets were dropped into Hungary by way of balloons. As of 1 October 1954, balloons were launched from the vicinity of Berchtesgaden with the twelve-point manifesto of a fictitious National Opposition Movement; the first drop consisted of 15 million leaflets printed in Munich. Austria had no possibility of preventing these flights over her airspace. By the fall of 1955, over 212 million leaflets or newspapers had been dropped into Hungary, Poland, and Czechoslovakia. The programs of RFE regularly discussed and commented on the action code-named Operation Focus as well as the contents of the various leaflets (with demands for rights and the condemnation of the party dictatorships). According to a 1957 RFE survey of Hungarian defectors, 15 percent of the population relied on these leaflets for their news.[3]

The Hungarian uprising came as a total surprise not only to the American government but to the Hungarian editorial office of RFE as well. Later the principal reproach against RFE was that by their misleading reports or hints, the staff of the Hungarian Desk incited the freedom fighters and unfairly encouraged them to persevere in a hopeless situation. Naturally the broadcasters and commentators of the Hungarian Service from Munich did not do this *expressis verbis*. However, the tone and the formulation of some of the commentaries did arouse this expectation. Even the politically better-informed Hungarians believed that the West would not leave them in the lurch and would persuade or even force the Soviets to give in, or at least to make concessions.

Moreover, the responsible heads of the Hungarian Desk, in contrast to their Polish colleagues, did not properly assess the split within the state party and shrilly attacked in particular the prime minister, even after his open stand on the side of the people and explicitly against the Soviets. On 30 October, for example, one of the commentaries sounded as follows: "This murderer of the people, Imre Nagy, does not have even enough humanity and Hungarian feeling in him to resign. The promise of a cease-fire by this government of the bloody hands was only a dastardly deception. The strike of our working brothers is the strongest weapon against this nation-extirpating government." And on 31 October: "The question now is, whether this heroic nation . . . has a leader. . . . The answer to this question is right here: [Cardinal] József Mindszenty. . . . The reborn Hungary and the leader appointed and sent by God meet each other in this hour."

On 1 November: "The Hungarian people do not want Nagy Imre's system. If Nagy Imre survives this situation, what is the guarantee that all the suffering of the past does not return?" On 3 November, the eve of the Soviet intervention: "We do not know whether it is his [Nagy's] fault that there is still a government behind him, whose members belong in the dock rather than on the ministerial benches." The emigrant and, later, consultant for RFE in Munich Zoltán Benkő, who had spent several years before his flight in the infamous labor camp at Recsk, has collected these quotations from twenty-four broadcasts from the time of the revolution. In a report to an international memorial conference in September 1996, he drew this conclusion: "What happened in those twelve days was not a mistake but a crime! The RFE broadcasts lagged far behind the events, not to mention their content and mentality. All the broadcasts that I made notes of have one trait in common: they attack, condemn and stigmatize Imre Nagy! Most of the broadcasts fulfill the criteria of incitement, interference and military advice." This stern judgment carried particularly great weight, as the speaker, himself a victim of the dictatorship, had no reason to gloss over the facts.[4]

The late George R. Urban, who was on the staff of the BBC and then RFE and was director of the Munich station between 1983 and 1986, dealt with the history of RFE in an entire book, of which a thirty-seven-page chapter is devoted solely to the station's role during and after the revolution. Using a number of quotations, this experienced journalist too sheds light on the flawed evaluation of the situation by the Hungarian Desk. The fact that RFE and its Hungarian Service represented a resolutely anti-Communist attitude was consistent with the prevailing Western atmosphere. However, consistently missing in that period were an appreciation of the complexity of the situation, sufficient knowledge about the political personalities in question, and professionalism in the day-to-day work.

It is worth noting that at the above-mentioned 1996 international conference, the former "gray eminence" behind the RFE-RL, William E. Griffith, later professor of political science at the Massachusetts Institute of Technology (MIT), tried to shift almost the entire responsibility for the mistakes of 1956 onto the Hungarian Desk. Urban was of the opinion that it was Griffith (also deceased a few years ago) and some other important American program controllers who were to blame for the grave political blunders. In his history of the RFE, Gyula Borbándi, who worked as editor of the Hungarian Service from its inception until the end of October 1993, shares the latter's views.

At any rate, a survey of 628 Hungarian refugees en route to the United States revealed that half of them had already expected American intervention before the revolution. It was, of course, impossible in the fifties to gather reliable data about political expectations behind the Iron Curtain. Reports by diplomats and the few qualified Western foreign correspondents, however, left no doubt about the exorbitantly exaggerated hopes nurtured about America's foreign policy concerning the satellite countries. In fact the situation was probably just as Alexis de Tocqueville described it 150 years earlier: "In politics everything is like in war. Appearances are often more important than reality." That is how it was with the effect of the RFE broadcasts on the Hungarian listeners. The great Hungarian émigré author Sándor Márai wrote in his diary on 22 November 1956, that is, after the crushing of the revolution: "It is not true that the radios incited to insurrection. That is stupid and evil gossip and is spread by the Russians. . . . But it is true that for many years every Western station, every newspaper and every statesman told us that there was such a thing as Western solidarity."

What was the course that the Eisenhower administration actually pursued between 1953 and 1956, and in particular what was its reaction during and after the Hungarian Revolution? Could there have been a chance for the success of the uprising if international conditions had been more favorable? Was the impending presidential election in the United States a decisive factor? Did the hospitalization of the American secretary of state, John Foster Dulles, and the absence of a U.S. minister in Budapest contribute to the conspicuous passivity in Washington? Or was it the simultaneous Suez crisis with the Israeli-British-French attack against Egypt that sealed the fate of the Hungarian people?

Following the opening of the American, British, and French archives and the publication of seminal Eisenhower biographies and monographs about his two administrations, we can now confirm the American historian H. W. Brand's assertion that the strident liberation rhetoric was often determined by anti-Communist ideology, while actual policies were usually affected by realistic geopolitical considerations.[5] Eisenhower's Hungarian policy is a classic example of his careful and peaceful Eastern European line. The president and his powerfully eloquent secretary of state kindled great expectations in the satellite states with their slogans of a "rollback" and "liberation." However, in crisis situations they did not take any action either in East Germany in 1953 or in Poland and Hungary in 1956. In the final phases of the Moscow preparations for crushing the Hungarian War of Independence, the United States and its allies gave the Soviets practically a free hand in dealing with Hungary. The condemnation of the intervention in the United Nations after the event was simply a face-saving exercise by the U.S. administration.

Since studying the documents that became accessible during the last decades, historians have evaluated the contradictions of Eisenhower's Hungary policy very critically. In their seminal works, two Hungarian historians, Csaba Békés and László Borhi,[6] have exposed the much-discussed liberation policy as idle rhetoric, just like the cynical tactic that was behind the contradictory messages to the Hungarian people on the one hand and the Soviet leadership on the other. Csaba Békés drew this conclusion: "Between 1953 and 1956 the Soviet Union never considered tolerating the desertion of the satellite states from the Soviet Bloc, nor did the West for a moment consider liberating these countries."

At no time during the Hungarian Revolution did President Eisenhower and Secretary of State Dulles consider supporting the insurgents with weapons or putting direct pressure on the Soviet leadership. The No. 5608 decision of the National Security Council of July 1956, which was "for internal use," already established that there was no short-term chance for the restoration of the satellite states' independence. On 26 October Eisenhower cautioned the chief of staff and the CIA leadership to act with the "greatest circumspection and attention" in the Hungarian crisis. All documents and information point to the fact that between 24 and 30 October the question of military countermeasures was not even raised. In reply to his brother Milton's question, the president repeatedly stressed as well that an intervention in Hungary was strategically impossible, as the country could not be approached by land and therefore was "just as inaccessible to us as Tibet."[7] There were many in the CIA who pressed for clandestinely arming and supporting the freedom fighters. Yet they could not win over either their chief, Allen Dulles (the brother of the secretary of state), or the president.

Instead of trying to deter the Soviets, they wanted rather to reassure them. For that reason, in a speech made in Dallas on 27 October, John

Foster Dulles declared: "We do not look upon these nations as potential military allies." To make sure that Dulles's message was heard in Moscow, the U.S. ambassador was instructed to repeat the crucial passage to Soviet leaders, which he did at a reception on 29 October. It was the Suez crisis and not the Hungarian Revolution that constituted the focal point of crisis management in Washington. As a result of Eisenhower's massive pressure, the British and French were eventually forced to withdraw. When the UN ambassadors of both states endeavored to have Nagy's declaration of neutrality and the threat to Hungary of a second Soviet intervention put on the agenda of the Security Council on 2 November, it was prevented by a directive from Dulles.

The above-mentioned Hungarian historians both point to a hitherto barely known fact: the U.S. administration regarded Nagy with mistrust and did not treat him—in crass contrast to Władysław Gomułka in Warsaw—as a potential negotiating partner. In a telephone conversation Dulles declared that Nagy's government was "not one we want much to do with."[8] Unlike the Polish leader Gomułka, Nagy was regarded with open hostility in Washington. Unlike Gomułka, Nagy was seen as insufficiently anti-Soviet, as he had spent a considerable time in the Soviet Union. Some Western observers made a similar mistake later in regard to the role of Alexander Dubček before the Prague Spring in 1968. Incidentally, Gomułka soon proved to be Moscow's reliable party follower, and as far as Poland's domestic policy was concerned, was blinkered and doctrinaire. These strange judgments were influenced by the traditional priority of Poland in America's East European policy. Before the improvement of the situation as a result of the Polish-Soviet compromise, the possibility of the United States applying force against the USSR was at least considered.

A bizarre footnote to the sad story of Western passivity, which has come to light as late as the 1990s, was the involvement of Franco's Spain during the last phase of the revolution.[9] On 4 November Otto Habsburg got in touch with the Spanish dictator Franco through an intermediary and requested that he send aid to the Hungarian freedom fighters. The Spanish government immediately decided to dispatch a volunteer unit, and Spain asked the United States for two airplanes for the transport of weapons and ammunition. Washington's response was unequivocal: The U.S. government could lend no support, overt or covert, to any military intervention in Hungary. The State Department also expressed its hope that Spain would take no precipitate action without consulting the United States.

Naturally not only Hungarian historians are critical of the American inaction. Even such a well-informed and cynical chronicler as the ex–secretary of state Henry Kissinger pillories the Eisenhower-Dulles administration in his important work *Diplomacy* for acting as if they were "bystanders, with no direct stake in the outcome" of the trial of strength in Hungary, and without even warning the Kremlin that repression in Hungary would involve "major political and economic costs."[10] During the revolution and after the second Soviet intervention, nothing happened! No diplomatic notes, no pressure, and no offer of mediation came from Washington. Kissinger also rightly notes the sad fact that the enthusiasm with which Imre Nagy's declaration of neutrality was greeted in Hungary was matched only by the indifference with which the so-called world community received it. Totally preoccupied with the matter of Suez, neither the United States nor Great Britain and France took any steps to induce the United Nations to deal with Nagy's message on an urgent basis.

The Western attitude during the entire history of the Hungarian Revolution was therefore a byproduct of the diplomatic maneuvers in the Suez crisis, which were played out behind the scenes in the Washington-London-Paris triangle. The Suez adventure was not the result of the Kremlin's concentration on Hungary, nor had the war in Egypt elicited the Soviet decision reached on 31 October for the second intervention. With the relevant archival resources at our disposal, we can unreservedly agree with the analysis of Csaba Békés, according to which, despite all the internal debates, in all likelihood the Soviet troops would have been deployed to crush the Hungarian uprising even without the Suez events, as they did twelve years later against the Czechoslovak reformers. Still, the Suez crisis did benefit the Soviet action politically and from a propaganda point of view.

These factors molded also the stance of the United Nations. A Security Council resolution of 4 November, asking the Soviet Union to withdraw, was promptly vetoed by the Soviets. It was significant that the Yugoslav representative abstained from voting. The special session of the General Assembly voted that same day on a similar resolution, which was passed by 50 to 8, with 15 abstentions. The resolution affirmed Hungary's right to independence, demanding the cessation of Soviet military action in Hungary, the withdrawal of troops, and the admittance of UN observers. On 10 and 20 November, the General Assembly called upon the Soviet Union to withdraw its forces without further delay and expressed the view that free elections should be held under UN auspices. Arguably the resolution that was most significant in the long run was taken on 10 January 1957 with the aim of setting up a five-nation special committee consisting of Australia, Ceylon, Denmark, Tunisia, and Uruguay. The committee was refused permission to enter Hungary. After hearing the testimonies of 111 witnesses in New York, Geneva, Vienna, Rome, and London, including Anna Kéthly, minister of state in the Nagy government, Major General Béla Király, military commander of the city of Budapest and commander in chief of the National Guard, and József Kövágó, mayor of Budapest (1945–1947 and again from 31 October to 4 November 1956), the committee submitted its unanimous report to the United Nations.

The report concluded that the events that took place in Hungary in October and November 1956 constituted a "spontaneous national uprising" and that "the present Hungarian regime had been imposed on the Hungarian people by the armed intervention of the Union of Soviet Social Republics." The four-hundred-page report was a scathing indictment of the Soviets and their puppets and was translated into a number of languages. On 14 September 1957 the UN General Assembly endorsed the report by a vote of 60 in favor, 10 against (the Eastern Bloc and Yugoslavia), and 10 abstentions (including India and Finland). Until the fall of 1962, the West placed the Hungarian question annually on the agenda of the UN General Assembly.[11] From 1957 onward the voting patterns showed that most of the African and Asian nations, under the influence of the Suez crisis, adopted a pro-Soviet stand and showed little or no interest in the fate of Hungary. The Syrian head of state epitomized their position; he did not mince his words: "The situation in Hungary is not our concern, and I don't give a damn whether fifty Budapests are destroyed."[12]

The mysterious suicide of the Danish UN employee and secretary of the Hungarian Committee, Povl Bang-Jensen, gave the rumors about Soviet infiltration of the UN apparatus added momentum, whose influence is felt to this day. Bang-Jensen had repeatedly refused to release the list of names of the witnesses, since to do so would have been to breach his promise to keep the names secret. He was fired for his refusal. A four-hundred-page docunovel by a well-known Hungarian dramatist was published in 2005 about the unexplained background of the case. Bang-Jensen had been personally strongly committed to the cause of the hamstrung Hungarian people. He did not conceal his distrust of some of his superiors and probably also of Secretary-General Dag Hammarskjöld. Bang-Jensen burned the envelope with the list of the endangered Hungarian witnesses, as a result of which he was suspended as psychologically unbalanced and finally fired in the summer of 1958. On 26 November 1959 the body of Bang-Jensen, a father of five, was found in New York. For the Hungarian and Soviet secret services it was of paramount interest to discredit the embarrassing report and to bring the witnesses into disrepute.[13] That is why the Kádár regime—by a carrot-and-stick method—organized the signatures of over two hundred writers, who in a resolution of September 1957 protested against the treatment of the Hungarian question in the United Nations General Assembly. Even so it took another five years before the Hungarian question was taken off the United Nations' agenda in December 1962 in exchange for a general amnesty announced by the Kádár regime for the following March.[14]

The Hungarian Revolution was the greatest challenge for the Soviet hegemony and a symbol of the Soviet Socialist model's bankruptcy. In the entire crisis history of the Soviet system before and after 1956, there had never been an armed uprising of this magnitude as in the fall of 1956 in Hungary. What frightened the ruling Leninist parties was the fact that it was a spontaneous revolution, fought exclusively for freedom, without any previous military defeat, without a putsch or a conspiratorial party. The global significance of this Hungarian fall was enormous precisely because this "anti-totalitarian revolution" (Raymond Aron)[1] did not aim at restoring the prewar feudal-capitalistic system, and the Communist system was swept away by those whom it purported to represent. Perhaps what shook the Soviet empire more than anything else was that for the first time since 1917 it transpired that communism could be rolled back into capitalism.

The Twentieth Party Congress of the CPSU and Khrushchev's secret speech, the turnabout in the "Polish October," and the revolution in Hungary shaped this decisive year in the history of communism. The year 1956 marked the beginning of the dissolution of the Eastern Bloc and the end of the collective myth that epitomized that bloc. The liberal British paper the *Manchester Guardian* compared the devastating effect of the crushing of the Hungarian freedom fight on the Western Left and the Communist parties to the Ribbentrop-Molotov Pact of August 1939.[2] Famous Communist sympathizers, such as Jean-Paul Sartre, Albert Camus, Pablo Picasso, and many others realized for the first time that they had been led astray. The French actress Simone Signoret, who had been a guest along with Yves Montand at the 1957 New Year's celebrations in Moscow, expressed the sentiments of many others about the situation in Budapest when she addressed her hosts by saying that the Soviet soldiers "in one short week stopped being only the heroes of 1917 and the victors of Stalingrad ... but had transformed themselves into imperial troops invading a colony. Those who condemn such acts when they occur elsewhere cannot close their eyes to these."[3]

The shock waves of the Hungarian uprising considerably accelerated the disintegration of the Western Communist parties. The Italian CP lost 10 percent (200,000) of its members. Peter Fryer, the special correspondent of the British Communist Party paper, *Daily Worker*, broke publicly with his employers in protest because his outspoken dispatches from Budapest, including a description of the suppression of the uprising by Soviet troops, were either heavily censored or suppressed.[4] Some eminent intellectual members left the British Communist Party. The Swiss one also shrank by half after 1956, and the Danish one practically fell apart. Otto von Habsburg aptly characterized the revolution as the "Stalingrad of Communism."[5] In his aforementioned speech made in Pula on 11 November 1956, Marshal Tito bluntly voiced the bitter fact that "Socialism has received a terrible blow. It has been compromised.... Just look at what a terrifying resistance a scantily armed people can offer with its bare hands, if its sole aim is only to be free and independent."[6]

In the wake of events during the de-Stalinization and as a result of the revolts in Poland and Hungary, the Chinese Communist Party began to play a significant role in international communism. Some commentators, especially in the *Peking People's Daily*, criticized Khrushchev's speech at the Twentieth Congress and cautioned against criticizing Stalin beyond a controllable measure. In his seminal work on the history of communism, the French historian François Furet rightly comments that "the Hungarian insurrection had confronted the entire Communist movement, whether Stalinist or anti-Stalinist, with the question of survival. It had overflowed its banks assigned to it by the Twentieth Congress— that of Communism regenerated.... Nagy [however] had illustrated a precedent even more alarming than nationalistic Communism—namely, suicidal Communism." [7]

As already mentioned, Milovan Djilas immediately recognized the world-historical significance of the Hungarian fall: "The world has rarely witnessed such unprecedented unity of the popular masses and such heroism ... the Hungarian Revolution blazed a path which sooner or later other Communist countries must follow. The wound which the Hungarian Revolution inflicted on Communism can never be completely healed."[8] Twenty-four years later, in a long conversation with George

Urban, Djilas again paid tribute to the Hungarian Revolution and made a comparison between the Prague Spring and the Hungarian Revolution in favor of the "strong and proud" Hungarian nation. Incidentally, in that interview for the first time he mentioned that Stalin had admired the Hungarians and Poles as strong nations.[9] That this fear of the two nations was more than justified was demonstrated by the consequences of de-Stalinization, that is, the denunciation of the crimes that Stalin had committed in the USSR, in Poland, and in Hungary. The repercussions in the countries over which he had ruled only indirectly and for a few years took on a far more dramatic character than in the Soviet Union itself.

Today we know quite a bit more about the echo that the events in Poland and above all in Hungary elicited immediately afterward in the former Soviet Union. In his unsparing analysis of the Bolshevik tyranny, Alexander Yakovlev, the intellectual force of the Gorbachev era, writes that "the events in Hungary threw the Presidium of the CC of the CPSU into total panic." On 19 December 1956 the leadership decided to send a third confidential letter (after two similar ones in April and July) to all party members "on the blocking of attacks by anti-Soviet, hostile elements." Yakovlev tells of a wave of arrests and sentencing for "slandering the Soviet system" and for "revisionism." "In the first few months of 1957 alone, hundreds of people were indicted. For believing Khrushchev and taking a stand on the side of reform, thousands were thrown into concentration camps." Yakovlev poses the question: Why did Khrushchev shift the course of de-Stalinization? The main reason seems obvious. After speaking the truth about Stalin's crimes, he himself became alarmed by the consequences of his unprecedented action.[10]

The Soviet intervention was particularly well received by the Communist potentates in Romania, because there (according to an in-depth analysis of Romanian-Hungarian relations) the situation, due to the large Hungarian minority, was dramatic, and the leadership lost its nerve. The Romanian party leader, Gheorghe Gheorghiu-Dej, had cleverly made the most of the Hungarian Revolution from the very beginning to strengthen his position at home and vis-à-vis Moscow. He even offered to send Romanian troops to Hungary to crush the revolution, and his emissaries played an important role in misleading Imre Nagy on the eve of the second Soviet intervention. Moreover, the Bucharest leadership made political capital of the undoubtedly existing fear of possible territorial demands by an independent

Hungarian neighbor. Due to the absence of de-Stalinization, the vigilance of the state security authorities, and the unchallenged structure of the party apparatus, the effect of the Hungarian events was spontaneous, unorganized, and of short duration. Nevertheless, there were meetings in Bucharest, Cluj-Napoca (Kolozsvár), and Timişoara (Temesvár), where demands were presented for the improvement of the university students' situation, the abolition of compulsory produce delivery, and equality in the political and economic sphere with the Soviet Union.

Dozens of people, especially the spokespersons of the student solidarity declarations for Hungary and the demands for democratization, were arrested in Cluj-Napoca, Timişoara, and Bucharest. After a protest meeting at the Technical University in Timişoara, some 2,500 students were arrested on 30 and 31 October. Thirty, mainly Romanian, students were later given prison sentences of three months to eight years. In a series of trials in Târgu-Mureş (Maros-Vásárhely), Cluj-Napoca, and Bucharest, numerous Hungarian and Romanian intellectuals were sentenced. There was also an unknown number of death sentences. It is said that between 1955 and 1958 a total of more than ten thousand people were detained, partly as a result of events in Hungary. The Romanian historian Mihail Retegan went even further in his assessment (at an international conference in September 1996 in Budapest): he spoke of forty thousand Hungarians, Romanians, and Germans who had been arrested in his country in connection with the Hungarian Revolution. However, no thorough investigations have been made so far into this question in Romania. What is certain, though, is that the Romanian leadership used the unrest as a convenient excuse to restrict the autonomy of the 1.5-million-strong Hungarian minority.[11]

In Czechoslovakia, too, especially in Slovakia with its dense Hungarian minority (some 600,000), the party organs tried to present the revolution in the neighboring country as a nationalistic-revanchist movement. Here too hundreds were arrested in October–November 1956 because they had, in some form or another, expressed sympathy with the Hungarian Revolution.

Nowhere in the world, however, did the public follow the triumph and tragedy of the Hungarian Revolution with as much solidarity and with such sympathy as in Poland. After the fighting in Budapest and the crushing of the revolution, in the atmosphere of the seemingly successful

Polish self-liberation, a nasty political joke was making the rounds: The Hungarians had behaved in October 1956 like the Poles, the Poles like the Czechs, and the Czechs like pigs. The miracle on the Vltava eleven years later proved to the whole world how hollow and profoundly unfair such generalizations are about a nation. Or as Schopenhauer put it once: "Every nation ridicules other nations, and all are right."[12]

Gomułka's return to power and the successful resistance of the Communist leadership against the enormous pressure by the Soviets were, as already portrayed in the first chapter, the actual triggers of the events in Hungary. Both factors had sparked off the demonstration of solidarity with Poland on 23 October and eventually the uprising and the revolution. The common Soviet threat against the parallel reform movements produced a particularly solid emotional bond between Warsaw and Budapest. Polish society in flux reacted totally differently to the dramatic happenings in Hungary than was the case in the other countries of the Eastern Bloc. Its pressure from below managed for a short while to force the new leadership under Gomułka to authorize truthful information to get through from Hungary. Ten committed Polish correspondents were in Budapest during the revolution and dispatched extensive reports about events as they unfolded. This continued at least until the Soviet invasion on 4 November, when the infamous Polish censorship went into action.

The appeals of the Polish Radio and some newspapers "to help the Hungarian brothers" elicited a surprising echo in this poor society. Lines formed at the blood donation stations, and the collection of food, medicine, and money was well under way. According to Polish sources, Poland had provided, from voluntary contributions, the equivalent of some $2 million by 19 November, twice as much as did the United States. There were also numerous demonstrations and mass meetings in Warsaw, Wrocław, and Kraków to stress "brotherhood with the Hungarians." The largest one took place in Olsztyn on 30 October. Tens of thousands of people took part in the demonstration of solidarity in the northern Polish town. The main slogans were "Down with the security forces!" and "Free Poland—Free Hungary!" The largest banner bore the legend "We call on the Soviet Union to leave Hungary!"[13]

During the revolution the Polish leadership even sent two high-ranking functionaries to Budapest, who conducted briefing conversations with Nagy and Kádár. At the same time the 28 October meeting of the Polish Central Committee declared its support for "Imre Nagy's path and his program," whose text was published in all Polish newspapers and in Hungarian party organs. Although, as already mentioned, Gomułka was informed on 1 November of the imminent second Soviet intervention, the Polish leadership found itself in a difficult situation due to the general outrage. The fact that in the UN General Assembly the Poles (together with the Chinese) voted against the U.S.-sponsored resolution condemning Soviet intervention provoked a sharp confrontation during an internal party consultation between the editors in chief of the most important papers, the electronic media, and Gomułka.

The eminent party journalists, who were supposed to explain the decision to the public, charged the surprised Gomułka with the "betrayal of the Hungarian nation" and even demanded the immediate resignation of Foreign Minister Adam Rapacki. The new head of the party, Gomułka, responded to his critics in a highly emotional tone (as he would frequently do in future crisis situations): "Comrades! You expect me to risk the fate of our nation. You want me to defend Nagy, although I do not know who he is and what his intentions are. I only know that there are practically no Communists in his cabinet anymore, and that members of reactionary parties are in the majority, while Communists are strung up on street lamps. If we defend this government, we shall suffer the same fate as Hungary. I shall never agree to that."[14]

As a convinced Communist, Gomułka was a determined opponent of Hungary's withdrawal from the Warsaw Pact and an advocate of Soviet military presence as a guarantee of Poland's western borders and the continuation of the Communist system. At the same time he considered himself beholden to the spirit of the "Polish October" as far as a limited liberalization (independence of the church, private ownership in agriculture, as well as, at the beginning, more freedom of the media and culture) was concerned. Yet as of December 1956, the Polish censors forbade any criticism of the Soviet intervention. Still, for a time Poland did not join the other Socialist states in applying the term "counterrevolution."

During the eighteen unforgettable days that I spent in Warsaw from 12 January 1957 as chief foreign columnist and special correspondent of the newly established Budapest daily, *Esti Hírlap*, I was in a position personally to experience the still prevailing dynamic atmosphere. It was on the eve of the parliamentary elections, which were also regarded as a touchstone for the success of Gomułka's reform wing. From the first minute to the very last I felt how committed the journalists and intellectuals were in Warsaw in their solidarity with the crushed and hamstrung Hungarians. Despite its defeat, almost all Poles expressed their admiration of the revolution. My trip was organized by Polish colleagues Marian Bielecki, a Polish Radio correspondent and contributor to the weekly magazine *Po Prostu* (Quite Simply), and the passionately pro-Hungarian Hanna Adamiecka of the Young Communists' weekly *Sztandar Mlodych*. It was with their help that the party paper *Trybuna Ludu*, which was then (still) headed by reformers, undertook to carry the expenses of my stay.[15]

The Hungarian Revolution had a particular meaning for the Poles, both in its moments of triumph and in those of tragedy. And the other way around: The Poles still seemed to offer a glimmer of hope for the Hungarian reporters in Warsaw. It was a land—or so it appeared to us at the time—where the peaceful transition from Stalinism to reform had indeed succeeded. Naturally we saw everything through the rose-colored spectacles of our glorification of all things Polish. It was not yet predicted that the Polish reforms would wither away in the desert of the Eastern Bloc's neo-Stalinism. The more than hundred foreign correspondents and exclusive reporters from all over the world still stressed the victory of the "Polish October" and the political and psychological significance of the thaw. Still, there and then it was already perceptible that the free and candid dissemination of news was becoming pretty much impossible even in Warsaw.

This was valid particularly as far as reports about the worrying developments in Hungary were concerned. The fact that after the elections in Poland the report volumes of Hanna Adamiecka and Wiktor Woroszylski were proscribed demonstrated that Polish censorship was also tightening the reins. After Bielicki and Woroszylski were dismissed as "supporters of the Hungarian Revolution," both of them left the party in the fall of 1957. The famous revolutionary weekly *Po Prostu* was later banned by the authorities. Gomułka was of the opinion that "the spirit of reform had gone too far." Woroszylski's *Budapest Diary 1956* could appear only in 1979, and by the end of the 1980s at least seven unofficial versions were in circulation; Hungarian translations followed rapidly.

Nowadays the *Diary* is regarded as one of the key sources of the dramatic events in Hungary. Woroszylski later became a pioneer of the

Solidarity movement. His fate symbolizes the profound bond between the happenings in Poland and Hungary. At first official Poland still kept away from the Budapest summit meeting of the Eastern Bloc countries (1–4 January 1957); Gomułka managed to delay visiting Hungary until May 1958 as the head of a delegation. However, at the end of June he made a dramatic volte-face: in a public speech given at the Gdansk shipyard (fraught with symbolism since 1980), he concurred not only with the intervention ("a correct and necessary step") but also with the execution of Imre Nagy and his associates ("Hungary's internal affair"). The Polish people again gave vent to their outrage. The party leadership, with Gomułka in the lead, adopted the time-tested tactic of silence about the entire complex of the revolution and the Nagy trial. The "normalization" in both countries eventually put an end to the awkward phase of Hungarian-Polish relations.[16]

Even those who had been closely affected in the "two weakest links in the Socialist chain" gave different answers at different times to the question as to who had won and who had lost in the critical year of 1956. This is how a well-known Polish writer described his impressions to me in the 1960s after his first visit to Hungary since 1956: "We won in October 1956, but in the long run we have lost. The Hungarians lost at the time, but in the end they have won."[17] In his above-mentioned work, François Furet compared the paths of the two countries in another way: "To draw a contrast between the 'liberal' solution of the Polish crisis and the catastrophic result of the Hungarian insurrection is misleading, not only because both the events exemplify Soviet geopolitical success that left the frontiers of the 'socialist camp' intact, but more especially, because the two Communist regimes that emerged from the uprisings of October 1956 would rapidly become more similar to each other than one might have predicted given the conditions of their birth. Gomułka turned out to be less liberal and Kádár less Stalinist than those who had put them in power."[18]

As in the case of the great freedom fights of the past—the Rákóczi uprising of 1704 to 1711 and the War of Independence of 1848–1849—victory on the battlefield, this time on the streets of Budapest, was also denied to this national show of strength. But the fame of this courageous small nation reverberated in the whole world. Tens of thousands took to the streets in Paris and London, Rome and Vienna, to protest against the brutal crushing of the revolution. However, no other Western country viewed events in Hungary with greater suspense and concern than neighboring Austria, a country that until recently had also lived under foreign occupation, having regained its full foreign political elbow room only by the State Treaty of 15 May 1955.

If one were to pose the tiebreaker question what the greatest influence on Austria's postwar history was, the overwhelming majority of answers would name the State Treaty and neutrality, wrote the Austrian historian Manfried Rauchensteiner twenty-five years ago.[19] And at the end of the treatise appended to his book, he immediately added: "This should, however, be supplemented by an event: the Hungarian Revolution." Today one would probably also mention Austria's entry into the European Union as a determining factor. Yet even in retrospect the effect of the Hungarian tragedy, and above all the ways and means by which the government and the people stood this historical test, remains a political and psychological watershed in the postwar history of Austria.

With the State Treaty signed and sealed, and after the withdrawal of the occupation forces from the country, Austria could at last act as a sovereign state. On 28 October 1956 the coalition government, consisting of the Austrian People's Party (ÖVP) and the Socialist Party of Austria (SPÖ) under Chancellor Julius Raab, addressed a dramatic appeal to the Soviet leadership: "The Austrian federal government observes with sorrowful sympathy the bloody and casualty-fraught events in neighboring Hungary. The government requests the government of the USSR to cooperate in putting an end to the fighting in order to stop the bloodshed. Based on the freedom and independence of Austria, ensured by her neutrality, the Austrian federal government advocates a normalization of conditions in Hungary with the aim that by the restoration of freedom in the spirit of human rights, the peace of Europe be strengthened and assured."[20]

No other neutral country took such an unequivocal stand on Hungary's human rights. In addition, Foreign Minister Leopold Figl expanded further on Austria's attitude to the newly appointed Soviet ambassador, Sergei G. Lapin. If, so Figl said, unarmed people crossed the border, they would be treated according to the Geneva Convention. "Should, however, fighting groups step on Austrian soil and not obey the challenge to lay down their arms, the Austrian military forces are instructed to break their resistance." The resolution of the Council of Ministers and the government's appeal were immediately conveyed to the Western embassies and the United Nations Security Council. The slightly indignant Ambassador Lapin described this verbal note as "unusual."

At the same time, Austria had to give serious thought to the question whether, in view of the expected wave of refugees, the 375-kilometer eastern border should be closed or left open. Since Switzerland was generally regarded as the model for a perpetually neutral state, the Austrian government sought answers in Bern. Max Petitpierre, the Swiss president, paid tribute to the Austrian ambassador in Bern, Johannes Coreth, for Austria's stance and the appeal to the Soviets. He added though that he had already "received reproaches from various sides that Switzerland had failed to lodge a similar diplomatic protest in Moscow." It was more in accordance with Switzerland's tradition, however, to stay strictly aloof in such cases. Despite the accolade, official Switzerland did not therefore consider Austria's example worthy of imitation. Still, to emphasize his understanding of Austria's stance, Petitpierre added that Austria, as a direct neighbor, was "more immediately affected by events in Hungary."

The Austrians, both the government and the people, behaved in an exemplary manner in 1956. In spite of warnings and broadsides from the Eastern Bloc media, the question never arose, not even in the form of the slightest hint, that Austria would consider closing her borders to the Hungarians or to conduct a selection of the refugees. Even after 4 November—the Soviet invasion of Hungary—the government decided without hesitation to keep the borders open and that all refugees, with or without papers, were to be accepted without any formalities. An unambiguous command was issued to the new, still weak Federal Army, whose first recruits had been drafted only on 15 October: "Whoever enters Austrian territory armed has to be disarmed; fire has to be opened on anyone who resists. That applies to Soviet Russian units as well." Hugo Portisch, the Austrian journalist and author of the famous TV series *Österreich II*, gave an account in his book of the same title about the criticism by leading (unnamed) contemporary Swiss politicians and military personalities of the Austrian attitude, which they believed the Soviets must have perceived as a "provocation."[21]

There were only a few hundred gendarmes, and until 2 November merely 1,537 army personnel were involved. There was also a lack of necessary equipment. All in all, at the time the army had 2,787 officers, noncoms, and men in deployment or in readiness. Despite this military limitation and due to the trauma of 1938, the authorities were determined that in case any Soviet units crossed the border, there should "at least be some resistance, a fight to gain time" (as General Scharff put it). At that time not a single shot had been fired against the troops of the Third Reich. In spite of the jubilant welcome given to Hitler, even a brief token resistance or a firing command would have counted in favor of the Austrians in the Allies' postwar assessment of their attitude. Erwin Fussenegger, general inspector of the troops, therefore gave a clear firing command: "There must never be another March 1938!"[22]

Instead of the dreaded panic atmosphere, there was growing indignation in Austria at the brutal tactics the Soviets used against their neighbors. Authentic news was rare, and the rival international correspondents frequently—as is their wont in similar crisis situations abroad—exorbitantly exaggerated the facts. Thus, for example, the headline of the *Neuer Kurier* (New courier) on 9 November reported that Budapest was a sea of flames and that the Soviets had killed sixty-five thousand Hungarians. It was not the rarely trustworthy reports of the penny press, but the sound editorials and commentaries of the quality papers that reflected the unbelievably strong sympathy and at the same time the deeply rooted historical solidarity of the Austrian public.

Thus, for instance, in a full-page article in *Die Presse* (The press) (on 28 October), entitled "Suffering and Greatness of the Hungarian Nation," the historian Adam Wandruszka posed the question: "Whence came the strength to defy the greatest military might?" And he promptly answered it in the subtitle: "The history of the Magyar people, a centuries-old epic of resistance and fighting for national self-preservation— isolated in the midst of a Germanic-Latin-Slavic environment." The Socialist *Arbeiter-Zeitung* (Workers' newspaper) wrote on the same day: "In Hungary, for the first time in the history of modern dictatorships, an entire people has risen up against the Communist tyranny and is in the process of ridding itself from it.... Burning and bloody, the proof stands clear in front of the eyes of the whole world: the Communist governments in the satellite countries of the East are upheld solely on Russia's command and by Russia's power." After the crushing of the revolution, the editorial of the *Salzburger Nachrichten* (Salzburg news) cried out with desperate indignation: "If the West does not hurry to the aid of the Magyars, thereby demonstrating the solidarity of the Free World, then life for free people will have lost its meaning!"[23]

The fact that Austria had escaped the fate of partition and subjection to a foreign dictatorship doubtless influenced the emotional reaction to the Hungarian tragedy. That a country after seven years of Anschluss and war, after almost twelve years of occupation, and so soon after the pullout of the last foreign soldier accommodated the Hungarian refugees so naturally, undauntedly, and magnanimously was and is a glorious chapter in modern Austrian history. As the political scientist Norbert Leser observed almost forty years later: "The popular uprising was for Austria and the Austrians a practical test of humanitarianism and a chance to let the living Hungarians benefit from their gratitude that Austria had fared so much better than Hungary."[24] They marked the length of the Austrian border with red-white-red flags. During the night, fires were lit. They wanted the refugees to know, be it day or night, where they could feel safe at last. Not since World War II had there been such a huge, spontaneous exodus of civilians. The Hungarians, many of them entire families, came by the thousands on that 4 November. The Bridge at Andau became a symbol for a bridging of East and West not only through James Michener's book of that name and the film based on it, but above all "through the experience of the people themselves." In the vicinity of Andau alone, where the so-called Einser Canal and other branch canals make up the border, some seventy thousand Hungarians entered Austria. Most of them used the narrow wooden bridge that became world famous as the Bridge at Andau. On 21 November Hungarian border guards blew up this little footbridge. Yet the influx continued.[25]

In November the number of Hungarian refugees totaled 113,810. The highest figure registered on a single day was 8,537, on 23 November. In December 49,685 refugees arrived. Even after the border had been hermetically sealed, the number for January totaled 12,882. In view of the never-ebbing stream of refugees through Yugoslavia as well (in 1957 alone 10,000 Hungarian refugees arrived in Austria from Yugoslavia), it is almost impossible to put an exact figure on the sum total of the refugee wave. By March 1957 the Austrian Interior Ministry counted 180,432 Hungarians who had found refuge in Austria. Hungarian statistics reported a total of 193,885 refugees; Yugoslavia accounted for 18,181 of these. More than 11,000 later returned to Hungary, so that the number of emigrants eventually amounted to 182,348. Intellectuals, among them students, comprised a quarter of the refugees.[26]

Behind these figures we have to see the generous and altruistic attitude and the enormous wave of spontaneous and improvised helpfulness of the entire Austrian people. One should not forget that at the time there were still tens of thousands of "old refugees" housed in camps and mass accommodations, and thirty thousand Austrians still lived in temporary lodgings and barracks. Yet in no time at all reception centers and larger camps were set up, first in Burgenland and later in all of Austria. They also filled the army's barracks. Money, clothes, and foodstuffs were collected everywhere for the Hungarians. Thousands of Austrians offered their own homes to accommodate refugees. A number of schools, and even some hotels and guesthouses, were transformed into emergency housing. There are no statistics about the extent of this unique helpfulness. Austrian pharmacists, for instance, donated 600 million units of penicillin, while the workers of the Böhler-Werke (one of the oldest manufacturers of stainless steel in Central Europe) each offered five hours' wages. In Vienna eight blood banks were set up, which operated day and night. In the words of the famous actress Johanna Matz, who, together with many other artists and writers, roamed the streets with collection boxes, it was "a totally amazing feeling of togetherness.... All of Austria was carried away by this wave."[27]

Naturally there were also instances of tensions and difficulties with some refugees, most of whom sought new homes as far away from Hungary and as soon as possible. By the end of November there was one refugee for every thirty Austrians (including the 114,000 so-called old refugees). The Austrian government launched appeals to twenty countries to open their frontiers and to accept refugee transports "without any formalities." An obvious sense of guilt by the Western governments that they had so miserably failed the Hungarians in those November days probably also accounted for the subsequent and never-to-be-repeated willingness of so many states, from Switzerland to the United States and Canada, to accept refugees. In the relatively short period until the end of 1956, almost 100,000, and until the end of 1957 practically all those who wanted to emigrate, a total of 160,000 left Austria. Most refugees wanted to find a new home in the United States or—as a second choice—in

Canada. According to final figures, every second refugee went overseas, with the United States taking 24 percent and Canada 16 percent of the total. The outpouring of U.S. sympathy for the Hungarian freedom fighters, mixed with a widespread feeling of remorse for the failure to help Hungary, forced President Eisenhower to act quickly and to prod Congress to increase the number of Hungarian refugees allowed to enter the United States. A three-day visit by Vice President Richard Nixon to Austria in mid-December 1956 brought a breakthrough: The quota for the Hungarian immigrants was trebled to 21,500. In the end, the UN High Commissioner for Refugees put the final figure at 40,650, while Austrian statistics refer to a total of 38,058 people admitted to the United States. The figure for Canada is 27,280, and for Australia 11,680. In all, thirty-seven countries were willing to accept refugees, with the U.K. admitting 20,990 and France 12,690. According to Austrian data, only about 8,000 refugees returned to Hungary. It is estimated that at the end of the day only some 10,000 Hungarian refugees remained in Austria, although their exact number can no longer be established.[28]

The conduct of Switzerland represented a particular chapter. In comparison to its size, the country exceeded all others in collections and the reception of refugees. Within a few short weeks, Switzerland took in fourteen thousand Hungarian refugees. As in other European countries, there were also numerous torch-lit processions and silent demonstrations followed by rallies. In Switzerland, as elsewhere, students and other youths attacked the buildings and printing presses of the Communist Party of Labor (PdA). It is well known that prior to 1945, Jews and anti-Nazis who tried to escape from the Third Reich to Switzerland were admitted only under the most stringent restrictions. The act of helping the Hungarians in 1956—according to a later study of the earlier code of refugee procedure—gave the Swiss the opportunity to "realign the refugee policy and to shore up the asylum tradition. This was expressed in the change of personnel in the highest echelon of the aliens branch of the Federal Police, as well as the broad-minded and unbureaucratic rapidity of accepting the refugees.... It is not widely remembered that this new, generous phase lasted for a mere seven weeks."[29]

The other primary destination of the refugee wave was the Federal Republic of Germany. A total of 14,500 Hungarians, approximately two-thirds of them under the age of thirty, found a new home there.

Only about 500 of these returned to Hungary. In 1959 some 1,200 young Hungarians were admitted to West German universities. "In no other country in the world," reported a young student at the Hungarian Youth Congress in Hennef an der Sieg, "have so many of our compatriots been admitted with such magnanimity to the universities as in the Federal Republic." As early as December 1956, the West German government made 25 million deutsche mark available for the care and support of Hungarian refugees. A noteworthy event was the establishment of a Hungarian high school with boarding facilities on the Klosterberg in the Bavarian township of Kastl, where two hundred boys and girls found a home and received an education.[30]

While Austria got much sympathy and recognition from the free world for its courageous and magnanimous actions, the government in Vienna became a favored target of sharp attacks from the Eastern Bloc. That Austria behaved in a manner "more Western than the West" (as an observer put it) was naturally regarded with as much disapproval by Moscow as the anti-Soviet and anti-Communist demonstrations, the attacks on party venues, and last but not least the passionate pro-Hungarian outlook of most of the media. The Austrian ambassador, Walther Peinsipp, was the only Western diplomat in Budapest who responded to the demands of the revolution with humanity and gallantry, concludes the extremely critical American correspondent Leslie B. Bain in his book. Peinsipp was "the Western hero" during the revolution and the dark days of its suppression. He rode from hospitals to battle stations distributing food and medicine (to the value of today's 1.4 million euros) and was accessible at all times to Hungarians and Austrians. The head of mission arranged for 650 people (among them many with dual citizenship) to go to Austria in convoys equipped with "diplomatic protection." In contrast, according to Bain, the American Legation seemed to have exhausted itself by extending political asylum to Cardinal Mindszenty.[31]

In the eyes of the Soviets and their stooges, all these were signs of conduct unbecoming to neutrality. On 4 December the Moscow *Pravda* alleged that the Austrian Embassy in Budapest had distributed weapons. Time and again the ridiculous fabrications of the Viennese Communist paper, the *Volksstimme* (The people's voice), were repeated and embroidered. A Bulgarian paper even claimed that sixty thousand emigrants inundated Hungary from West Germany via Austria. One of the most embarrassing and at the same time farcical stories was played out at the General Assembly of the United Nations in New York. On 21 November 1956, the Soviet foreign minister D. T. Shepilov attacked Austria. He recounted that Austrian-made pistols of the Gasser brand were found on Hungarian insurgents. A short while later, Federal Chancellor Raab explained that the Gasser Company had ceased producing their eight-millimeter revolvers in 1917! No ammunition had been manufactured for that revolver since. The Gasser Company had been transformed, in conjunction with the Rast Company, into a sewing-machine factory. Raab then asked somewhat sarcastically whether the insurgents might have shot at the Soviets with sewing machines, and whether it could be a case of some new secret weapon.[32]

A byproduct of the Austrian reaction to the crushing of the Hungarian Revolution was the irrevocable end of the small Communist Party. At the next parliamentary elections in 1959, the Communists failed to get a single seat. Chancellor Raab took an interesting, but in the event ineffective, initiative when he suggested in a radio address of 20 January 1957 that Hungary too should become neutral like Austria. Yet by then Hungary was already in the throes of the process of "normalization." Three months later the Soviet leadership reacted to this provocative proposal. It happened in April 1957, when Anastas Mikoyan made up for his canceled October 1956 visit to Austria. The five-day visit improved the rather resentful relationship between the two countries. At any rate Mikoyan gave an unmistakable reply to Raab's suggestion of Hungarian neutrality: Austria's neutrality was a special case, irreproducible under the current conditions.[33] Hungary, the source of infection, had to remain in quarantine.

In November 1956 János Kádár was forty-four years old. In that zero hour he had to start to rebuild the state party from scratch and without any illusions. In some respects the years following the installation of the Kádár government were almost as important and revealing, if at first less noted, than the revolution itself. Undoubtedly the Communist regimes in Central and Eastern Europe (with the exception of Yugoslavia) had come into being essentially "in the shadow of the Soviet military might." But only in Hungary did a spontaneous and unprepared national and anti-Communist uprising virtually destroy the power monopoly. Only in that country did it come to pass that the unprecedented attempt to secede from the Warsaw Pact as a neutral state was suppressed with open force by the same military might that had stood godfather at the birth of the system. First and foremost, however, only in Hungary did a tiny ruling class try to build up a fundamentally unchanged Communist Party dictatorship after it had been destroyed and discredited before the whole world. The conflict that emerged repeatedly (if often only covertly) in the ensuing period between the forces of inertia and renewal bore specific traits because of the popular uprising in 1956.

The fact that at the time the West did not give a helping hand—moreover, with the Suez adventure in the eyes of the Hungarians it even gave the decisive impetus for the victory of the hawks in the Moscow leadership—caused the elite and the man in the street profound disappointment. Political resignation born out of salutary disenchantment has perhaps contributed even more in the long run to the consolidation of the regained power than the shattering of the opposition. Despite the retribution against the active or putative opponents, the systematic use of the old carrot-and-stick method helped Moscow's hated procurator slowly to gain at least the acquiescence of the broad masses.

It soon became apparent that the puppet government was not going to keep its political promises, such as the negotiations regarding the withdrawal of Soviet troops or the accreditation of other political parties in the framework of a coalition. On the other hand, the realistic concessions for the peasants (retention of the abolition of mandatory produce deliveries decreed by the Nagy government), as well as the middle class (private businesses and tax relief) and industrial workers (in 1957 real wages were increased by 17 percent!), were maintained. With the help of a $600 million loan from the Soviet Union and other Eastern Bloc countries, small-scale industry was cranked up, and the real wages of workers, but also of other strata of society, were substantially increased through tax relief. Privatization and depoliticization proved for a long time to be the most important pillars of the system.

However, in view of the profound distrust of workers and intellectuals, the fundamental question arose from the very beginning: Which groups *actually* supported the despised and isolated regime, thus becoming the ruling class of postrevolutionary Hungary? In the first weeks after their inglorious entry in Soviet tanks, Kádár and his clique operated in a political vacuum. On the one hand there were the vengeful Stalinists in their Moscow exile and their hell-bent followers in Hungary, and on the other the larger group of partly hostile, partly mistrustful, and at best indifferent inner-party reformers. At the same time it was absurd to suppose that months later a "handful of puppets by the grace of the Soviets" could still direct the entire state apparatus. Although the party, government, and military bureaucracy, namely the "privileged class" of the allegedly classless society or the apparatus itself, was small in relation to the total population, it was still a monopoly of considerable size. Above all, the loyalty of the apparatchiks, whose personal well-being and security were intrinsically tied to the party's monopoly of power, played a crucial role in the relatively rapid reorganization of the Communist control system.

Nonetheless, the rebuilding of the state party proceeded only very laboriously. This was shown by the extremely low membership figures of the newly founded Hungarian Socialist Workers' Party. Only 103,000 people joined the new party by the end of December 1956.[1] Behind the scenes of ostensible unanimity, bitter battles were fought for the leading positions, above all regarding the question of the critical assessment of the past. All the concessions made to win the citizens' consensus did not alter the fact that the so-called Revolutionary Workers' and Peasants'

Government had been born on 4 November by way of a constitutional fiction. Not only during the subsequent critical months, but over three decades the regime had to uphold that fiction from which it originated. It was a time of illusions and lies, of promises and pitfalls, of tragedies and treachery. People who had been thrown into jail by Rákosi during the early fifties and sometimes shared a cell, or even the young spokesmen of the Petőfi Circle, changed within days into embittered opponents, and after the second Soviet intervention split up into victims and victors.

Those Communists who at the time had "pulled the chestnuts out of the fire" refused to cooperate with those who had "vacillated" or were in opposition in 1956. Old fighters soon complained that in many respects nonparty people received preferential treatment. What was left for the "several ten thousand" party, state, and economics functionaries? Power! The critical fall of 1956 demonstrated that when it comes to the crunch, the people in charge of the bureaucracy are the most reliable reinforcements of the power system. They were the ones who in the course of the reorganizations occupied the key positions, and in the spirit of the famous "two-front war" against Stalinists and "revisionists," persecuted as collaborators of the "counterrevolution" those members who wanted to bring about a limited relaxation of the Communist system—albeit without the abolition of the party's monopoly of power. The result was a renewed top leadership with a basically unchanged apparatus. The argument about the causes of the uprising, the character of the October events, and the extent of the old leadership's responsibility was carried on below the surface even directly after the consolidation. The attitude in the fall of 1956 counted primarily as the benchmark, and not the fight against Stalinism. While thousands of "revisionists" were arrested, dismissed, or demoted, only in 1962 did Kádár strike a blow against those top functionaries and high-ranking officers of the State Security forces whose services he had used for the concerted reprisals between 1956 and 1961.

After the period in which old party members could be readmitted came to an end on 1 May 1957, the head count was fewer than 300,000. These Communists were the "pillars" of the regime. As late as the spring of 1958, Deputy Minister of the Interior László Földes[2] estimated that the number of genuine "class enemies," those elements which "were ready at any minute to fight against the people's democracy" (former landowners and wealthy peasants, wholesalers and priests, officers and officials), amounted to 700,000. Thus, according to official admission, the number of "active enemies" far exceeded that of the regime's convinced followers.

The ferocious settling of scores with those who were made responsible for the "counterrevolution" or who had attempted to organize the resistance after 4 November was undoubtedly the most important aspect of Hungary's postrevolutionary development. The true dimension and the unbelievable brutality of the campaign of vengeance became known only after the change of regime. The collections of documents, which the researchers of the 1956 Institute could process in their entirety almost forty years after the events, as well as the memoirs and interviews of survivors and their families, demonstrate the hypocrisy and duplicity of even the consolidated Kádár regime.

The first government declaration still guaranteed freedom from prosecution for participants of the revolution. Kádár spoke of the justified dissatisfaction of most of the participants. There were consultations with representatives of the workers' councils; the deportation of groups of young insurgents to the Soviet Union was rescinded after Kádár and Münnich managed to convince General Serov and the Soviet "supervisors" that such measures were counterproductive, particularly as far as normalization, namely breaking the resistance, was concerned. During the first weeks the Soviet commanders and essentially Suslov, Malenkov, and Aristov were responsible for the "restoration of order." On the eve of the important Central Committee meeting of the newly founded state party (2 and 3 December 1956), the three Soviet top functionaries "persuaded" Kádár—as they had already done before the kidnapping of the Imre Nagy group—that it was necessary to adopt a harsher course and to denounce the popular uprising from the start as a "counterrevolution."[3]

The provisional Central Committee's fundamental resolution stated four reasons for the breakdown of the Communist system: (1) the grave mistakes and transgressions of the Rákosi-Gerő clique (this point was mentioned less and less as time went on), (2) the activities of the inner-party oppositional circle around Imre Nagy and Géza Losonczy, (3) the activities of the Horthy Fascists and Hungarian capitalist-landowner counterrevolutionaries, and (4) the interference of international imperialism. This resolution was to serve for thirty-three years as the cornerstone of the Kádár regime's "legitimization."

After the adoption of this resolution, the instruments of retribution were organized in an accelerated tempo. After December the arrests and interrogations were conducted no longer by the Soviet colleagues but by the Hungarian State Security organs. At the same time they established special emergency police units, called in popular parlance "quilted jackets" (*pufajkások*) because of their characteristic Russian uniform. This new police force was formed from former State Security personnel, army officers, and armed party functionaries driven from their positions during the revolution. These commandos went about it with particular brutality in the provinces and beat people, for instance the specially active students of the Technical University in the town of Miskolc, within an inch of their lives.[4] Although the torture methods of the Stalinist era were officially prohibited and were not employed against well-known prisoners, in the case of thousands of young workers and apprentices, insurgents and postrevolutionary resisters, beatings and torture continued with gay abandon everywhere, and later in the prisons as well.

The vengeance of the victors by the grace of Khrushchev was gruesome and lasted several years. Hand in hand with the formation of the operative organizations, they began to create the legal prerequisites for the impending avalanche of trials and proceedings. Concurrently, politically unreliable judges and prosecutors, those who had learned from the lawlessness of the Rákosi era and had therefore voiced their reservations, were dismissed or suspended from service. Special lists of "trustworthy" attorneys were compiled for political proceedings. On 11 December the government declared a state of emergency, and in the first of December days it arrested two hundred leading representatives of the workers' and revolutionary councils. Soon the first death sentences were announced as a deterrent. Martial law was invoked for murder, arson, robbery, sabotage, and concealment of weapons. The sentences pronounced by the summary courts could be carried out within two hours of a rejection of clemency pleas. The twenty-nine-year-old shoemaker József Soltész became the first victim of summary justice for the unauthorized possession of a firearm. He was sentenced to death on 15 December 1956 in Miskolc and shot ninety minutes later at the infantry's firing range. The reason: In the course of a police raid, he was found to be carrying a pistol.

The researchers of the 1956 Institute estimate that between 1956 and 1961 a total of 350 to 400 people were executed.[5] Some among them were allegedly sentenced to death as common criminals or for political crimes committed prior to 1956, in part during World War II. Since the regime constantly tried to equate insurgents with common criminals, there could have been revolutionaries among those executed. Two hundred and twenty-nine people, including six women, were executed because of their participation in the revolution or the resistance. Almost one in three of these was under the age of twenty-four, and three-quarters of them were younger than thirty-four. Most of them were workers, peasants, apprentices, and soldiers. Three people, among them Géza Losonczy, the minister of state in the Nagy government, died in prison in unexplained circumstances. Even if, among the 341 people who were confirmed to have been executed, one takes into account only those 229 people who were victims of the 1956–1961 campaign of vengeance, one finds that their number exceeded the 123 condemned to die after the War of Independence of 1848–49, the 65 dead after the fall of the Communist Soviet Republic of 1919, and the 189 people executed after 1945. Hence the vengeance of the victors went far beyond all the earlier ones in modern Hungarian history.

However, the bare figures and the various categories of charges should not obscure the unbelievable cruelty of the retaliation as mirrored in the terrifying fates of individuals.[6] People were sentenced to death totally gratuitously or under specious pretexts. Ferenc Fáy, the commander of the National Guard of Nagytétény, on the outskirts of Budapest, ended his life on the gallows only because he had filled that position, although there had not been any fighting or acts of violence in the locality. Or let us take the shocking case of the Protestant minister Lajos Gulyás. He had saved an officer of the border guard from being lynched after the massacre at Magyaróvár and almost fell victim to the enraged crowd for his intervention. He was executed just like a worker called Imre Farkas, who had tried to prevent a fatal act of vengeance in Csepel. The fact that he had a pistol on him was enough justification for the death sentence.

The execution of intellectuals who—although they filled leading positions during the revolution—personally never did anything that could have been held against them belongs to another category. A characteristic example was the case of Dr. Árpád Brusznyai. The thirty-two-year-old high school teacher of classical philology in the town of Veszprém became a member of the county revolutionary council and was elected its chairman on 1 November. The leading intellectual light of the council, he always took up the cudgel for discipline and public order, and on several occasions used his influence to prevent acts of violence. Arrested in April 1957, Brusznyai was condemned to life imprisonment by a military court, whereupon the party secretary of Veszprém County, János Pap, in a letter to the president of the Supreme Court, demanded that Brusznyai be given the death sentence in the second instance. On 7 January 1958 the Special Council of the Military College of the "independent" Supreme Court complied with the powerful party functionary's demand and increased the sentence to death. Brusznyai was executed two days later. The informer was later appointed minister of the interior, and for a while he was even deputy premier. After the change of regime, he committed suicide, together with his wife.[7]

An unusual case was that of Major Antal Pálinkás, who was ordered by the government to escort the recently freed Cardinal József Mindszenty to Budapest. Pálinkás was a scion of the margravial Pallavicini family. He took part as a professional officer in the anti-Fascist resistance during the German occupation of Hungary. After the arrest of his superiors, he joined the Red Army. However, his deployment never came. After the war he was decorated with the Freedom Medal, changed his name to Pálinkás, and joined the Communist Party. On 30 October the Revolutionary Military Council of his armored regiment elected him its chairman. On 4 November his unit became involved in a military action. The court of first instance sentenced him to life imprisonment in 1957, but two months later the Special Council of the Military College of the Supreme Court altered this to a death sentence. Before his plea for clemency was rejected, Major Pálinkás is said to have made a gallows humor remark in his prison cell: "Surely they won't miss the opportunity of hanging a Margrave Pallavicini!"[8]

Tragic too was the fate of Gábor Földes, director of the State Theater in Győr. One of the most talented theatrical figures in Hungary, he was a convinced reform Communist and follower of Imre Nagy. As chair of the Constituent Council of the Intelligentsia and the Petőfi Circle in Győr, he played an important role in trying to restrain the crowd from committing violent acts and at Mosonmagyaróvár saved the lives of several officers of the border guard. Because of an anti-Semitic demonstration, Földes had to resign on 28 October 1956, but he wrote articles in the spirit of the revolution even after 4 November. He was arrested in May, sentenced to death in June by the court of first instance, and in December 1957 the death sentence was upheld in the second instance. Although leading Communist actors personally appealed to Kádár for clemency, Földes was executed on 15 January 1958, after his appeal for clemency was rejected by the Presidential Council. According to a well-informed civil rights activist, Földes ended up on the gallows despite the known facts and the intervention of his colleagues because in the Presidential Council's view it would not have made a good impression if among all the persons condemned to death in Győr they would have given a reprieve to a Jew.[9]

During the revolution, Földes was sent to Mosonmagyaróvár by Attila Szigethy, the chairman of the Győr National Revolutionary Council, to restore order and prevent further bloodshed after the massacre at the barracks of the border guard. Szigethy was later elected chairman of the Trans-Danubian National Council, in which capacity he played a prominent part in the endeavors to bring about full social reconciliation. During the German occupation he gave refuge to several fugitives, including the later crypto-Communist state president István Dobi. After the war he was an independent member of Parliament from 1947 to 1957. As a keen supporter of Imre Nagy, he was dismissed from his position as deputy chairman of the Győr-Sopron County Council in 1954 and later appointed manager of a state farm. After the defeat of the revolution, the Kádár government tried unsuccessfully to recruit Szigethy as a government commissioner or a minister. In February 1957 he could still travel to Bulgaria with a Patriotic People's Front delegation. In early May he was arrested and stripped of his mandate. After two unsuccessful attempts, Szigethy committed suicide on 12 August 1957 while on remand, before his trial could have commenced.[10]

The target groups for retaliation were not only those that took part in the armed struggle or participated actively in the resistance even after 4 November, but also people who played any sort of role in the revolution or were involved in its "preparation," namely in the inner-party opposition. The prosecutors and courts, diminished by the purges, were overtaxed. In 1957 alone more than 20,000 people were subjected to court proceedings on political grounds, but only 6,000 cases ended in a sentence. Altogether 26,000 people were arrested, of whom 22,000 received valid sentences. Some 13,000 people landed in internment camps for a longer or shorter period without any legal procedure. The camps that were abolished in 1953 by the Nagy government were reopened and new ones set up by decree no. 31/1956. The percentage of internees who were forced to cooperate with the authorities was exceptionally high.[11]

One of the most shocking chapters of the reprisals concerns those victims who, hoodwinked by Kádár's promise of an amnesty, returned to Hungary from Austria, Germany, and Switzerland only to disappear in prison or end their lives on the gallows. Agents planted among the emigrants, such as Miklós Szabó and his ilk, betrayed dozens of refugees, who undertook to go back to Hungary to organize the resistance or to help people across the border. One must not forget those people who, after an interrogation or in prison under pressure or tempted by promises, could be persuaded to cooperate as informers with the Secret Police. Some well-known intellectuals and artists, whose careers were later discreetly facilitated by the Kádár regime, were suspected of collaborating with the Secret Police soon after their release. Others were exposed only four or five decades later on the basis of files that became accessible after the change of regime.

The phases of repression were of unequal duration and intensity. The first partial amnesty was decreed in April 1960 for all those whose terms were shorter than five years. At the same time the government abolished the internment camps. However, here too the regime operated with a double standard. Gábor Péter, the highest-ranking Stalinist torturer and the party representative in the Secret Service, and ex-minister of defense Mihály Farkas, together with his son Vladimir, who as a lieutenant colonel had been personally responsible for the torture of many innocent people, were released in 1959–1960. According to the memoirs of the son, the two Farkases lived in a prison as comfortable as a two-star hotel![12] As three and a half years after the revolution there was still no sign of a general amnesty, some outraged political prisoners in the Vác penitentiary held a hunger strike, which soon developed into a large prison revolt. The incident was kept secret and was brutally put down.[13] Only in March 1963 did the government (in return for having the "Hungarian question" taken off the UN's agenda) announce a general amnesty, even if several hundred prisoners ("recidivists," people convicted for murder, high treason, or espionage) were not released.

Those who had tried, through the diplomatic missions of foreign countries or by letters, to alert world opinion to the real conditions behind the ostensive consolidation had to reckon with lengthy prison sentences. My former colleague and friend, the journalist Péter Földes, who had fought in the French Resistance during the war, was sentenced to thirteen years in 1960 because of a letter of protest written to the French Embassy!

According to the available documents, the last execution probably took place on 26 August 1961. The victim was the precision mechanic László Nickelsburg, who during World War II eked out a miserable existence as a Jewish forced laborer and whose entire family perished in the gas chambers of Auschwitz. He was a much-decorated ace worker and party member. During the revolution he joined the National Guard on 31 October and soon became leader of the group at Baross Square, in the vicinity of the Eastern Railway Station. His principal aim was to prevent violence and looting. After the futile resistance against the Soviet tanks on 4 November, Nickelsburg joined the voluntary emergency medical service, and he himself sustained injuries. He fled to Vienna on 25 November but returned to Budapest on 5 December. Arrested soon after, Nickelsburg refused to collaborate with the State Security forces after his release. For this he was taken into custody again in February 1957 and sentenced to life imprisonment. While serving his term in the Vác prison, a supplementary investigation was initiated in the case of the Baross Square group. Nickelsburg was retried on the charge of leading a conspiracy and after four years in prison was sentenced to death without recourse to an appeal.

Hundreds of trials took place in the course of the bloody reprisal, and besides those executed and arrested, several thousands were placed under police surveillance for longer or shorter periods. Historians of the period estimate that at least 100,000 people were directly affected by the repressive measures (dismissals, demotions, exclusion from higher studies, and so on), and this figure does not even include the affected family members.[14] The children of the condemned grew up stigmatized. Two Hungarian sociologists have published forty-two extensive interviews with children affected by their parents' execution and imprisonment and described their harrowing personal experiences against the background of the Kádár system's hushed-up history.[15]

The retaliatory actions reached their culmination with the trial of Imre Nagy and his associates—a trial that was denounced all over the world. In view of the extraordinary significance of this criminal procedure against the legitimate Hungarian prime minister, it appears appropriate at the end of this chapter to give a more detailed picture of the campaign of vengeance against Nagy and the road leading to his execution.

The preparation, the inquiry, and the trial itself were carried out in absolute secrecy. By violating all the norms of legality and the much-vaunted inner-party democracy, a small circle (Kádár, Münnich, Interior Minister Béla Biszku, and Minister of State Gyula Kállai)—in constant consultation with the Soviet leadership—wrote the scenario for settling the score with the Nagy group. Kállai, as special emissary, held fruitless talks with Nagy in Romania as late as 25 January 1957. After his return, he was the first top politician to suggest at the meeting of the party's executive committee that Nagy should be brought to trial. During Kádár's visit to Moscow at the end of March, the matter was resolved in principle with the Soviet leadership. On 14 April 1957 a delegation of the Hungarian State Security forces arrested Nagy and the other members of the group at Snagov and flew them back to Budapest in shackles and blindfolded as if they were dangerous criminals. Here is a macabre footnote to the hypocritical vileness of the Hungarian and Romanian leaderships: On 5 April 1957 Kádár, as prime minister, requested the Romanian prime minister, Chivu Stoica, to rescind the right of asylum and to extradite the Nagy group, because "new facts about their criminal activities" had come to light. The request was immediately complied with. Seven months after the Nagy trial, on the occasion of the repatriation of the last deported member of the group at the beginning of 1959, Kádár as party chief thanked his colleague Gheorghe Gheorghiu-Dej on behalf of the Central Committee in a cordial letter for "the international help." "We know how much work, effort and cost the accommodation and care of this group has entailed for you."[16]

In August Interior Minister Biszku informed the Soviet leadership about the preparations.[17] On 21 December 1957 the Hungarian Central Committee gave the green light for the criminal proceedings. Kádár kept the minutes of the closed sitting locked in his safe until the end of his life. Although the indictment had been prepared a long time ago, the trial had to be postponed twice at the express wish of the Soviets for foreign policy considerations. The entire trial, the indictment and the verdict, were built on a lie: Imre Nagy and his codefendants had to bear the chief responsibility for everything that had happened in Hungary between 23 October and 4 November 1956. Before the revolution their aim was to seize power by force through their "illegal antistate group" organized in December 1955, and by their treachery they "smoothed the way for the reactionary forces." "They [also] bent their efforts directly toward disrupting the alliance of Socialist states." The finishing touches to this barbarous vendetta were supplied by the fact that during a year and a half not a single communiqué appeared about the whereabouts and fate of the Nagy group, and even their closest relatives, still interned in Romania, could not find out anything about the defendants until after their secret trial.

The secret trial took place in Budapest from 9 to 15 June 1958. Imre Nagy, Defense Minister Pál Maléter, and the journalist Miklós Gimes were sentenced to death. They were executed on 16 June. Nagy's close associate, the prewar Communist József Szilágyi, refused to cooperate and answer his investigators. He was therefore tried separately and was executed earlier, on 24 April 1958. The mentally ill Géza Losonczy perished in remand on 21 December 1957 in unexplained circumstances. Of the other defendants, Ferenc Donáth, member of the party's executive committee, was sentenced to twelve years, Minister of State Zoltán Tildy to six, the Budapest chief of police Sándor Kopácsi to life, the son-in-law of Nagy, Ferenc Jánosi, to eight, and Miklós Vásárhelyi to five.

Nagy became a tragic hero of Hungarian history. He, who knew better than anyone how in Moscow and later in Budapest tens of thousands got caught up in the ever-turning wheels of the purging machinery, and how prosecutors and Communist journalists could fabricate cases built on nothing but lies, remained steadfast until the end. Perhaps he could have saved his life by a timely resignation or a later self-criticism. By his stance in that historic moment he wanted to remain true to himself and *his* notion of October. He had lost fifteen kilos, but the politician with heart disease professed his innocence all through the interrogations and the secret trial. He considered himself a Communist to the last, challenged the competence of the court, and declared that he was willing to answer ideological-political questions only before an expert party forum.

In his political testament, titled *Thoughts, Memories*, which he wrote during his internment in Snagov, Nagy repeatedly attempted to combine the "national liberation revolution" with the defense of the "Socialist achievements."[18] He expressed similar views in a series of political letters addressed to Tito, Khrushchev, Gomułka, and Togliatti, to the Romanian party leadership, and to the Hungarian Central Committee (these were never passed on by the Secret Service). The revolution's prime minister has often been criticized for not having been a "real politician" because instead of taking control of the centers of power, he merely made speeches. The Marxist philosopher Georg Lukács also voiced this opinion in confidential conversations with his students. However, Nagy's followers, for instance the philosopher Agnes Heller and the poet István Eörsi, admired him for acting like a democratic politician by implementing the people's wishes of withdrawing from the Warsaw Pact and changing from the dictatorship of the party to a democratic multiparty system.[19]

It was these practical political steps during the revolution and his unswerving allegiance to these convictions to the very end and not his theoretical-political writings that determine the role of Imre Nagy. He was neither a charismatic figure nor a wily party politician. But even with his last words after his sentence had been pronounced, he acted as a statesman of admirable moral fiber. He considered the death penalty "unjust, unfounded and unacceptable"; however, he was convinced that sooner or later the Hungarian people and the international working class would acquit him of the grave accusations. The time would come when he would be judged fairly. He was the victim of a grave mistake, of a miscarriage of justice. His closing words were: "I do not ask for mercy."[20]

After Nagy's execution by hanging at 5:09 a.m., Pál Maléter and Miklós Gimes were hanged. The three coffins were buried in the courtyard of the prison. To make the freshly dug soil inconspicuous, a truckload of old office furniture and junk was heaped over the mounds. On 24 February 1961 the three coffins were exhumed under the strictest secrecy. They were then reinterred—rolled in tar paper, in an unmarked grave among the remains of hundreds of other hastily buried victims of the retaliation—in Plot 301 of the nearby cemetery. All three of them were registered under false names in the cemetery's records; Imre Nagy as a woman called Piroska Borbíró.

The executions of Nagy and his friends, which the Chinese CP's central organ, the Peking *People's Daily*, hailed as "welcome news," elicited general outrage in the free world. Most of the commentators held Khrushchev and the Soviet leadership responsible for the judicial murder.[21] However, the documents from the Hungarian archives, which meanwhile have become accessible, particularly the minutes of the deliberations of the state party's highest bodies, indicate that in fact Kádár was the moving force behind the trial. It was he and no one else who uttered the decisive words, especially concerning the levels of penalty for Nagy, Szilágyi, Maléter, and Gimes. For Kádár and his regime a live Imre Nagy meant a personal and political threat of the first order. Precisely because Nagy had rejected any acknowledgment of guilt as an anti-Stalinist, but as a convinced Communist, his existence became the embodiment of Kádár's missing legitimization.[22]

The trial of Nagy was, as we have seen, neither the beginning nor the end of the Soviet-backed victors' vengeance. Up to the very end, the Kádár regime had to bear the indelible moral burden for the breaches of repeated promises of safe conduct and impunity and the secret trial and the executions of Nagy, Maléter, Gimes, and others. Until the end of his time in power, a conspiracy of silence surrounded the truth about the events of 1956 and Kádár's multiple acts of treachery against Imre Nagy, as well as about his real role behind the scenes of the Rajk case. The circle was closed only more than three decades later with the dramatic reassessment of the Nagy trial and the posthumous ceremonial funeral of the four executed victims on Heroes' Square in Budapest in the presence of more than 200,000 people.[23]

Imre Nagy went down in history as a man who was transformed from a servant of evil into the martyr of a nation and of the fight for freedom. In a strange transformation, Kádár, the hated stooge of Moscow, became over the years and decades the "father of the nation" even in the eyes of some of his opponents. Yet Hungary's longest-ruling politician of the twentieth century could never rid himself of Imre Nagy's shadow.[24]

The memory of how the West left the small country to its fate after the crushing of the revolution, just as it had in 1849 and after 1945, determined the state of mind of the defeated nation as much as did the trauma of repeated instances of Russian repression. The recent defeat opened up old wounds. The disconsolate situation in the period of the revenge campaign recalled the bitter outcry by the great poet Mihály Vörösmarty in 1849: "No more hope! No more hope!" Just as it did a hundred years earlier, all that the oppressed and gagged country received was rhetorical comfort, particularly from the hypocritical political theater of the United Nations.

In this ostensibly unpromising situation, the outside world recognized with amazement during the sixties that Hungary began to change from the "Sick Man" to the showpiece of the Eastern Bloc. Taking stock of the previous ten years and comparing the situation with the pre-1956 state of affairs and conditions prevailing in the other "fraternal countries," many Hungarians aptly summarized their thoughts: "It could have been far worse." In view of the surprising development in a country that had become depoliticized by indifference and at least partly "sated," some observers at that time posed the question that would be frequently asked later: Although the popular uprising had been defeated by the force of arms, had it at the end of the day gained a victory after all?

In hindsight and on the basis of documents available today, this question can definitely be answered in the negative. Given the realities in the Eastern Bloc, Kádár could *not* achieve what Imre Nagy had stood and died for—a democratic multiparty system and genuine independence—but then, he had not striven for that. The fact that the regime owed its existence to a constitutional fiction remained just as much of a taboo topic until the end of the Kádár regime as his treachery vis-à-vis Imre Nagy.

Nonetheless, this professional functionary with his dark and unresolved past has become—according to all public opinion polls—arguably one of the most successful and to date most popular politicians in Hungarian history. In a survey conducted in 2002 (thirteen years after the change of regime and his death!), Kádár achieved fourth place on the list of most admired historical figures with 65 points. The list was headed by the great figures of the revolution of 1848: Count István Széchenyi (95 points) and Lajos Kossuth (90). Kádár lagged behind Imre Nagy (68) only by a slender margin. To the question about his role in 1956, only 23 percent replied that he had betrayed the revolution. In contrast, 56 percent believed that he had been forced to call in the Russians, and a mere 8 percent of the polled blamed him for the defeat of the revolution.[1]

From the Budapest of 1956 a long and convoluted, often covert and tacit, path led to the stage when Kádár's Hungary became "the merriest barrack in the Socialist camp." The trendy clichés in the public mood reports and in the judgments based purely on appearances peaked in the summer of 1983 in a book published by *Spiegel* with the lurid title *Hungary: A Communist Wonderland?* In his introductory essay György Konrád warned: "It is an impossibility to want anything basically different from the present government in power," only to call Kádár—whom he does not mention by name—"moderate and paternal," comparing him to Emperor-King Franz Joseph. The oppositionist author who was time and again criticized, but at the same time tolerated, by the regime provided the key to an understanding of the audacious tightrope dance of the Kádár regime. He wrote that the leadership "wanted to avoid two dangers: Moscow's wrath and the wrath of Hungarian society," and at the same time act as "mediators ... appeasing both partners."[2]

The interaction of various factors—the merciless crushing of the opposition, the unlimited Soviet support (after March 1957), together with Khrushchev's victory over his Stalinist rivals in June 1957 who from their exile had openly supported the Rákosi groups against the "suspect" Kádár, and, last but not least, the widespread apathy of the people provided the Hungarian Communists with time, opportunities, and the necessary elbow room for a complete "overhaul" of the party and the state. The leadership tried, with tangible material concessions, to neutralize important elite groups and to win them over for compromises. The arrested writers and intellectual spokespeople of the revolution, as, for instance, the poet István Eörsi, reacted with bitterness when they learned that as early as the fall of 1957 more than two hundred writers and the bishops had distanced themselves from the revolution in a public declaration and spoke out against the "meddling" of the United Nations and the West.[3]

All that happened in Hungary then and later was, in a deeper sense, a reflection of the historical experiences of the year 1956. Therein lay the additional implication of the brutally and rapidly strangled revolution. A Communist functionary once put that to me succinctly: "The party and the non-Communist population have become realists." That tacit modus vivendi, in which both the party and the people were equally conscious of the limits of latitude, enabled the survival of a Hungarian brand of communism. The decisive significance of the popular uprising in Hungary is that it brought the process of disintegration of the Soviet Union's East European empire hitherto to the furthest point. However, it also showed that the status quo hallmarked by Soviet hegemony in Eastern Europe could not be fundamentally altered single-handedly. From the sixties onward that country once again became the touchstone for how much freedom a Communist system can grant and tolerate without dramatic upheavals and a consequent Soviet intervention.

The peculiar truce reached its apparent peak as early as 18 October 1964, when, after the unexpected fall from power of his "paternal friend and older brother" Khrushchev, Kádár returned from an official visit to Warsaw. On his arrival at the railway station in Budapest, he paid warm tribute to the deposed ruler of the Kremlin and explained in a famous speech that the Hungarian CP's moderate political line would not change one iota. Kádár's statement was a sensation at the time, strengthening his popularity. Nothing could illustrate the process of change better than the fact that the two most hated men of 1956 were regarded as the guarantors of relaxation eight years later.[4]

Then—and not for the first time—the sorely tested Hungarians looked to Moscow with uncertainty and concern. The escape into a sense of humor, jokes, and anecdotes is a national trait of Hungarians and especially of those living in Budapest. Some authors consider it a characteristic of Hungarian frivolity. At any rate, Hungarians reacted to Khrushchev's fall with their usual gallows humor. Bets were made in jest, such as: Who will come back sooner, the hated Rákosi from Soviet exile or Kádár from his state visit to Poland?[5]

Even during the period of retaliation, that is, between November 1956 and about mid-1962, the artful tactic of carrot and stick bore relatively plentiful fruit within a relatively short time. By 1960 per-capita incomes were already 20 to 25 percent higher than in 1956. During the first decade after the October revolution, real wages rose by a phenomenal 47 percent.[6] The marginal concessions (occupational advancement without party affiliation, greater tolerance in cultural life, and the abatement of day-to-day harassment) gradually made life easier for citizens. This policy of alliances—initiated in December 1961—of constant improvisations, of cautious reforms within the framework of monopolistic power, satisfying the people's need for more affluence and a *little* more freedom, the policy with the motto "He who is not against us is with us"—all that was later to be called Kádárism—began only in 1962–1963. It led to a process of consolidation and normalization no one would have dared to envisage in 1956. Kádár's crew had, from the very beginning, employed the recipe that the French statesman François Guizot had formulated after the revolutions of the nineteenth century: "Enrichissez-vous!" (Enrich yourselves!).

After he was released from prison by the amnesty at the end of March 1963, György Krassó, one of the most radical and courageous freedom fighters and oppositionists, reacted to this with bafflement. In an interview in 1990, more than twenty-five years later, he could still describe his feelings very graphically:

> The country had changed terribly. On the one hand that was
> good, because, compared with the memories of the tanks and
> the destruction in Budapest, conditions were almost Western.
> On the other hand the atmosphere of utter political torpor
> and intimidation in which the people lived was very sad. Being
> intimidated wasn't even that sad; what was sadder was that the
> people had not only begun to accept the Kádár regime, but even
> to like it. They didn't show any animosity toward the 56ers, but
> they said—and that was the typical attitude—you fell for the
> thing. They didn't say whether that thing was a revolution or
> a counterrevolution, they just said you fell for it; OK, that was
> then, now forget it. Do something . . . try to get into some busi-
> ness. Everything is possible, forget the whole thing, in a year or
> in five years' time you won't even remember it. And let's not talk
> about it. That is how it went on for decades. All they asked about

prison was: How did you manage without women, what was the chow like, and how often did you get a beating? That was all they were interested in. Nor is it much different today. The people have pushed the whole topic away from themselves. If one started to talk about the executions, they didn't want to hear it. That was buried somewhere in their consciousness. In short, that was a very bad thing, and it went from bad to worse.... They helped me wherever they could at the lower level. But this help was not because of enthusiasm for the revolution, but because it was a decent cause—but it was a naïveté, suicide, let's forget it.[7]

The psychologically immensely important freedom to travel to the West greatly contributed to the acceptance and growing popularity of the regime. In 1954, 3,040 Hungarians (functionaries, officials, and sportsmen) were permitted to travel to the West, but, believe it or not, only 95 of these were private individuals. In 1958 the number had grown to 28,000, in 1962 to 65,000, and in 1963 to more than 120,000. The number of travelers to the West rose in 1986 to 708,000. At the same time the number of travelers to Yugoslavia and the Eastern Bloc countries rose from some 250,000 to almost 5 million in 1980.[8] Hungarians in exile in Vienna, Munich, and Zurich called the fact that more and more of their friends and relatives turned up on their doorsteps "Kádár's revenge." Hungary was also far ahead of the other Eastern Bloc countries in its access to tertiary study, priority of specialized knowledge over the red party book for various positions in industry and administration (of course, not for the highest positions), as well as a tolerable climate for small enterprise. Naturally, the central party organs reserved the right of choice for the 1,500 to 3,000 leading positions. These comprised the so-called *nomenklatura*, or the ruling class. In addition, there were some 80,000 to 100,000 leading positions in whose choice the lower party organs also had a say.[9]

These were the years when the successful petit bourgeois was born, whom the astute political scientist László Lengyel dubbed the "homo kadaricus," as against the "homo sovieticus." According to Lengyel's analysis, the former lived in both the state and the so-called second economy and profited from these extra incomes. In the "heyday of high Kádárism," the system consisted of the following pillars: separation of public and private life with the motto "We worry about politics at the top—you live down there"; transition from a centralized to an indirect and decentralized economy; an increase in consumerism and the living standard as the basis for the regime's acceptance; and a lasting compromise with elite groups and total loyalty to the Soviet Union alongside a cautious and step-by-step opening toward the West.[10]

Many people began to perceive the expanded elbow room with a sense of relief and hope. "I have no love lost for communism, and I don't pay any attention at all to politics. You ask whether I have any regrets that during my so-called flight I turned back at the outskirts of Budapest in November 1956 and remained here. I don't know. Frankly, this question doesn't interest me any longer. What is important is that I didn't have to write a new CV since 1958; that I can work undisturbed and—most important—they let us make money. We all want something from life at last—and not the day after tomorrow, but today."[11] Not only my childhood friend, a thirty-four-year-old engineer, but also the people whom I met later in Budapest, in the country and also in Vienna, exhibited this attitude in various shapes and forms: some serenely and with satisfaction, others cynically and full of sarcasm. The memory of the fifties' naked terror and the tragedy of October was still so fresh in the minds of people that despite a number of limitations and some deprivations, they preferred silent appeasement of the regime to any new adventures.

The constant changes in the eyes of an outside observer brought Montaigne's words to mind: "The world is but a perennial see-saw. All things in it are in constant motion.... I am not portraying being but becoming.... This is a register of varied and changing occurrences of ideas which are unresolved and, when needs be, contradictory."[12] However, one thing had to be understood even at the zenith of the Kádár era: The changes for the better, namely the moderate policy of live and let live, took place within the Communist system. Admittedly it was a more mellow and tolerable system, but its nerve center was still in party headquarters (and in the Interior Ministry, controlled by the party's leadership).

From the beginning to the end of the Kádár regime, there were three basic taboos that no one could query: the one-party system, namely the party dictatorship; loyalty to the alliance with the Soviet Union, that is, foreign rule; and the appraisal of the 1956 uprising as a counterrevolution, namely the legitimacy of the retaliation, including the Nagy trial. Political prisoners released after lengthy sentences and relatives of the executed were tailed, discriminated against, and harassed for decades. Judith Gyenes, the widow of Maléter, for instance, could find only a modest job as a librarian a full twenty years after the events, and was granted a passport only twenty-five years after her initial application. The Security Service took every opportunity to intimidate and hassle the survivors of the trial, such as Miklós Vásárhelyi, Sándor Kopácsi, and Ferenc Donáth; the former presidents of the Budapest Central Workers' Council Sándor Rácz and Sándor Bali; and the freedom and resistance fighters Imre Mécs and Jenő Fónay, who had originally been sentenced to death—just to mention a few of the many who were affected. Thus, for example, at her late husband's funeral, the widow of Sándor Bali was coerced into asking the civil rights activists and friends not to give funeral orations, else her son, suffering from leukemia, would not be granted an exit visa to receive treatment abroad!

Nonetheless we have to agree with the diagnosis of Péter György: "The first true victory of the Kádár era was the transformation of the shared silence into a collective amnesia. The silent resistance became first a forced silence and then a silent resignation."[13] The source of Kádár's power could not be separated from the construction of the house of lies. In contrast to Khrushchev and Gorbachev, who had settled the outstanding accounts of their predecessors and their transgressions, Kádár could not expose himself in relation to the Nagy trial. From his own standpoint, Kádár did the right thing, believes Péter György. The overwhelming majority of society, even the younger generation, barricaded itself behind a collective amnesia. However, even in hindsight, one should not underestimate the enormous significance of the leadership style molded by Kádár. Even today I still clearly remember my first glimpse of Kádár in Parliament. Together with many of my friends, I hoped at the time that the resistance of the intelligentsia and the workers, coupled with pressure from outside, could, after all, open the way to a tolerable compromise. We were in the process of carrying out preliminary talks concerning the founding of a newspaper to be called *Esti Hírlap*. We were therefore discussing some details of the new paper with a few colleagues and with István Szirmai, the former editor in chief of *Esti Budapest* (the paper where I had been employed shortly before the revolution) and the liaison between the isolated leadership and the mistrustful journalists. As we were leaving Szirmai's office in the Parliament Building on that late afternoon in December 1956, I caught a glimpse of a small group scurrying past in a corridor; it was Kádár, shielded by four bodyguards armed to the teeth in the near-empty Parliament, although the massive building was even more heavily protected than before on all sides. Indeed, this was an emblematic encounter with the head of the party and the government by the grace of Moscow.

Following the wave of arrests of writers and journalists and the proscription of the Journalists' and the Writers' Unions, I took off from Warsaw in early 1957 and applied for political asylum in Vienna. Some seven years later, as an Austrian citizen and correspondent of the *Financial Times* and the Viennese *Die Presse* (The press), I unexpectedly received an entry visa in the spirit of the "diplomacy of smiles" toward the Austrian neighbor. I was permitted to accompany the then foreign minister Bruno Kreisky and to take part in the congress of the Patriotic People's Front, a Communist Party–led mass organization. There I could observe Kádár from close by. His style as an orator was a welcome respite from the tone of Stalinist times and differed conspicuously from the speechifying of the top leaders in Prague, Warsaw, and East Berlin. In place of overpowering political jargon, he used normal, everyday expressions, often mentioning the break with the past; he would chat, exhort, mock, and tell anecdotes.

His main achievement as a politician was that, without ever questioning the basis of a one-party dictatorship or absolute loyalty to the Soviet power structure, he was able to obtain in part active cooperation and in part benevolent toleration of the regime by wide sections of society. He became popular because he could get the party to accept the principle that one should not promise the people a bed of roses but—apart from the three above-mentioned taboos—tell the truth, even if it was unpalatable. He was a cautious reformer, a tactician with an uncanny political instinct, a gifted technician of power, who understood that despite its monopoly of power and Soviet backing, the party could not in the long term operate in a political vacuum.

His almost puritanical lifestyle, his personal modesty and sense of humor even gained him the temporary favor of the great national poet Gyula Illyés. Kádár succeeded in winning the people's confidence by his "objectivity, modesty, and achievements" (as Illyés told me during a personal conversation in 1982). At the same time Kádár was a publicity-shy man who did not like to talk about himself; nor did he abide being flattered by others. In contrast to the other leaders in the Eastern Bloc, Kádár was averse to any form of personality cult. No pictures of him hung in public offices; nor were his likenesses carried aloft during parades. In the apt words of the political scientist Mihály Bihari, Kádár was "a typical Bolshevist Party soldier. As a captive of an ideology, he was at the same time the system's proconsul, hands-on manager and its victim.... A dictator without any personal dictatorial inclinations."[14]

It is less well known that Kádár could implement his moderate course only by a dogged running battle against the resistance of the resentful representatives of the old guard, whose support was still indispensable in 1957. Even in a Communist Party dictatorship the power of a party chief is not necessarily steady, but often fairly indefinite, fickle, and fluid. The top party body, the twelve- to thirteen-member Politburo, seemed remarkably stable from the outside. There were only thirty-three members in it between 1957 and 1988. According to the compilation of a Hungarian-born U.S. political scientist, in the next thirty-three years of the Kádár regime, 1,270 Politburo meetings, 260 Central Committee meetings, 7 party congresses, and 2 national party conferences were held.[15] The strategy of power creation, the intensity with which the "Number One" exercises that power, the structure of distributing the spheres of authority among colleagues and covert rivals, the development of constantly changing centers of power in the party and state apparatus—all these are, however, often more important in the understanding of events than isolated statistics or superficial explanations.

For thirty-two years Kádár managed with matchless skill and subtlety, cynically and—if necessary—brutally to neutralize his potential rivals; to appease the Kremlin's Hungarian "moles," only to boot them out at lightning speed; and to encourage and defend the most important reformers, only to abandon them as fall guys under Moscow's pressure. That is also valid for the ups and downs of his relationship with Leonid Brezhnev and the Soviet leadership during the eighteen years of immobilism in Moscow. It is unclear to this day to what extent Kádár encouraged and supported or criticized and, according to the latest Russian sources, betrayed the Prague Spring and specifically Alexander Dubček, whom he had met on nine occasions between January and August 1968. The invasion of Czechoslovakia on 21 August 1968, in which Hungary participated with two divisions, meant only a temporary reversion of the encouraging economic reforms.

However, in February 1972 the entire reform program and Kádár himself became the targets of a campaign orchestrated by Soviet and local "blockheads"—some of it, of course, conducted surreptitiously. The concessions in the field of the "small freedoms," which gratified the "homo kadaricus," sounded the alarm bells in the Kremlin. For thirteen hours, Kádár negotiated with Brezhnev in a hunting lodge at Zavidovo, near Moscow. The Hungarian had to listen to accusations of "dangerous right deviations, petit bourgeois tendencies in culture, reestablishment of smallholder capitalistic conditions in the countryside, the disregard of social justice, the slackening of vigilance." He could save his position and basically the substance of "Kádárism" only because he had offered to the party leadership and the Kremlin to resign before his sixtieth birthday. As a result, "although the czar remained, the Boyars had to go," as Rezső Nyers, the economic reformer and Central Committee secretary, relieved of his position, put it thirty years later. Despite the later course correction and the neutralization of the "moles," the consequences of obstructing the reform course at the time and the removal of the most important reformers from key positions contributed considerably to the intensification of the economic crisis to the point where it became unbearable.[16]

Maybe the time is not yet ripe for a balanced judgment in the form of a biography about the illusions and lies, promises and traps, tragedies and treacheries, successes and finally failure, of this unusual man, who, longer than anyone else, helped to shape the modern history of Hungary. Kádár's victims and unforgiving opponents see him solely as the executioner and jailer of the first four years and regard the rest as more or less clever camouflage. On the other hand, even today the "homo kadaricus" or "the significant majority" of society sees in retrospect only the positive sides of the Kádár era. One-third even identify themselves with the Kádár regime in every respect, treating it as a golden era. Only one-fifth of those polled express a negative opinion. Actually only 4 percent of people disapprove consistently of both the Horthy and the Kádár regimes. These astonishing figures, analyzed by Maria Vásárhelyi in a new study,[17] seem to confirm the parallels drawn at the end of December 2003 by the two outstanding authors Péter Nádas and György Spiró between the mentalities and attitudes under the Horthy and the Kádár regimes.

In the biographical articles and studies about Kádár's politics and personality, his most important and closest adviser, György Aczél, the Politburo member in charge of ideological-cultural questions, is sometimes quoted. According to Aczél, there were five questions about which Kádár was not willing to talk even to him: the dissolution of the Communist Party in 1943; the Rajk affair; his own arrest in 1951 and the three years he spent in prison; the days in Moscow on 2 and 3 November 1956; and the trial of Imre Nagy. In his masterly sketch of the "only significant Hungarian Communist labor politician," the historian and resistance fighter György Litván, who himself had spent four years behind bars (1958–1962), refers to the legends about Kádár, which, for instance in the warped portrayal of his first Western biographer, cause him to appear virtually as a "tragic hero."[18]

To these legends belongs the yarn about how he was tortured in prison (according to which a secret policeman had torn out his fingernails and urinated into his mouth), or the claim that he had tried to help his friend Rajk (in reality it was Kádár as interior minister who ordered Rajk to be beaten within an inch of his life to make him confess), or that it was the Kremlin that ordered Imre Nagy to be executed. In fact, at the time it was Kádár—and he alone—who was the driving force behind the trial and the death sentence. However, Litván also acknowledged that thanks to his political successes, Kádár could completely conceal and efface his ruthless side. He was ready to grant any concession, precisely to prevent the realization of the substance of 1956.

In spite of setbacks, at the beginning of the eighties, János Kádár stood at the height of his popularity. László Lengyel was right when he wrote that had he died or retired in 1981, the entire country would have mourned him. In a memorable and already quoted speech on his sixtieth birthday in May 1972, he spoke for the first time of 1956 not as a "counterrevolution" but as a "national tragedy; a tragedy for the party, for the working class, for the people and for every single person." The ensuing period brought an opening in foreign policy toward the West, and after numerous tactical maneuvers, Hungary became the first Eastern Bloc country to join the International Monetary Fund.

Yet in the early eighties, due to a failed economic policy and a large foreign debt, the country slid into an acute financial crisis. In that situation the Austrian government and financial world played a particularly helpful role.

The pun invented by a Hungarian television speaker, "K.u.K." ("Kreisky and Kádár"—as formerly in the Austro-Hungarian monarchy "Kaiserlich und Königlich"), was characteristic of the relaxed atmosphere. It put its stamp on the close rapport between the two politicians to whom, despite the difference in systems, the special relationship between Vienna and Budapest meant a great deal. That is why the previously unthinkable could happen. During a visit by Kreisky to Budapest between 18 and 20 November 1981, the party chief granted me—on the intercession of the Austrian chancellor—a lengthy, exclusive filmed interview. It was the first time that he agreed to do so with a Hungarian exile who had defected as a journalist a quarter of a century ago.[19] At the time I was editor in chief of the Austrian Radio and TV's eastern editorial office and was in the process of preparing a TV documentary on the changes in Hungary. After the initial protocolary questions about the bilateral relationships, I asked the laid-back and friendly seeming sixty-nine-year-old Kádár about his passion for chess. He told me that since his early teens he had been a regular chess player. Chess is not only beneficial for one's character and mind; "chess teaches one how to put up with defeat, and later how to accept victory." To my interjected question of what happened if the game was a draw, the laughing Kádár answered quick as a flash: "Then one has to start a new game."

During the interview, when Kádár talked about the economic reforms, he repeatedly emphasized that he was a committed Communist, a follower of Socialist concepts, and naturally a "son of the Hungarian people" and that he was acting according to his own convictions. "I have always racked my brains, how one could progress so that the people should never have to suffer more than necessary," he added. This basic position had guided him also when judging certain questions in 1956. When I obliquely asked him about his memories of 1956, he pensively replied: "From a certain standpoint twenty-five years ago—not today—it was a stroke of fate that I was free of the grave mistakes of the personality cult. A fairly broad circle of people had known me already for a long while, and therefore I enjoyed certain reserves of trust, which was extremely important at that time." During our conversation I hinted at the marginal age difference between him and the Austrian chancellor. Kádár became brooding and edgy at the same time. He had never given any thought to age. "When I am working, then I haven't got the time to think about it, and when I am not working, then I don't feel like it.... People tell me: 'You have to stay healthy, because we need you.' That is all I can say about the question of age. One has to work a lot, and I am preoccupied with work and not with the passing of time." That was all Kádár had to say in November 1981. The fact that at the 1985 party congress and afterward he still shirked the question of age greatly contributed to the remarkable circumstances of his departure. What Paul Valéry once wrote about the exercise of power was also valid for the aged Kádár: Every ruler knows how fragile the authority of rulers is; he just does not know it about his own.

What were the reasons for the positively dramatic change in the political climate of 1987–1988 and finally of the peaceful collapse of "Kádárism"?

1. An acute economic crisis increasingly eroded the confidence, the basis of the regime's legitimacy, and the compromise between the state party and the people.
2. The dynamic Gorbachev line created a new situation, in which Kádár, almost twenty years older, seemed no longer the guarantee of stability but the stumbling block of progress.
3. Kádár's tragedy was that he had gambled away the chance of determining the timing and form of his retirement. The decline of his authority, made evident to the population in his television appearances, which produced a catastrophic impression, opened the way to a putsch against Kádár.
4. The looming battle for the succession coincided with a renewed intensification of the discussion about the political relevance of the revolution's thirtieth anniversary, and with the democratic opposition's reaction to the renewed campaign against the "counterrevolution."

The man of the hour was the professional functionary Károly Grósz, whom Kádár had promoted to prime minister in June 1987. After a clever mobilization of the apparatus and Kádár's outmaneuvering at the preliminary discussions, a political earthquake erupted at the extraordinary party conference in May. During the elections of the new Central Committee (CC), the five members of Kádár's closest leadership circle were pushed aside so radically that they were denied seats on the CC. Yet only this body could elect the members of the Politburo. Thus, although Kádár became honorary president and officially a member of the Central Committee, he remained without any direct access to power, as he had been deprived of his allies. This signified an unexpected break with the past; not a single member of the new Politburo had belonged to that body prior to the last party congress in 1985.

The combined resources of party secretary and prime minister tended to confer exceptional powers on the person of Károly Grósz. He was extraordinarily gifted and a wily schemer, but not a visionary or strong leader. With the appearance of the new political alignments and the decline of "Real Existing Socialism" all over the Eastern Bloc, Grósz gambled away his authority and power barely within one year. Incidentally, he retired entirely from politics after the liquidation of the party.[20]

In the atmosphere of the intraparty faction fights, the serious economic crisis, the shattering effect of the Hungarian minorities' situation in Romania—highlighted by the largest-ever mass demonstration in Heroes' Square in June 1988—and the campaign against the Hungarian-Czechoslovak Bős-Nagymaros barrage project, tackling the events of the fall of 1956 acted as a virtual catalyst for the peaceful collapse of the gutted one-party dictatorship. The state minister and Politburo member Imre Pozsgay, at the time the best-known Hungarian politician in the West, was the first to grasp the nettle of the 1956 events. In January 1989—preempting the final report of a Central Committee team—he publicly described what had happened then as a "popular uprising" and no longer as a "counterrevolution" or a "tragedy." Yet subsequently Pozsgay proved to be a bad tactician who at the crucial moment probably lacked the nerve to split the party.

Now it was the radical reformers who set the pace toward a multiparty system and free elections. Miklós Németh (the forty-year-old economic expert, elected prime minister in November 1988), Rezső Nyers (the initiator of the "new economic mechanism" of the sixties), whom Kádár had demoted in 1974 on Moscow's demand, as well as Foreign Minister Gyula Horn, were the ones who in the year of transition to Western democracy set the agenda for two events that had worldwide political ramifications: the dismantling of the Iron Curtain along the border with Austria in May 1989 and, in the face of furious protests by East Berlin, the promulgation of a government resolution on 11 September

1989, which allowed all East German citizens who had fled to Hungary free passage to West Germany. It was a courageous and farsighted move, which at the same time marked the beginning of the end of the East German state, the GDR.

The irreversible break with the party dictatorship enabled a peaceful system change by means of a "roundtable discussion" with the opposition (just as in Poland), which opened the way to free and secret elections. A Center-Right coalition presided over by the historian József Antall won the elections and, backed by a parliamentary resolution reached by an overwhelming majority, terminated Hungary's membership in the Warsaw Pact and finalized agreements for the withdrawal of Soviet troops. Ten years later the new Hungary became a member of NATO and in 2004 joined the European Union.

The funeral service for Imre Nagy and his four companions in misfortune on Heroes' Square on 16 June 1989, the thirty-first anniversary of their execution, was attended by some 200,000 people. This mass demonstration and their reinterment in heroes' graves in Plot 301 of the cemetery where they had been unceremoniously dumped into unmarked mass graves marked a symbolic change in Hungary's modern history. Only since 1989 has it been possible to speak of the 1956 revolution as a "victory in defeat."

And what of János Kádár? On 12 April 1989 the aging honorary party president, suffering from advanced dementia, surprised everybody by making a rambling, totally confused speech of apology before the Central Committee. His allusions to his role in the Rajk trial, frequently interspersed with digressions and stereotyped phrases, and especially to his responsibility for the volte-face in November 1956 and the execution of Nagy, warrants a psychoanalytic study. Kádár could not rid himself of the shadow of his actions; nor was he a figure of Shakespearean cut. The analysis of Kádár's last public appearance and its intrigue-filled side effects by the political scientist László Lengyel is probably the most perceptive and empathic of all. Lengyel has compared the not entirely compos mentis Kádár to a figure from Ionesco or Gombrowicz rather than to Macbeth or Richard III. Be that as it may, Kádár died on 6 July 1989, the very day on which Imre Nagy was rehabilitated by the high court. More than 100,000 people paid their last respects by filing past his coffin, which lay in state in the entrance hall of the then party building.[21]

Quite a few historians, political scientists, and writers compare Franz Joseph I, Regent Horthy, and Kádár with each other—comparisons that naturally provoke sharp disapproval. Despite the differences of times and particularly of personalities, all of them began their long rules as hated executioners and finished them as widely respected father figures. The economist Sándor Kopátsy wrote in a provocative volume that he, just as 90 percent of the population, had at one stage morally despised Kádár, but as time went by he gradually came to understand him more and more.[22] Today the former Peasant Party politician believes that after November 1956 any other solution, any other "procurator" accepted by the Russians, would have been worse. Kádár's greatest sin was that he had hundreds of young people hanged; but one must realize that any other leader would have drowned the resistance in an even more horrible bloodbath. Under the very restricted circumstances of the time, no one could have been more advantageous than Kádár. Kopátsy draws the following bold conclusion at the end of his analysis: "Kádár will go down in Hungarian history as the most significant politician of the twentieth century. The Hungarian people will always think back to him with affection and a certain nostalgia."

Fifty years after the revolution and seventeen years after the death of János Kádár, we still do not know enough to form a conclusive judgment about this key figure of Hungarian, and to an extent also of European, history.

Epilogue: Whose 1956?

The historical categorization of the events of 1956 set the scene for the end phase of the development that led to the bloodless change of the system. The posthumous funeral on 16 June 1989 in Heroes' Square, with the sixth coffin symbolizing *Time* magazine's "Man of the Year for 1956," the unknown freedom fighter, marked the zenith of the consensus between the democratic and the post- and reform-Communist forces. This appearance of unity in diversity, however, was deceptive.

The façade cracked in 1990 with the adoption of the First Act of Parliament commemorating the revolution. The original bill had recognized Imre Nagy's role as prime minister, but in a last-minute amendment his name was removed, and it was only after the formation of a left-wing coalition government by the Socialists and Free Democrats in 1996 that an official bill naming Imre Nagy a martyr of the nation was enacted, with numerous members voting against the proposal. Many observers regarded it as symbolic when on one of the anniversaries Prime Minister Gyula Horn and Erzsébet Nagy, daughter of the revolutionary prime minister, jointly laid a wreath at Nagy's grave.[1]

Each election campaign served, of course, as an opportunity for settling old and new accounts between the parties and the various factions. These related above all to the role of the reform Communists in the fall of 1956, with special emphasis on the writers and intellectuals, and beyond that to the nature of the events. Was it an uprising? A national war of independence? A left-wing revolution? Did a unique national unity actually exist, and if so, how long would it have lasted?

"Temetni tudunk!" is a laconic expression in Hungarian, which in English would translate into something like "What we are really good at is burying people"—in other words, arranging funerals. The political cult of death had played an important role in the time of the monarchy—one need only recall the 1894 repatriation of the remains of the revolutionary hero Lajos Kossuth, who had died in Turin after forty-six years in exile.

And after the ceremonial farewell from Nagy, attended by some 200,000 people, the mortal remains of Cardinal József Mindszenty, dead since 1974, were also brought back from Austria to Hungary and laid to rest in 1991 in the Cathedral of Esztergom. The militant church dignitary had spent fifteen years in political asylum in the U.S. Embassy before he was permitted—following extremely complicated negotiations—to leave his country. Barely a month after Mindszenty's funeral, the reinterment of Oszkár Jászi, the great liberal thinker and politician in exile since 1919, took place, albeit in the presence of far fewer people.

Politically, the most controversial reburial was that of Miklós Horthy. In September 1993 the mortal remains of the regent, who had died in 1957 in Portuguese emigration, were interred on his family estate of Kenderes in the presence of thousands of people. While Jászi's memory was honored by the liberal and left-wing intellectuals, the funeral of Mindszenty, and even more so of Horthy, mobilized the conservative and Christian-nationalist forces. At public ceremonies commemorating the revolution, even at the famous martyrs' Plot 301 of the Central Cemetery, there were recurring spiteful incidents, which sometimes even degenerated into violence organized by extreme nationalist and right-radical groups against such outstanding figures of the revolution as the former state president Árpád Göncz and the liberal parliamentary deputy Imre Mécs, both of whom had spent close on six years in prison.[2]

It is always difficult to draw the line between remembering and forgetting. In Hungary the consolidation of the Kádár regime meant the revolution's *damnatio memoriae*. In the course of this historical loss of memory,[3] everything was proscribed that evoked the triumphal and tragic days of the revolution. Then, after more than three decades of collective amnesia, at the memorable funeral service for Imre Nagy on 16 June 1989, there suddenly appeared the adulterated, marginalized, and forgotten history of 1956 as *the* glorious and defeated revolution, and with it the surviving actors once again stepped onto the stage of history.[4]

Not only my personal experiences, but all the available documents cited here in detail confirm the thesis that the events of October–November 1956 were a spontaneous and unexpected revolution in the true meaning of the word. Twenty years later, István Bibó emphasized the "unique character" of the Hungarian Revolution: there were no structures or leadership (neither revolutionary nor counterrevolutionary); it lacked a scientific or at least a consciously formulated ideology; and there was no personnel echelon that was ready to fill the power vacuum.[5] The spontaneous uprising aimed not at reforming but at shaking off Stalinist rule, enforcing the withdrawal of Soviet troops and the establishment of workers' councils and organs of local government. In his (left-socialist and syndicalist) work *Hungary 1956*,[6] Bill Lomax argued that it was a social revolution aimed not at restoring a previous regime but at creating a radically new social order, one that would be both more democratic than the capitalist West and more Socialist than the Communist East. The objection that the popular uprising was not a revolution because it failed in its aims of establishing a new political system and restructuring the social order lacks credence; the point can be made that the revolutionary movement of 1956 did succeed, only to be defeated after outside military intervention.

It is a different matter as far as the heritage of the glorious thirteen days is concerned. While incredible national unity existed in the fight against the Communist dictatorship and Soviet domination, that unity even then consisted of a coalition of diverse forces ranging from Communist reformers and democratic Socialists to national conservatives and elements of the Far Right. Between 1956 and 1989 forgetting became the citizens' prime duty. The changeover in the winter of 1989–1990 was a peaceful compromise and not a "second" revolution. Still, characteristic features of a new memory emerged in quick succession, and the conditions of the collective memory's social framework became transformed. Yet not even the symbolic recognition of the revolution could eradicate the Kádár regime's flawed legacy.[7]

That is why the struggle for a dominant interpretation of the revolution, accompanied by individual personal lies and tactical maneuvers, in some respects resembles the historical disputes about the War of Independence of 1848–1849 and the Austro-Hungarian Compromise (*Ausgleich*) of 1867. The controversies about the assessment of the bourgeois revolution of 1918 and its consequences, from the Hungarian Soviet Republic to the Horthy era, all fit into this framework as well.[8]

Imre Nagy and his associates have for decades been castigated for having provoked the Soviet leadership and thereby the second intervention by their rash and reckless decisions (authorization of a multiparty system, neutrality, and renunciation of the Warsaw Pact). Following the publication of the Soviet secret documents—analyzed in earlier chapters—and based on my own conversations with the former head of the KGB, Vladimir Kryuchkov, I have no doubts whatsoever that at the time the Nagy government was ensnared in hopeless contradictions and irresolvable alternatives between the dynamics from below and the threat from outside. Of course, there is always the temptation to attract attention by writing counterfactual history, which explores events the way one would wish them to have occurred, that is, which deals with how "it actually should not have happened." There is no indication that Khrushchev and the majority of the party Presidium (with the special exception of Mikoyan) and the Chinese leadership, which was involved in the decision making, would have been willing to offer a Yugoslav or Polish way to a mutinous Hungary.[9] Imre Nagy certainly was no Lajos Kossuth or Ferenc Deák (the architect of the 1867 *Ausgleich*), else he would never have survived the purges, nor could he have become prime minister of a Communist satellite state twice. However, under the given international and domestic political conditions—irrespective of his government's miscalculations—the national fight for independence did not have the ghost of a chance.

As the historian Thomas Nipperdey wrote about German history in his essay collection *Nachdenken über die deutsche Geschichte* (Reflections on German History): "The virtue that we learn is compassionate, understanding, realistic skepticism; skepticism of anything that oversteps the limits of humanity, of claims of perfect conclusions and perfect planning; skepticism of the absolutism of all 'new men' and of radical idealists; skepticism of our own absolutism, of a sentimental view of a better future and—this also has to be spelled out—a better past."[10] In Hungary too there was and is an accrued need for skepticism in dealing with the past.

Who then owns 1956—the uprising, the revolution, and the National War of Independence? No one, not a single group can and should expropriate the memory of 1956 for itself; no one must monopolize it. Without the reformers in the apparatus of the state party and without the disillusioned, conscience-stricken Communist intellectuals determined to make amends, a popular uprising would have been unthinkable in the first place. And *after* the invasion, the instruments of the resistance were the workers' councils, the democratically elected representatives of the working class.

Yet the spearheads of this revolution were the "Pest Lads," the armed young workers and apprentices, soldiers and students, that "nameless ragtag" in whose honor István Angyal had wished—in his last letter written before his execution—for a large rustic stone as a memorial. There it stands now, forty-two tons of simplicity, without names and symbols—a memorial stone designed by the sculptor György Jovánovics—in Plot 301, the last resting place of the executed victims.[11]

Regardless of the dispute between the Left and the Right, the liberal and conservative groupings and their mouthpieces, the Hungarian uprising of 1956 remains part of the entire nation's heritage. Edmund Burke's saying that the state includes the dead, the living, and the coming generations conveys to us that 1956 belongs to that heritage of Hungarian history of which the present generation cannot take sole possession.[12] Even after half a century, William Faulkner's timelessly valid words apply to our reflections about the fainthearted and the innocent victims, the barbarous victors and the heroic defeated of the revolution and the resistance of 1956–1957: "The past is not dead. In fact, it's not even past."

Acknowledgments

This book would never have materialized in time without the encouragement and without the intellectual and practical support of my wife, Zsóka Lendvai. My heartfelt gratitude goes to her first and foremost.

I have received invaluable help from the Austrian ambassadors in Moscow and Budapest (Dr. Martin Vukovits and Dr. Ferdinand Mayrhofer-Grünbühel) in arranging contacts with the former head of the KGB, Vladimir Kryuchkov; and the Russian ambassador in Budapest, Valeri Musatov.

I owe particular gratitude to the founding and present directors of the Institute for the History of the 1956 Hungarian Revolution, the late György Litván and János M. Rainer, as well as the historian Tibor Huszár for their advice in the evaluation of controversial situations and the clarification of sources.

My special thanks go to Katalin Havas of the Ervin Szabó Library and my stepdaughter, Fanni Borbiró, as well as to Georg-Paul Hefty, editor of the *Frankfurter Allgemeine Zeitung*, for their assistance in procuring important books and texts. Thanks are due also to Katalin Jalsovszky of the Hungarian National Museum's picture archive for her unfailing and resourceful help in gaining access to important photographs.

Chronology

1920   Peace Treaty of Trianon reduces Hungary to one-third of the Lands of the Crown of Saint Stephen: loss of Croatia, Transylvania, and Slovakia.

1938   According to the "Viennese Award" by the Axis foreign ministers, reannexation of southern Slovakia and southern Carpatho-Ukraine. First anti-Jewish laws.

1939   Signing of the Anticomintern Pact with Germany, Italy, and Japan. Hungarian troops march into the rest of Carpatho-Ukraine. Quitting of the League of Nations. Electoral gains for the Arrow Cross. Harsher anti-Jewish laws.

1940   Second "Viennese Award": reannexation of northern Transylvania and the Székely region by Hungary.

1941   Germans invade Yugoslavia; three days later Hungarian troops occupy the previous Magyar regions in Yugoslavia.

         Hungary declares war on the USSR. Third anti-Jewish law. Great Britain declares war on Hungary, Hungary on the United States.

1944   19 March: German troops occupy Hungary.
A total of 437,000 Jews are deported to Auschwitz.

         15 October: Horthy attempts "defection" and asks the USSR for a cease-fire. German "protective custody." Terror regime of the Arrow Cross under Ferenc Szálasi.

1945   13 February: Red Army takes Budapest.

         4 April: End of hostilities in Hungary.

         November: Smallholders' Party wins parliamentary majority. Coalition government.

1946   1 February: Hungary becomes a republic.

1947   Peace treaty is signed in Paris.

Manipulated elections in the multiparty system.

Rejection of the Marshall Plan.

1948   February: Treaty of friendship with the Soviet Union.

June: Liquidation of the Social Democrats ("Unification Congress"): Hungarian Workers' Party (MDP).

Communist takeover—Secretary-General Mátyás Rákosi.

December: Cardinal Mindszenty is arrested.

1949   February: Cardinal Mindszenty is put on trial.

September: Foreign minister László Rajk is accused of "Titoism" and executed.

Hungary becomes a people's republic.

1952   Rákosi becomes prime minister (until July 1953).

1953   Death of Stalin. Popular uprising in Berlin.

Imre Nagy becomes prime minister (until April 1955).

Amnesty, internment camps closed. New course.

1955   Nagy branded deviationist and purged from the party. His successor is András Hegedüs.

Signing of Warsaw Pact.

Austrian State Treaty.

Hungary admitted to the United Nations.

1956   14–15 February: Twentieth Congress of the Communist Party of the Soviet Union, Stalinism condemned.

Following Khrushchev's speech, Rajk is rehabilitated.

28 June: Uprising in Poznán, Poland.

17 July: Rákosi relieved as head of party and replaced by Ernő Gerő.

6 October: Funeral of László Rajk and his associates.

15 October: Hungarian party and government delegation in Yugoslavia.

19 October: Gomułka elected first secretary in Warsaw.

23 October: Student demonstrations. Siege of Radio Building. Gerő calls in Soviet troops. Popular uprising.

24 October: Nagy, once again prime minister, announces martial law. Strikes begin in most Budapest plants. Fighting with Soviet troops. Soviet Politburo members Suslov and Mikoyan in Budapest.

25 October: János Kádár replaces Gerő as first secretary. Massacre of unarmed demonstrators by Soviet tanks and State Security forces. Over one hundred dead and wounded. Protest demonstration.

26 October: Armed clashes at the Kilián Barracks, the Corvin Passage, and so on, in Budapest and throughout the country. Workers' and revolutionary councils form in most localities.

27 October: Imre Nagy announces his new government.

28 October: Gerő and Hegedüs go to Moscow. Negotiations with insurgents.

Nagy announces cease-fire over the radio.

The uprising is acknowledged as a national-democratic revolution; promise of Soviet troops' withdrawal.

The United Nations' Security Council places the Hungarian question on its agenda.

29 October: The State Security (ÁVH) is dissolved. New Imre Nagy government. Beginning of Suez crisis.

30 October: The Soviet government announces its willingness to negotiate on the removal of Soviet troops.

Armed groups storm the Budapest headquarters of the MDP at Republic Square. Lynch justice.

Cardinal Mindszenty is freed. Alteration of government on the basis of the 1945 coalition. New parties and independent newspapers.

31 October: The Revolutionary Defense Committee names Béla Király commander of the National Guard. Pál Maléter is named deputy defense minister. In Moscow the Soviet leadership decides on the second intervention. Soviet troops in Romania and the Ukraine move toward Hungary.

1 November: Hungary renounces the Warsaw Pact in protest against the renewed Soviet troop movements. The government declares Hungary's neutrality. The Hungarian Socialist Workers' Party is founded, with János Kádár as its leader. Late in the evening Kádár's recorded speech is broadcast. Kádár and Interior Minister Münnich enter the Soviet Embassy and are flown to Moscow to discuss the formation of a counter-government.

2 November: Khrushchev's secret trip to Bucharest. Informing the Romanian, Bulgarian, and Czechoslovak leaders about the intervention. At the secret meeting on the island of Brioni, Tito supports intervention. Imre Nagy protests to the secretary-general of the United Nations against the Soviet invasion; notes of protest.

3 November: Third Nagy government with the participation of all postwar democratic coalition parties. Arrest of General Maléter and his team during negotiations about withdrawal of Soviet troops.

Radio speech by Cardinal Mindszenty.

4 November: Soviet troops begin their attack on Budapest.

Imre Nagy broadcasts the announcement of the Soviet attack and takes refuge in the Yugoslav Embassy.

Broadcast announcement (from Szolnok or probably Uzhgorod) about the formation of the Revolutionary Workers' and Peasants' Government.

Minister of State István Bibó composes an official protest against the forcible removal of the legitimate government.

5 November: Fighting in Budapest.

7 November: Arrival and swearing-in of the Kádár government.

9 November: The armed resistance is brutally crushed.

12 November: Founding of the Central Workers' Council of Greater Budapest.

22 November: The abduction of the Nagy group to Romania.

4 December: Women's demonstration on Heroes' Square.

8 December: Massacre by Soviet troops and Security Service forces in Salgótarján; numerous dead and wounded.

11 December: Martial law is declared.

16 December: The first death sentence is given for hiding weapons.

1957   1–4 January: Summit meeting of East European Communist leaders (without Poland) in Budapest.

11 January: United Nations fact-finding commission in Hungary.

March: Kádár is in Moscow. Agreement over Soviet troops stationed in Hungary. Negotiations about the Nagy trial.

March–April: Imre Nagy and his group are arrested in Romania and transported to Budapest.

13 November: Sentence in the writers' trial.

1958   9–15 June: Secret trial of the Nagy group.

16 June: Imre Nagy, Pál Maléter, and Miklós Gimes are executed in the prison yard.

1961   László Nickelsburg, the last 1956er, is executed.

1962   August: Resolution on terminating the political trials.

1963   March: Amnesty for most political detainees (in exchange the United Nations' General Assembly removes the Hungarian question from its agenda).

1968   Participation in the military intervention by the Warsaw Pact in Czechoslovakia.

1971   Amnesty and exile for Cardinal Mindszenty.

1974   Several top reformers removed. Setback suffered by reform course.

1987   Károly Grósz becomes prime minister.

1988   Putsch at an extraordinary national conference of the party against the Kádár group. Grósz takes on post of secretary-general as well.

1989   Imre Nagy is rehabilitated and ceremoniously reburied. Freedom of assembly, press, and to demonstrate. Multiparty system.

         Border opening for GDR (East German) citizens. Miklós Németh is prime minister.

1990   First free elections are held. József Antall of the MDF (Hungarian Democratic Forum) becomes the first non-Communist prime minister. Agreement on the withdrawal of Soviet troops.

Notes

Introduction

1. Bain, *Reluctant Satellites*, p. 97.
2. The bibliography contains a list of works and research findings about the revolution publishe d prior to 1996 (predominantly in Hungarian). The 1956 Institute has issued more than ninety books since 1991 and some one thousand interviews (audio recordings lasting more than ten thousand hours) collected in the Oral History Archive.
3. The title of the original French edition of the history of the revolution by Miklós Molnár: *Victoire d'une defaite* (Paris, 1968).
4. The title of the introduction by Raymond Aron for the French edition of the collection of documents titled *La Revolution Hongroise*, eds. M. L. Lasky and François Bondy (Paris, 1957).
5. The expression originates with Edgar Morin, quoted by François Fejtö in *Magyar füzetek* [Hungarian pamphlets] (Paris, 1981), nos. 9–10.

Chapter 1
A Day That Shook the Communist World

1. Jacob Burckhardt, *Reflections on History*, trans. by M.D.H. from the German original *Weltgeschichtliche Betrachtungen* (London, 1950), pp. 25, 142.
2. Cf. Kecskeméti, *Unexpected Revolution*.
3. Tischler, *Lengyelország és Magyarország.*
4. Interview with the author, Budapest, 25–26 May 2005.
5. Varga, *Az elhagyott tömeg*, pp. 88–89.
6. See his complete report in *Hiányzó lapok 1956 történetéből: Dokumentumok a volt SZKP KB levéltárából* [Missing pages from the history of 1956: Documents from the archive of the former CPSU CC] (Budapest, 1993), pp. 83–90.
7. Ibid., pp. 92–99.
8. Ibid., p. 90.
9. See Ripp, *A pártvezetés végnapjai*, pp. 169–90.
10. See Hegedüs, *A történelem*, p. 289. Cf. also "A kormány és a part vezetö szerveinek dokumentaiból, 23.10.1956–4 November" [From the

documents of the government's and party's leading organs, 23 October 1956 to 4 November], *Historia* (Budapest), nos. 4–5 (1989).

11. Lasky, *Hungarian Revolution*, pp. 51–52.

12. For the course of events, see ibid.; Litván and Bak, *Hungarian Revolution*, pp. 51–52; Alföldy, *Ungarn 1956*; Paul Lendvai, *Blacklisted: A Journalist's Life in Central Europe* (New York, 1998); 1956 *Kézikönyve: Kronologia* [1956's handbook: The chronology] (Budapest, 1996); Varga, *Az elhagyott tömeg;* Gyurkó, *1956;* Ripp, *A pártvezetés végnapjai;* idem, *1956.*

13. V. I. Lenin, *Der "linke Radikalismus": Die Kinderkrankheit im Kommunismus,* Ausgewählte Werke in 2 Bänden (Moscow, 1947), pp. 729–30; translated as "Left-Wing Communism: An Infantile Disorder," in *Lenin: Selected Works,* 2 vols. (London, 1947), 2:621.

14. Rainer, *Nagy.*

15. Vásárhelyi, *Ellenzékben;* Julius Hay, *Born 1900;* Eva Hay, *Auf beiden Seiten;* Méray, *Thirteen Days;* Molnár, *Budapest 1956.*

16. Istvan Zador, "Visiting Imre Nagy," *Irodalmi Ujsag* [Literary gazette], London, 1 August 1958.

17. See Rainer, *Nagy;* Fazekas, *Forró ösz Budapesten;* Kövér, *Géza Losonczy;* Méray, *Thirteen Days.*

18. The expression originates with the aged Marxist philosopher Georg Lukács, who was informed by his student and demonstrator Miklós Krassó in the evening of 23 October about the day's events after the armed conflict in front of the Radio Building had begun. "We are at the mercy of an unknown force," said the professor, to which Krassó remarked: "This unknown force is the Hungarian people." Cf. Zoltán Szabó, *Terepfelverés,* p. 239.

19. See Rainer, *Nagy,* 2:243–46; Fazekas, *Forró ösz Budapesten,* pp. 89–94; Méray, *Thirten Days;* pp. 77–82; Gyurkó, *1956,* pp. 64–67.

20. Cf. *Aforradalom hangja* [The voice of the revolution], radio broadcasts, 23 October–4 November 1956 (Budapest, 1989).

21. See Rainer, *Nagy,* p. 249.

22. Cf. Kövér, *Géza Losonczy,* p. 270; Gyurkó, *1956,* p. 81; Lendvai, *The Hungarians,* p. 139.

Chapter 2
The Road to Revolution

1. See Paul Lendvai, "The Admiral on a White Horse," in *The Hungarians,* pp. 373–76.

2. Ibid. Cf. Romsics, *Magyarország története a XX. Században.*

3. Braham, *Politics of Genocide*. See also László Varga, "Ungarn," in Benz, *Dimensionen des Völkermordes*, pp. 331–43.

4. Cf. Gyula Juhász in *Historia* (Budapest) 92, no. 1:8–10.

5. Cf. Borhi, *Magyarország a hidegháborúban*. See also Balázs Illényi, "The Soviets in the Hungarian Economy, 1945–1948," *HVG (Budapest)*, 2 April 2005 (in Hungarian).

6. Quoted in Arpád von Klimko and Alexander M. Kunst, "Die ungarische Parteiführung und die Systemkrisen 1953, 1956 und 1968" [The Hungarian party leadership and the system crises 1953, 1956 and 1968], in Bispinck et al., *Aufstände im Ostblock*, p. 290.

7. Katalin Sinko, "Zur Entstehung der staatlichen und nationalen Feiertage in Ungarn (1850–1991)" [On the origin of state and national holidays in Hungary (1850–1991)], in Brix and Stekl, *Der Kampf um das Gedächtnis*, pp. 265–71.

8. Pünkösti, *Rákosi*.

9. Ibid. See also János M. Rainer, telegram to Comrade "Filipov." Rákosi's dispatches to Stalin's secretariat, in *Évkönyv 1998* [Yearbook 1998], 1956 Institute, pp. 103–19.

10. Lendvai, *The Hungarians*, pp. 433–34.

11. Cf. Hodos, *Schauprozesse*; Lendvai, *Auf schwarzen Listen*, pp. 91–134; Farkas, *Nincs mentség*.

12. Cf. Szakasits, *Fent és lent*.

13. Pünkösti, *Rákosi*.

14. Gyurkó, *Arcképvázlat történelmi háttérrel*; Huszár, *Kádár*; Molnár, *De Béla Kun à János Kádár*, pp. 105, 115.

15. Lendvai, *The Hungarians*, p. 434.

16. Ripp, *Forradalom és szabadágharc Magyarországon*, pp. 23–24.

17. Lendvai, *Auf schwarzen Listen*, p. 93; Romsics, *Magyarország története a XX. Százsadban*, p. 344; Ripp, *1956*, pp. 38–41; *Rubicon*, nos. 6–7 (2002): 26–29; Kiszely, *ÁVH*, pp. 318–22.

18. Molnár, *Short History*, p. 75.

19. For details, see Pünkösti, *Rákosi*, pp. 471–85.

20. For Péter's biography, see Györgyi Gyarmati, "Péter Gábor fiatalsága 1906–1945" [Gábor Péter's youth, 1906–1945], in *Yearbook 2000–2001*, Historical Institute (Budapest, 2002), pp. 25–79 (in Hungarian).

21. Elias Canetti, *The Conscience of Words*, trans. Joachim Neugroschel (New York, 1979), p. 22.

22. Cf. Lendvai, *Antisemitismus ohne Juden*.

23. For the full and authentic text, see T. Varga György, ed., *Jegyzőkönyv a szovjet es a magyar párt- és állami vezetők tárgyalásairól 1953 junius 13–16*

[Proceedings of the negotiations between the Soviet and Hungarian party and state leadership (13–16 June 1953)] (Multunk, 1992); issues 2–3.

24. Cf. Rainer, *Nagy*. For the number of the released, see Kiszely, *ÁVH*, p. 321.

25. See Rainer, *Nagy*. The author's interview with Kryuchkov, 26 September 2005, Moscow, and with Ambassador Valeri Musatov, 16 September 2005, Budapest.

26. Cf. Rainer, *Nagy*; Ripp, *A pártvezetés végnapjai*; and Lendvai, *Antisemitismus ohne Juden*.

Chapter 3
A Night of Cataclysmic Decisions

1. See Valeri Vartanov, "Die Sowjetunion und die Ereignisse in Ungarn im Herbst 1956" [The Soviet Union and the events in Hungary in the fall of 1956], in Schmidl, *Die Ungarnkrise 1956*, pp. 73–88; Horváth, *1956 hadikrónikája*; Alexander Kirov, "Á szovjet hadsereg és a magyar forradalom" [The Soviet Army and the Hungarian Revolution], in *Évkönyv* [Yearbook] *1996–97*, pp. 76ff.

2. For all notes about the sessions of the Soviet party Presidium from 9 July 1956 to 27 November 1956 and the relevant documents, see Vyatcheslav Sereda and János M. Rainer, eds., *Döntés a Kremlben, 1956: A szovjet pártelnökség vitái Magyarországról* [Decision in the Kremlin, 1956: The debates of the Soviet party Presidium on Hungary] (Budapest, 1996), pp. 26–27.

3. For Khrushchev's speech on 24 October 1956 in Moscow, see Sereda and Rainer, *Döntés*, pp. 173–81; see also the analysis by Rainer in *Nagy*, pp. 120–23, and Rákosi, *Visszaemlékezések*, pp. 1032–33. For the tug-of-war about the signature under the "cry for help," cf. Hegedüs, *A történelem*, pp. 290ff.

4. For the mood and course of the meetings, see Ripp, *A pártvezetés végnapjai*, pp. 169–315. Cf. also *Historia* (Budapest), nos. 4–5 (1989).

5. See Ildikó Zsitnyanyi, "A Magyar Néphadsereg karhatalmi célu alkalmazása az 1956-os forradalom kezdetén" [The deployment of the Hungarian People's Army at the beginning of the revolution of 1956], in *A Történeti Hivatal Évkönyve* [Yearbook of the Historical Bureau] *2000/2001*, pp. 257–65; Horváth, *1956 hadikrónikája*, pp. 17–45 and 137–67.

6. Vartanov, "Die Sowjetunion"; Horváth, *1956 hadikrónikája*; Ripp, 1956, pp. 93–100.

7. Cf. the report by Mikoyan and Suslov on 24 October 1956 from Budapest in *A "Jelcin-Dossie": Sowjet dokumentumok 1956-ról* [The "Yeltsin dossier": Soviet documents about 1956] (Budapest, 1993), pp. 47–50.

8. For details, see Ripp, *1956*, pp. 190–210.

9. Földes, *A második vonalban.*

10. Donáth, *A márciusi Fronttól Monorig,* pp. 99–125.

Chapter 4
The Legend of the Corvirists

1. For the speeches and communiqués, see Lasky, *Hungarian Revolution;* United Nations Report of the Special Committee on the Problem of Hungary, New York, 1957; cf. also *A forradalom hangja—Magyarországi rádioadások* [The voice of the revolution—radio broadcasts in Hungary], 23 October 1956–9 November 1956 (Budapest, 1989).

2. Hannah Arendt, *Die Ungarische Revolution* (Munich, 1958), p. 37.

3. UN Report, paragraph 396, p. 68.

4. Cf. for the day-to-day course of events between 23 October 1956 and 12 December 1956: *1956 Kézikönyve Kronológia* [Handbook of 1956, chronology] (Budapest, 1996).

5. See *Corvinisták 1956, a VIII. Kerület fegyveres csoportjai* [Corvinists 1956, the armed groups in the eighth district] (Budapest, 2001). Cf. also László Eörsi, *Ferencváros 1956*; Horváth, *1956 hadikrónikája*; Szűcs, *Ezredes voltam 1956*; Gyurkó, *1956*. For the role of Gergely Pongrátz, see his highly subjective memoirs: *Corvin köz 1956.*

6. Cf. Gyurkó, *1956*, p. 223.

7. Politburo meeting, 28–29 October, cited in *Historia* (Budapest), nos. 4–5 (1989): 38.

8. *Hiányzó lapok 1956 történetéböl* [Missing pages from the history of 1956] (Budapest, 1993), p. 118; cf. also Sereda and Rainer, *Döntés a Kremlben, 1956: A szovjet pártelnökség vitái Magyarországról* [Decision in the Kremlin, 1956: The debates of the Soviet party Presidium on Hungary] (Budapest, 1996), p. 43.

9. Cf. Földes, *A második vonalban.*

10. For testimonies of the officers, see László Eörsi, *Ferencváros 1956*, pp. 49–57.

11. See György Litván, "Mitoszok és legendák 1956-rol" [Myths and legends about 1956]," in *Évkönyv* [Yearbook] 2000, p. 207.

Chapter 5
Wrestling for the Soul of Imre Nagy

1. See Ripp, *1956,* pp. 237–45.

2. *1956 Kézikönyve Kronológia* [Handbook of 1956, chronology] (Budapest, 1996), pp. 95–96, 106; cf. also Lasky, *Hungarian Revolution,* pp. 93–94.

3. *Kronológia*, pp. 113–17, 129; Horváth, *1956 hadikrónikája*, pp. 89, 152–53, 164. For the "military dictatorship," see Ripp, *1956*, pp. 263–64, 273–76.

4. Ripp, *1956*, pp. 132–37.

5. Ripp, *1956*, Rainer, *Nagy*.

6. Rainer, *Nagy* 2:264–70.

7. Donáth, *A márciusi Fronttól Monorig*, pp. 114–15.

8. Rainer, *Nagy* 1:83ff., 175.

9. *Hiányzó lapok 1956 történetéből* [Missing pages from the history of 1956] (Budapest, 1993), p. 115.

10. Hegedüs, *A történelem*, p. 292.

11. For details, cf. Ripp, *1956*, pp. 267–68; Rainer, *Nagy* 2:271–75.

12. Horváth, *1956 hadikrónikája*, pp. 16–173.

13. Cf. Fazekas, *Forróőzs Budapesten*, pp. 94–102. For Kopácsi's life, cf. *Életfogytiglan*.

14. For a description, see Rainer, *Nagy*, and Ripp, *1956*.

15. The members were (26–28 October) Antal Apró, András Hegedüs, János Kádár, Ferenc Münnich, Imre Nagy, Zoltán Szántó. Then (28–31 October) Hegedüs was replaced by Károl Kiss and Kádár appointed chairman.

16. Ripp, *1956*, pp. 271, 284–85.

17. For writers, cf. Standeisky, *Az írók és a hatalom*, p. 47. For Nagy, see party documents in Ripp, *1956*, pp. 98–106.

Chapter 6
Deadlocked

1. *A "Jelzin-Dossie": Sowjet dokumentumok 1956-ról* [The "Yeltsin dossier": Soviet documents about 1956] (Budapest, 1993), pp. 47–50.

2. *A forradalom hangja* [The voice of the revolution], radio broadcasts, 23 October–4 November 1956 (Budapest, 1989), p. 36.

3. Donáth, *A márciusi Fronttól Monorig*, pp. 97, 104–5; Rainer, *Nagy* 2:259.

4. Rainer, *Nagy*.

5. On the course of events and speculations, see Horváth, *1956 hadikrónikája*, pp. 74–85; László Varga, *Az elhagyott tömeg*, pp. 19–126; Gyurkó, *Arcképvázlat*, pp. 153–59; András Kő and Nagy J. Lambert, *Kossuth tér 1956* [Kossuth Square 1956] (Budapest, 2001).

6. Bain, *Reluctant Satellites*, pp. 115ff. See also Lasky, *Hungarian Revolution*, pp. 71–72.

7. Rainer, *Nagy* 2:261–62. Cf. also Bindorffer and Gyenes, *Pesti Utca 1956*, p. 187.

8. See *A "Jelzin-Dossie,"* pp. 50ff.; for Suslov's report, cf. also Hegedüs, *A történelem*, pp. 75ff., as well as Ripp, *A pártvezetés végnapjai*, pp. 222–26.

9. Lasky, *Hungarian Revolution,* p. 72.

10. In contrast to the eyewitness Hegedüs and to Ripp, *A pártvezetés végnapjai,* Rainer believes that the massacre was the reason for Gerő's quick replacement; see Rainer, *Nagy* 2:259–60.

11. For the abridged text of both speeches, see Lasky, *Hungarian Revolution,* pp. 73–74. The full text is in *A forradalom,* pp. 71–72.

12. Rainer, *Nagy* 2:261.

13. Cf. the report in *A "Jelzin-Dossie,"* pp. 50ff.

14. Cf. the report of 26 October in *Döntés a Kremlben, 1956: A szovjet pártelnökség vitái Magyarországról* [Decision in the Kremlin, 1956: The debates of the Soviet party Presidium on Hungary] (Budapest, 1996), pp. 189–93.

15. See Ripp, *1956,* pp. 132–33.

Chapter 7
A Turnaround with a Question Mark

1. For the English text, see Lasky, *Hungarian Revolution,* pp. 115–16.

2. *Consolidation* was the term used during the 1956 revolution for the period between 28 October and dawn on 4 November, when armed combat had ceased and life had returned to normal, after the political demands of the rebels (and the Hungarian nation) had been met. The Kádár government that gained power after 4 November applied the same term to the period up to about 1963. This period, marked by terror and reprisals against those who had taken part in the revolution, allowed the Kádár government to cement its initially tenuous hold on power, with the military help of the Soviet Union.

3. Méray, *Nagy Imre élete és halála,* p. 215.

4. Cf. Mikoyan's verbal reports at the meeting of the Politburo on 28 October, documented in Ripp, *1956,* p. 101.

5. *Döntés a Kremlben, 1956: A szovjet pártelnökség vitái Magyarországról* [Decision in the Kremlin, 1956: The debates of the Soviety party Presidium on Hungary] (Budapest, 1996), pp. 35–46.

6. György Litván, "Myths and Legends about 1956," in *Évkönyv* [Yearbook] *2000,* pp. 5–18.

7. Horváth, *1956 hadikrónikája,* pp. 135–36, 167; Litván and Bak, *Hungarian Revolution,* pp. 81–84; Lasky, *Hungarian Revolution,* pp. 111ff.

8. Litván and Bak, *Hungarian Revolution,* p. 86.

9. Donáth, *A márciusi fronttól monorig,* p. 117.

10. Rainer, *Nagy* 2:286.

11. For the reports, see *Hiányzó lapok 1956 történetéből: Dokumentumok a volt SZKP KB levéltárából* [Missing pages from the history of 1956: Documents from the archive of the former CPSU CC] (Budapest, 1993), pp. 123–26; and *Döntés,* pp. 61–62.

Chapter 8
The General, the Colonel, and the Adjutant

1. The full text of the speeches is in *A forradalom hangja* [The voice of the revolution], radio broadcasts, 23 October–4 November 1956 (Budapest, 1989), pp. 226–29; the abbreviated English text is in Lasky, *Hungarian Revolution,* pp. 155–56.

2. *1956 Kézikönyve, Kronologia* [1956's handbook, chronology] (Budapest, 1996), p. 129; for detailed information on the released prisoners with differing figures, cf. Horváth, *1956,* pp. 217–28.

3. The full text is in Lasky, *Hungarian Revolution,* p. 163; for Kéthly, see Rainer, *Nagy* 2:301.

4. Cf. Király, *Honvédségből Néphadsereg;* Gyurkó, *1956;* pp. 266–71.

5. Gyurkó, *1956,* p. 269.

6. For details see Horváth, *1956,* pp. 255–356; Király, *Honvédségből Néphadsereg.*

7. Gyurkó, *1956,* pp. 268ff. Oláh was sentenced to eight years' imprisonment after the defeat of the revolution; he passed away in the meantime (information from Gyurkó in conversation with the author).

8. A description of the "Maléter legend" by Miklós Horváth is in *Maléter Pál* (Budapest, 1995) (in Hungarian.); cf. also Gyurkó, *1956,* pp. 222–36. This version was also confirmed in an interview of 26 May 2005 with his widow, Judith Gyenes.

9. Cf. Lajos Csiba, "Napló" [Diary], in *Szivárvány-Szemle* (Chicago, 1988).

10. For the spiteful attitude of Pongrátz even twenty-five years after the execution of Maléter and of László Iván Kovács, see his memoir, *Corvin Köz 1956;* cf. also the critical obituary by András Kő in *Magyar Nemzet,* 28 May 2005.

11. Király, *Honvédségből Néphadsereg,* pp. 259–60, 269.

12. Cf. Horváth, *Maléter,* pp. 162–66. For another version of the planned action against Király, cf. Szűcs, *Ezredes voltam 1956,* pp. 104–20; Rainer, *Nagy* 2:325–26.

13. See the Introduction by Imre Mécs in Horváth, *Maléter,* pp. iv–v; cf. also Alföldy, *Ungarn 1956,* pp. 90–91.

Chapter 9
The Dams Are Breaking

1. Cf. Rainer, *Nagy* 2:299–304; Huszár, *Kádár*, 2:316ff.

2. For the whole text, see *A forradalom hangja* [The voice of the revolution], radio broadcasts, 23 October–4 November 1956 (Budapest, 1989), pp. 292–93; Rainer, *Nagy* 2:308–9.

3. *Khrushchev Remembers*, trans. and ed. Strobe Talbott (London, 1971), p. 418.

4. Gyurkó, *Arcképvázlat*, p. 167; Varga, *Kádár*, pp. 25ff; Hungaricus, *A Magyar nemzeti-demokratikus forradalom néhány tanulságáról*, p. 95.

5. Donáth, *A márciusi Fronttól Monorig*.

6. Quoted in Gyurkó, *Arcképvázlat*, p. 167.

7. Vlado Teslic in *Borba*, 1 November 1956, and Djuka Julius, *Politika*, 1 November 1956, quoted in Lasky, *Hungarian Revolution*, pp. 153–54, 159–60.

8. Wiktor Woroszylszki, *Nowa Kultura* (Warsaw), quoted in Lasky, *Hungarian Revolution*, pp. 158–59.

9. For the background and the course of the siege and occupation, see Horváth, *1956*, pp. 275–80; Gyurkó, *Arcképvázlat*, pp. 271–81.

10. For the fictitious stories of Republic Square, among them that "154 prisoners died in the underground prison under the theater," see George Mikes, *Revolution in Ungarn* [The Hungarian Revolution] (Stuttgart, 1957), p. 130. For quotes from Budapest newspapers, cf. Gyurkó, *Arcképvázlat*, p. 280.

11. *Kézikönyv 1956: Megtorlás és emlékezés* [Handbook 1956: Reprisal and memory] (Budapest, 1996), p. 304. For the number of ÁVH men in protective custody, cf. Kiszely, *ÁVH*, p. 355.

12. For details of my adventures then and later, see Paul Lendvai, *Blacklisted: A Journalist's Life in Central Europe* (New York, 1998), pp. 100–132.

13. For the biography of ÁVH's head, General Gábor Péter, see György Gyarmati, "Péter Gábor fiatalsága, 1906–1945" [Gábor Péter's youth, 1906–1945], in *Yearbook of the Historical Institute, 2000–2001* (Budapest, 2002), pp. 4–10; for his article about Péter, see idem, pp. 25–79.

14. Ibid., p. 246.

15. Horváth, *1956*, pp. 188–89.

16. Kiszely, *ÁVH*, p. 346.

17. Lomax, *Hungary 1956*, p. 128.

Chapter 10
The Condottiere, the "Uncle," and the Romantics

1. Baudy, *Jeunesse d'Octobre*, p. 383.

2. László Eörsi, *A Széna tériek*, pp. 286ff.; *Kézikönyv 1956: Megtorlás és emlékezés* [Handbook 1956: Reprisal and memory] (Budapest, 1996), p. 23; Gyurkó, *Arcképvázlat*, pp. 287–92; Lomax, *Hungary 1956*, pp. 129–32.

3. The text is in Ernő Nagy, ed., *A forradalom sajtója* [The press of the revolution], 2nd exp. ed. (Giromagny, 1984).

4. Cf. Rainer, *Nagy* 2:301–2; Gyurkó *1956*.

5. The text is in *A forradalom hangja* [The voice of the revolution], radio broadcasts, 23 October–4 November 1956 (Budapest, 1989), p. 236.

6. The English text is in Lasky, *Hungarian Revolution*, p. 196.

7. László Eörsi, *A Széna tériek*, pp. 8–10.

8. Ibid., p. 288.

9. Ibid., pp. 263–68.

10. Ibid., pp. 3–10.

11. Ibid., pp. 241–42; *Kézikönyv 1956*, p. 155.

12. For Angyal, Szirmai, Csongovai, and their group, see László Eörsi, *Ferencváros 1956*; idem, *A Tüzoltó utcai fegyveres csoport a forradalomban*.

13. Cf. György Litván, "Zsidó szerepvállalás a Magyar kommunizmusban, antisztálinizmusban és 1956-ban" [The Jewish role in Hungarian communism, anti-Stalinism and 1956], *Szombat*, no. 8 (1992): 14–17; Éva Standeisky, "Antiszemitizmus 1956," *Évkönyv* [Yearbook] 2004, pp. 147–85. For personal impressions, see also Lendvai, *Auf schwarzen Listen*, pp. 17–149.

14. Gyurkó, *Arcképvázlat*, pp. 434–37.

15. For Angyal, see also István Szigetvari and Olaf Per Csongovai in Bindorffer and Gyenes, *Pesti Utca 1956*, pp. 67–87 and 183–203.

16. Quoted in Litván and Bak, *Hungarian Revolution*, p. 70.

17. Csongovai, pp. 187–88; László Eörsi, *Ferencváros*, p. 60.

18. *Rubicon*, nos. 1–8 (2000): 82; Csongovai; Huszár, *Kádár*, 2:317–18.

19. *Kézikönyv 1956*, pp. 141, 148.

20. Ibid., p. 153; Bindorffer and Gyenes, *Pesti Utca 1956*, pp. 15–30; Péter Tamáska, ed., *Mária Wittner, Ellenörizve* [Monitored] (Budapest, 2002); László Eörsi, *A Széna tériek*, pp. 243–44.

21. Paul Valéry, "Vor der Zukunft" [Before the future], in *Werke* [works], vol. 7, *Zur Zeitgeschichte und Politik* [On history and politics], ed. Jürgen Schmidt-Radefeldt (Frankfurt am Main, 1995), p. 536.

Chapter 11
Decision in the Kremlin: The End of Patience

1. *Döntés a Kremlben, 1956: A szovjet pártelnökség vitái Magyarországról* [Decision in the Kremlin, 1956: The debates of the Soviet party Presidium on Hungary] (Budapest, 1996).

2. Ibid., pp. 7–16.

3. Csaba Békés, "Szovjet Döntés hozatal és az 1956-os magyar forradalom" [Soviet decision-making and the Hungarian Revolution of 1956], in *Európából Európába*, pp. 162–70.

4. Ibid.; cf. also András B. Hegedüs and Manfred Wilke, eds., *Satelliten nach Stalins Tod* [Satellites after Stalin's death] (Berlin, 2000), pp. 250–53.

5. *Khrushchev Remembers*, trans. and ed. Strobe Talbott (London, 1971), p. 418.

6. *Döntes*, pp. 62–68.

7. Chen Chsien, "Beijing und die Ungarnkrise von 1956" [Beijing and the Hungarian crisis of 1956], in *Évkönyv* [Yearbook] *1996–97*, pp. 186–94.

8. János Tischler, *Lengyelország és Magyarország*, pp. 32–54.

9. For the following, cf. Veljko Mićunović, *Moscow Diary*, trans. David Floyd, with an introduction by George Kennan (London, 1980), pp. 131–40.

10. For his letters, see *Évkönyv* [Yearbook] *1996–97*, pp. 252–53.

11. For the Soviet reply, see A *"Jelzin-Dossie": Sowjet dokumentumok 1956-ról* [The "Yeltsin dossier": Soviet documents about 1956] (Budapest, 1993), p. 69.

12. Békés, "Szovjet Döntés hozatal," pp. 171–222.

Chapter 12
Double Dive into Darkness

1. Huszár, *Kádár* 1:321–24; Rainer, *Nagy* 2:305–6; Ripp, *1956*, pp. 303–14.

2. *Döntés a Kremlben, 1956: A szovjet pártelnökség vitái Magyarországról* [Decision in the Kremlin, 1956: The debates of the Soviet party Presidium on Hungary] (Budapest, 1996), p. 77.

3. Arthur Koestler, *Darkness at Noon*, trans. Daphne Hardy (Hardmondsworth, Middlesex, 1972), p. 32.

4. Huszár, *Kádár* 1:324.

5. Ibid.; Ripp, *1956*, p. 311.

6. Ripp, *Ötvenhat*, p. 302.

7. Molnár, *Budapest 1956*, p. 167; Ripp, *Ötvenhat*, pp. 301–2.

8. Litván and Bak, *Hungarian Revolution*, p. 128. For the articles by Németh, cf. Irodalmi Ujság and Uj Magyarország, both 2 November 1956, and Anna Kéthly, Népszava, 1 November 1956, in *A forradalom hangja* [The voice of the revolution], radio broadcasts, 23 October–4 November 1956 (Budapest, 1989).

9. Huszár, *Kádár* 1:330.

10. Cf. the full text in *A forradalom hangja*, pp. 370–71; the abbreviated English extract is in Lasky, *Hungarian Revolution*, pp. 179ff.

11. Körösi and Tóth, *Pártok 1956*.

12. András Kovács, "A magyar szociáldemokrácia és az 1956-os forradalom" [Hungarian social democracy and the 1956 revolution], ibid., pp. 185–203.

13. Cf. also Ripp, *1956*, pp. 170–89.

14. The text is in *A forradalom hangya*, pp. 461ff.; the English abbreviation is in Lasky, *Hungarian Revolution*, p. 216.

15. Litván, *Októberek üzenete*, pp. 347–59.

16. Szabó, *Politikai kultúra Magyarországon*.

17. Lasky, *Hungarian Revolution*, pp. 217–18.

18. For Nagy's motives, see Rainer, *Nagy* 2:313–29; Ripp, *1956*, pp. 165–66. For Poland, cf. Tischler, *Lengyelország és Magyarország*, pp. 32–56; for the general situation, cf. Csaba Békes, "Szovjet Döntés hozatal és az 1956-os Magyar forradalom" [Soviet decision-making and the Hungarian Revolution of 1956], in *Európából Európába*, pp. 142–223.

19. Rainer, *Nagy* 2:313.

20. Cf. Ildikó Lipcsey, *Einleitung zu: Magyar-román kapcsolatok, 1956–1958, Dokumentumok* [Introduction to Hungarian-Romanian relations, 1956–1958, documents] (Budapest, 2004), pp. 6–46.

21. For details, see the next chapter.

Chapter 13
The Puppeteers and the Kádár Enigma

1. For Münnich, see www.rev.hu (1956 Institute Budapest); Gyurkó, *Arcképvázlat történelmi háttérrel*, p. 390; and interviews with Hungarian personalities.

2. Cf. Rainer, *Nagy* 2:323; *Rubicon*, nos. 7–8:85. Huszár, *Kádár* 1:333–34. Gyurkó, *Arcképvázlat történelmi háttérrel*, pp. 388–91.

3. Huszár, *Kádár* 1:335.

4. Ibid., p. 334.

5. Cf. András B. Hegedüs and Manfred Wilke, eds., *Satelliten nach Stalins Tod* [Satellites after Stalin's Death] (Berlin, 2000), pp. 262ff.

6. Gyurkó, *Arcképvázlat történelmi háttérrel*, pp. 396–96; Huszár, *Kádár*, p. 337.

7. The speech was made on 12 April 1989 at the meeting of the Central Committee. The text is in *A Magyar Szocialista Munkáspárt Központi Bizotságának 1989. évi jegyzökönyvei I* [Minutes of the Central Committee of the Hungarian Socialist Workers' Party, 1989, vol. 1] (Budapest, 1993), pp. 758–66.

8. Miklós Szabó, "A jellem és a szerep" [The character and the role], *Rubicon* (2000–2006): 32–33.

9. Quoted from *The Measures Taken,* in Bert Brecht, the minstrel of the GPU, http://members.optushome.com.au/spainter/Brecht.html.

10. Interviews with Musatov in Budapest on 16 September 2005 and with Kryuchkov in Moscow on 26 September 2005; cf. also Kryuchkov, *Personal Matters,* pp. 37–80, as well as *Personality and Power,* pp. 134–42 (both in Russian).

11. Arbatov, *Das System,* pp. 290–93.

12. Quoted in Shevchenko, *Breaking with Moscow,* p. 104.

13. Andrew and Gordievsky, *KGB,* p. 399.

14. Ibid.

15. *Döntés a Kremlben, 1956: A szovjet pártelnökség vitái Magyarországról* [Decision in the Kremlin, 1956: The debates of the Soviet party Presidium on Hungary] (Budapest, 1996), p. 69.

16. Ibid., pp. 71–72.

17. Ibid., pp. 75–85.

18. Ibid., pp. 88–95.

19. Cf. János M. Rainer, "Kísérlet a feljegyzések értelmezésére" [Attempt at interpreting the notes], in *Döntés,* pp. 111–51; Huszár, *Kádár,* pp. 337–48; *A "Jelzin-Dossie": Sowjet dokumentumok 1956-ról* [The "Yeltsin dossier": Soviet documents about 1956] (Budapest, 1993), pp. 87–93.

Chapter 14
Operation Whirlwind and Kádár's Phantom Government

1. For details, see Valeri Vartanov, "Die Sowjetunion und die Ereignisse in Ungarn im Herbst 1956 [The Soviet Union and the events in Hungary in the fall of 1956], in *Die Ungarnkrise 1956 und Österreich* [The Hungarian crisis 1956 and Austria] (Vienna, 2003), pp. 73–86; Alexander Kirov, "A szovjet hadsereg és a Magyar forradalom" [The Soviet Army and the Hungarian Revolution], in *Évkonyv* [Yearbook] *1996–97,* pp. 67–73; Horváth, *1956,* pp. 415–59; Király, *Honvédségből Néphadsereg,* pp. 279–96.

2. The reports are in *A "Jelzin-Dossie": Sowjet dokumentumok 1956-ról* [The "Yeltsin dossier": Soviet documents about 1956] (Budapest, 1993), pp. 95–103.

3. Cf. *1956 Chronology,* p. 204. For the arrest, see Horváth, *Maléter Pál* (Budapest, 1995); Szűcz, *Ezredes voltam 1956,* pp. 125ff.

4. Valeri Musatov, "Szovjet politikai beavatkozás és katonai intervenció Magyarországon 1956-ban" [Soviet political interference and military intervention in Hungary, 1956], in *Multunk* (Budapest, 1991), pp. 159–71.

5. Ember, *Menedékjog 1956,* pp. 135–59.

6. For a summary, see Rainer, *Nagy* 2:330–36; for quotes, cf. also *A forradalom hangja* [The voice of the revolution], radio broadcasts, 23 October–4 November 1956 (Budapest, 1989), pp. 487–93. The English text of Nagy's declaration is in Lasky, *Hungarian Revolution,* p. 228.

7. See the critical analysis in Rainer, *Nagy,* vol. 2.

8. The English text is in Lasky, *Hungarian Revolution.*

9. See ibid. for the English text, p. 234 (abbr.), and in Litván and Bak, *Hungarian Revolution* (full text), p. 105. In Hungarian: Bibó, *1956,* pp. 57–60. For the background and course, see Huszár, *István Bibó,* pp. 143–59.

10. An English summary is in Litván and Bak, *Hungarian Revolution,* pp. 115–16; the complete original text is in Huszár, *István Bibó,* pp. 276–80.

11. Bibó was arrested in May 1957 and, together with the future head of state Árpád Göncz, sentenced to life imprisonment in August 1958. Granted amnesty in March 1963, he was not permitted to leave Hungary in spite of invitations from abroad. He died in May 1977.

12. See Huszár, *István Bibó,* pp. 143–59.

13. Cf. the series of articles in *Népszabadság* about 1956 (Budapest, 1981), pp. 56–57.

14. Marosán, *A tanuk még élnek.*

15. Ibid.

16. Vyacheslav Sereda and Alexander Stikalin, eds., *Hiányzó lapok: Dokumentumok a volt SzKP KB Levéltárábol* [Missing pages: Documents from the archive of the former CC of the CPSU] (Budapest, 1993), pp. 143–44.

17. Ibid., pp. 161–64.

18. For Baikov, see Marosán, *A tanuk még élnek,* pp. 125–26. András B. Hegedüs in *Satelliten nach Stalins Tod* [Satellites after Stalin's death], ed. András B. Hegedüs and Manfred Wilke (Berlin, 2000), p. 264.

19. Huszár, *Kádár* 2:7–80. For Baikov's influence, cf. his report about the tensions and pecking-order fights in the Hungarian leadership in *A "Jelzin-Dossie,"* pp. 204–8.

Chapter 15
The Yugoslav-Soviet Conspiracy

1. See *Döntés a Kremlben, 1956: A szovjet pártelnökség vitái Magyarországról* [Decision in the Kremlin, 1956: The debates of the Soviet party Presidium on Hungary] (Budapest, 1996), pp. 101–4.

2. Cf. Szántó's memorandum in *Top Secret,* ed. Kiss, Ripp, and Vida, p. 228.

3. The details are in Rainer, *Nagy* 2:332–36.

4. Varga, *Kádár,* p. 154.

5. Ember, *Menedekjog 1956.*

6. See the directive of the party Presidium to the Soviet ambassador in Belgrade for passing on to Kardelj in Vyacheslav Sereda and Alexander Stikalin, eds., *Hiányzó lapok: Dokumentumok a volt SzKP KB Levéltárábol* [Missing pages: Documents from the archive of the former CC of the CPSU] (Budapest, 1993), pp. 224–25.

7. Cf. Ember, *Menedekjog 1956;* Rainer, *Nagy* 2:339–54.

8. Cf. Varga, *Kádár,* pp. 168–98.

9. For the decision, cf. *Top Secret,* ed. Kiss, Ripp, and Vida, p. 195. For Nagy's faltering, see Rainer, *Nagy* 2:344–45.

10. The full text is in *Top Secret,* pp. 204–10.

11. For the protest, cf. ibid., pp. 226–27.

12. Bozóky, *Zord idök nyomában,* pp. 285–86.

13. For letters and minutes between Kádár and the Yugoslavs, cf. *Top Secret,* pp. 241–75.

14. See Malekov, Suslov, and Aristov, letter to the Soviet CC, in Sereda and Stikalin, *Hiányzó lapok,* pp. 235–36.

15. Rainer, *Nagy* 2:350–51; Ember, *Menedekjog.*

16. The description is in Ember, *Menedekjog;* Rainer, *Nagy* 2:354–58.

17. *1956 Kézikönyve, Kronologia* [1956 Yearbook, chronology], p. 257.

18. *Top Secret,* pp. 291–305.

19. The text is in Lasky, *Hungarian Revolution,* p. 270. For Djilas's admiration for the Hungarians, see also the interview in Urban, *Stalinism,* pp. 200–201; *Top Secret,* pp. 291–305.

20. Cf. Gasteyger, *Die feindlichen Brüder;* Dusko Doder, *The Yugoslavs,* pp. 177–95; Bass and Marbury, *Soviet-Yugoslav Controversy.*

21. Huszár, *Kádár* 2:16–19.

22. Ibid., pp. 10–14; *Top Secret,* pp. 286–89.

23. The memo about the sitting of the party Presidium on 27 November 1956 is in *Döntés,* p. 108.

24. *1956 Kézikönyve, Kronologia,* p. 259.

Chapter 16
The Second Revolution

1. Vyacheslav Sereda and Alexander Stikalin,eds., *Hiányzó lapok: Dokumentumok a volt SzKP KB Levéltárábol* [Missing pages: Documents from the archive of the former CC of the CPSU] (Budapest, 1993), p. 166.

2. Ibid., p. 169.

3. András B. Hegedüs, in *Satelliten nach Stalins Tod* [Satellites after Stalin's death], ed. András B. Hegedüs and Manfred Wilke (Berlin, 2000), p. 270.

4. *Magyar ifjuság* [Hungarian youth], 2 February 1957.

5. Cf. Litván and Bak, *Hungarian Revolution*, p. 115.

6. Julius Hay, *Born 1900*, p. 320.

7. Molnár, *Budapest 1956*, p. 247.

8. Cf. Sereda and Stikalin, *Hiányzó lapok*, pp. 168, 184–87.

9. Varga, *Kádár*, p. 212.

10. István Örkény, *Noteszlapok 1956-ból* [Pages from a notebook] (Holmi, 1991), pp. 1354–64.

11. Quoted in Lasky, *Hungarian Revolution*, pp. 295–96.

12. Cf. *A "Jelzin-Dossie": Sowjet dokumentumok 1956-ról* [The "Yeltsin dossier": Soviet documents about 1956] (Budapest, 1993), pp. 133–37.

13. The Kádár speech is in *MSzMP ideiglenes vezetö testületeinek jegyzökönyvei I.* [Minutes of the provisional leading bodies of the Hungarian Socialist Workers' Party 1], p. 143.

14. Varga, *Kádár*, pp. 230–33.

15. *1956 Kézikönyve, Kronologia* [Yearbook, chronology], pp. 278–81.

16. Litván and Bak, *Hungarian Revolution*, pp. 133ff.; *1956 Kézikönyve, Kronologia*, pp. 278–79.

17. *Borba* (Belgrade), 12 December 1956; the English version is in Lasky, *Hungarian Revolution*, p. 296.

18. *1956 Kézikönyve, Kronologia*, pp. 278–81.

19. Quoted in Lasky, *Hungarian Revolution*, p. 296.

20. Ripp, *1956*, pp. 233ff.

21. Quoted in Varga, *Kádár*, p. 235.

22. Litván and Bak, *Hungarian Revolution*, p. 117; *1956 Kézikönyve, Kronologia*, pp. 267–68; *Borba*, 6 December 1956; the English version is in Lasky, *Hungarian Revolution*, p. 299.

23. Molnár, *Budapest 1956*, pp. 280–81; Litván and Bak, *Hungarian Revolution*, p. 119; Ripp, *1956*, pp. 242–43; for the full text, see Hungaricus.

24. For a brilliant summary and analysis of the attitude of the writers before, during, and after the revolution, see Standeisky, *Az irók és a hatalom*. See also Ripp, *1956*, pp. 239–43, and Molnár, *Budapest 1956*, pp. 249–50.

Chapter 17
The Moral Bankruptcy of the U.S. Liberation Theory

1. Quoted in László Borhi, "Liberation or Inaction? The United States and Hungary in 1956," in Schmidl, *Die Ungarnkrise 1956*, pp. 129–30.

2. Cf. Urban, *Radio Free Europe*, pp. 211–49; Lendvai, *Der Medienkrieg*, pp. 146–70; Borbándi, *Magyarok az Angol Kertben*.

3. Borbándi, *Magyarok az Angol Kertben*, pp. 169–82. Borhi, *Magyarország*, pp. 292ff.; Rauchensteiner, *Spätherbst 1956*, pp. 23–24.

4. For the quotations, see Zoltán Benkő in *Yearbook 1996/97*, pp. 284–87; Urban, *Radio Free Europe*, pp. 217–22; Borbándi, *Magyarok az Angol Kertben*, pp. 228–50.

5. Quoted by Günter Bischof, "Eindämmung und Koexistenz oder 'Roll-back' und Befreiung?" [Containment and coexistence, or "Rollback" and liberation?], in Schmidl, *Die Ungarnkrise 1956*.

6. For all quotations, cf. Békés, *Európából*, pp. 142–222; idem, *Az 1956-os magyar forradalom*. Cf. also *Yearbook 1996/97*, pp. 201–13; Borhi, *Magyarország*.

7. Quoted by Bischof, "Eindämmung," p. 126.

8. For quotations and discussions, see Borhi, *Magyarország*, pp. 305–18; Békés, *Európából*, pp. 171–86. Cf. also Raymond Garthoff, "A magyar forradalom és Washington" [The Hungarian Revolution and Washington], in *Yearbook 1996/97*, pp. 214–28; and Urban, *Radio Free Europe*.

9. For details, see Borbándi, *Magyarok az Angol Kertben*, pp. 223–26, and Borhi, *Magyarország*, p. 309.

10. Kissinger, *Diplomacy*, pp. 550–68.

11. See Váli, *Rift and Revolt in Hungary*, pp. 485–89; Békés, *Európából*; Borhi, *Magyarország*; UN Report of the Special Committee on the Problem of Hungary, New York, 1957.

12. Kyle, *Suez*, p. 486, quoted in Alföldy, *Ungarn 1956*.

13. András Nagy, *A Bang-Jensen ügy*; Békés, *Európából*, pp. 209–19. For the infiltration of the UN, see the memoirs of Arkady Shevchenko, undersecretary-general (USG) of the United Nations, who defected in 1978: *Breaking with Moscow*. And for the activities of the Hungarian secret agents in Vienna, see Miklós Szabó, *Foglalkozásuk*.

14. See Standeisky, *Az írók és a hatalom*, pp. 275–87.

Chapter 18
Worldwide Reactions

1. The title of the introduction by Raymond Aron for the French edition of the collection of documents, *La Révolution Hongroise*, ed. M. L. Lasky and François Bondy (Paris, 1957).

2. *Manchester Guardian*, 12 November 1956.

3. Litván and Bak, *Hungarian Revolution*, p. 155.

4. Fryer, *Hungarian Tragedy*.

5. Quoted in *Magyar Hirlap*, Budapest, 22 October 1992.

6. Quoted in *Top Secret*, ed. Kiss, Ripp, and Vida, p. 209.

7. Furet, *Passing of an Illusion*, p. 463.

8. Quoted in Lasky, *Hungarian Revolution*, p. 270.

9. Urban, *Stalinism*, pp. 200–201.

10. Yakovlev, *Century of Violence*, pp. 11–12.

11. Lipcsey, *Magyar-Román kapcsolatok*, pp. 5–45; *Yearbook 1996/97*, pp. 132–37; Mihail Retegan, *Yearbook 1996/97*, p. 197; Ghita Ionescu, *Communism in Rumania, 1944–1962* (London, 1964), pp. 257ff., 267–73.

12. Arthur Schopenhauer, *Aphorismen zur Lebensweisheit* (Frankfurt am Main, 1976), p. 67.

13. Cf. Bogdan Goralczyk, "Die Ereignisse in Ungarn 1956 aus polnischer Perspektive" [Events in Hungary from a Polish perspective], in Schmidl, *Die Ungarnkrise 1956*, pp. 187–200; Litván and Bak, *Hungarian Revolution*, pp. 149–50; Tischler, *Lengyelország és Magyarország*, pp. 13–112.

14. Quoted in Tischler, *Lengyelország és Magyarország*, pp. 53–54, from Andrej Werblan, in *Prawo i Zycie*, no. 43 (1991). Cf. also Goralczyk, "Ereignisse," p. 192.

15. Lendvai, *Auf schwarzen Listen*, pp. 150ff. For the story of the founding of this paper and the decision not to return to Budapest from my first trip abroad and to seek asylum in Vienna, see ibid., pp. 146–55.

16. Cf. Tischler, *Lengyelország és Magyarország*; Goralczyk, "Ereignisse."

17. Paul Lendvai, "Zehn Jahre danach" [Ten years later], *Der Monat* (October 1966).

18. Furet, *Passing of an Illusion*, p. 459.

19. Rauchensteiner, *Spätherbst 1956*, p. 101.

20. Ibid., p. 44. For the Swiss attitude, see p. 45.

21. Portisch, *Österreich II*, pp. 48ff.

22. Ibid., p. 51. Cf. also Rauchensteiner, *Spätherbst 1956*.

23. Ernö Deak, "Die ungarische Revolution in den österreichischen Medien" [The Hungarian Revolution in the Austrian media], in *Die ungarische Revolution 1956* [The Hungarian Revolution 1956] (Vienna, 1995), pp. 52, 57.

24. Norbert Leser, "Zwei 'Herrenvölker' zahlen Lehrgeld" [Two master races learn the hard way], *Europäische Rundschau*, no. 2 (1995): 9.

25. Rauchensteiner, *Spätherbst 1956*, p. 93.

26. Lendvai, *Auf schwarzen Listen*, pp. 156ff. For the Hungarian statistics, see *1956 Kézikönyve* [1956 Yearbook], 3:310–11.

27. Portisch, *Österreich II*, pp. 50–51; Rauchensteiner, *Spätherbst 1956*, pp. 84–87. Cf. also Kern, *Österreich*; Michael Gehler, "The Hungarian Crisis

and Austria," in *Contemporary Austrian Studies* (New Brunswick, 2001),
9:160–213.

28. Bundespressedienst [Federal news service], "Österreich als Asylland"
[Austria as asylum country], Vienna, 1896; Portisch, *Österreich II*, p. 56;
Stanek, *Flüchtlinge in Österreich*. See also the special reports "Fifty Years On,"
in *Refugees*, the publication of the UN Refugee Agency, no. 2 (2006): 4–23;
and Ibolya Murber and Zoltán Fonagy, *Die ungarische Revolution und Österreich* [The Hungarian Revolution and Austria] (Vienna, 2006), pp. 335–86.

29. For the help to the Hungarians in Switzerland, see the article by Rita
Lanz in *Schweizer Monatshefte* (February 2006): 34–37.

30. *Süddeutsche Zeitung*, 14 March 1958 and 24 February 1959; *Die Welt*, 23
February 1959; *Frankfurter Allgemeine Zeitung*, 28 May 1958.

31. Bain, *Reluctant Satellites*, pp. 183–84. I extracted the description, with
thanks, from the as-yet-unpublished manuscript of legation counselor
Dr. Martin Pammer in the Federal Ministry of Foreign Affairs about the
humanitarian actions of the Austrian legation in Budapest in the late fall
of 1956. For the quote "more Western than the West," cf. Thomas O.
Schlesinger, *Austrian Neutrality in Postwar Europe* (Vienna, 1972), p. 52.

32. *Wiener Zeitung*, 11 December 1956. Cf. also Rauchensteiner, *Spätherbst
1956*, pp. 99–100.

33. Cf. Portisch, *Österreich II*, pp. 62ff.; Rauchensteiner, *Spätherbst 1956*, pp.
107–8.

Chapter 19
The Barbarous Vendetta of the Victors

1. For membership figures, see Paul Lendvai, *Die Grenzen des Wandels*
[The limits of change] (Vienna, 1977), pp. 63–78. During the years before
the uprising the membership numbers fluctuated between 800,000 and
almost 900,000!

2. See his article in *Társadalmi Szemle* (Budapest, April 1958).

3. Huszár, *Kádár* 2:20ff.

4. For the incidents at the University Rudolf Ungváry, see *Élet és Irodalom*
[Life and literature), Budapest, 7 April 2006, pp. 4–5.

5. Cf. Litván and Bak, *Hungarian Revolution*, pp. 138ff.; *1956 Yearbook III, Retribution and Remembrance* (Budapest, 1996); Attila Szakolczai, "Über die
Hingerichteten während der nachrevolutionären Vergeltung" [About the
executed during the postrevolutionary retaliation], in *Évkönyv* [Yearbook]
1994, pp. 237–56. For individual cases, see the biographical notes in
Handbook III.

6. Some tragic cases have already been described in chapter 10 of this book.

7. Cf. Frigyes Kahler, *A Brusznyai per* [The Brusznyai trial] (Budapest, 1998); András B. Hegedüs, in *Satelliten nach Stalins Tod* [Satellites after Stalin's death], ed. András B. Hegedüs and Manfred Wilke (Berlin, 2000), p. 276.

8. *Handbook III*, p. 71. *Halottaink* [Our dead] (Budapest, 1989), pp. 32, 187–88.

9. Ferenc Köszeg, in *Halottaink*, p. 33.

10. *Handbook III*, pp. 521–23.

11. Litván and Bak, *Hungarian Revolution*, pp. 143ff.; *Handbook III*, pp. 7–12. Hegedüs, in *Satelliten*, pp. 273–79.

12. For the revelation, see Reinhard Olt, "Die legendäre Karton-Nummer sechs" [The legendary carton number 6], *Frankfurter Allgemeine Zeitung*, 9 May 2006, p. D/10. Cf. also Lendvai, *The Hungarians*, pp. 454–55.

13. Dezsö Kertész and György Litván, "Váci börtönsztrájk 1960" [The prison strike at Vác, 1960], in *Évkönyv 1995*, pp. 196–235.

14. Litván and Bak, *Hungarian Revolution*, p. 143.

15. Körösi and Molnár, *Mit einem Geheimnis leben*.

16. Quoted from *Kedves, jó Kádár elvtárs! Válogatás Kádár János levelezéséből 1954–1989* [My dear comrade Kádár! Extracts from the correspondence of János Kádár, 1954–1989], ed. Tibor Huszár (Budapest, 2002), pp. 78–79.

17. For the preparation and the course of the trial, cf. esp. Rainer, *Nagy* 2:355–441; Huszár, *Kádár* 2:27–37, 58–77. Cf. also the Soviet documents in *A "Jelzin-Dossie": Sowjet dokumentumok 1956-ról* [The "Yeltsin dossier": Soviet documents about 1956] (Budapest, 1993); "The Truth about the Nagy Affair, London, 1959," *Minutes of the CC of the Hungarian Socialist Workers' Party, 1957/58* (Budapest, 1997); Miklós Horváth, *Maléter Pál* (Budapest, 1995); Vásárhelyi, *Ellenzékben*, pp. 179–80; Kövér, *Losonczy*, pp. 337–54.

18. The five-hundred pages of handwritten notes—almost completely destroyed by Nagy—were copied beforehand by the Romanian Secret Service. Nagy's daughter, Erzsébet Nagy, did not permit publication of the text for many years, and agreed to have the text prepared for printing only in the spring of 2006 on the occasion of the fiftieth anniversary of the revolution and her father's 110th birthday. A Romanian edition had been published earlier. The daughter's negative attitude was due to several sharp attacks in the writing by Imre Nagy against the "Jewish Rákosi clique" and allusions to the Jewish origins of eight top functionaries, whom he named. "The broad masses of Hungarians hated and rejected these Jews, most of whom came from Moscow; they were not willing to accept these as representatives of the Hungarian national interests, let alone as their leaders." Nagy reproached "the Jew Rákosi and his clique" particularly for "wanting to be more Hungarian than the Hungarians"

and therefore [for] having represented a "chauvinistic and nationalistic" line vis-à-vis the friendly neighbors Romania and Czechoslovakia. For the complete text, see Nagy, *Snagovi jegyzetek,* pp. 93–96. His biographer Rainer emphasizes that he could not detect any anti-Semitic attitude while working on Nagy's biography. See Zsolt Gréczy, "Mit gondolt Nagy Imre az '56-os forradalomról?" [What did Imre Nagy think of the 1956 revolution?], interview in *Népszabadság,* 7 September 2005.

19. See Georg Lukács, *Record of a Life: An Autobiographical Sketch,* ed. István Eörsi, trans. Rodney Livingstone (London, 1983), pp. 129–34. Cf. also Agnes Heller, in Paetzke, *Andersdenkende in Ungarn,* pp. 112–13. See also Eörsi's earlier cited TV interview with the author, May 2005. For a comparison of Nagy with Kossuth, see István Deák, in *Évkönyv* [Yearbook] *1996/97,* pp. 129–32.

20. Rainer, *Nagy* 2:430–31.

21. Cf. "The Truth," pp. 180–215.

22. Rainer, *Nagy* 2:386–91; Huszár, *Kádár* 2:66–69. See also Kádár's earlier cited last befuddled speech on 12 April 1989 before the CC of the Hungarian Party, *Minutes.* Cf. also the witty commentary by Mihály Kornis, Kádár, and notes to Kádár's monologue, in *Bridge of Sighs* (Budapest, 1997), pp. 91–174 (in Hungarian). See the meeting of the Presidium of 5 February 1958: Agreement on court proceedings against the Nagy group without death sentence or death sentence with subsequent clemency, in Archives of the Kremlin, Presidium of the CC of the CPSU, 1954–1964, Moscow, 2004, p. 293. I am indebted for this helpful advice to the former Russian ambassador to Budapest Valeri Musatov.

23. Litván and Bak, *Hungarian Revolution,* pp. xii–xiii; András B. Hegedüs, *Satelliten nach Stalins Tod,* pp. 277–78.

24. Károly Grósz, Kádár's successor, in a posthumous interview, in *Magyar Nemzet,* Budapest, 20 August 1994, quoted in Alföldy, *Ungarn 1956,* p. 153.

Chapter 20
1956–1989: Victory in Defeat?

1. Data from the opinion pollster Maria Vásárhelyi, 9 February 2006.

2. Futaky, *Ungarn.* For Konrád, cf. pp. 20–21.

3. Standeisky, *Az írók és a hatalom,* pp. 276–79. István Eörsi, *Népszabadsag,* 1 March 2005.

4. Paul Lendvai, "Zehn Jahre danach" [Ten years later], *Der Monat* (October 1966): 18–28.

5. Paul Lendvai, *Das eigenwillige Ungarn* [Headstrong Hungary] (Osnabrück, 1968), p. 66.

6. Ivan T. Berend, *Gazdasági útkeresés 1956–1965* [Search for new ways in the economy, 1956–1965] (Budapest, 1983), pp. 179–93.

7. Interview with György Krassó (András Bozóki), January 1990, in Ervin Csizmadia (ed), *A magyar demokratikus ellenzék* [The Hungarian democratic opposition], *1968–1988* (Budapest, 1995), pp. 60–61.

8. Lendvai, *The Hungarians*, p. 459. See also Romsics, *Magyarország története*, p. 422.

9. Romsics, *Magyarország története*, p. 423.

10. László Lengyel, "Akádárizmus alkonya" [The twilight of Kádárism], in Rácz, *Ki volt Kádár?* pp. 155–65.

11. Lendvai, *Das eigenwillige Ungarn*, pp. 64–65.

12. *The Essays of Michel de Montaigne: Of Repentance,* trans. and ed. M. A. Screech (Harmondsworth, Middlesex, 1991), pp. 907–8.

13. György, *Néma hagyomány*, p. 76.

14. Mihály Bihari, "Kádár és rendszere" [Kádár and his system], in *Ki volt Kádár?* ed. Rácz, p. 154.

15. Tőkés, *Hungary's Negotiated Revolution*, p. 37.

16. Huszár, *Beszélgetések Nyers Rezsővel*, pp. 322–70.

17. See Csaba Gombár and Hedi Volosin, eds., *Két Magyarország* [Two Hungaries] (Budapest, 2005), pp. 166ff.

18. Shawcross, *Crime and Compromise.*

19. The following quotations are from the transcript of the interview. Cf. also Lendvai, *Das eigenwillige Ungarn*, and idem, "Auf dem Schachbrett kommunistischer Politik" [On the chessboard of Communist politics], *Der Bund* (Bern), 1 December 1981.

20. For details, cf. Lendvai *Das eigenwillige Ungarn;* Huszár, *Kádár* vol. 2; and László Lengyel and Imre Pozsgay, in *Ki volt Kádár?* ed. Rácz, pp. 155–65 and 208–20.

21. The text of the entire speech is in *Ki volt Kádár*, pp. 213–16.

22. Sándor Kopátsy, *Kádár és kora* [Kádár and his times] (Budapest, 2002).

Epilogue
Whose 1956?

1. Horn, whose brother was killed after the intervention under unexplained circumstances, was a member, from December 1956 to June 1957, of the new armed security forces, dubbed by the people as the "quilted jackets" (pufajkás) because of their Soviet-type uniforms. Cf. his memoirs: *Cölöpök* [Stilts], (Budapest, 1991), pp. 106–10.

2. Attila Pók, "Geschichte im Transformationsprozess Ungarns" [History in Hungary's transformation process], in *Gegen Erinnerung: Geschichte als politisches Argument* (Munich, 2006), pp. 173–90.

3. Cf. Harald Weinrich, *Lethe, Kunst und Kritik des Vergessens* [Lethe, art and the critique of forgetfulness] (Munich, 1997), p. 144.

4. György, *Néma hagyomány*, p. 21.

5. Huszár, *István Bibó*, pp. 160–61.

6. Lomax, *Hungary 1956*, p. 17.

7. György, *Néma hagyomány*, pp. 19ff. Cf. also István Deák, "1956 in Hungarian Memory and Public Consciousness," in Schmidl, *Die Ungarnkrise 1956*, pp. 89–100.

8. Gábor Gyani, "Az '56-Mitosz, az emlékezet tere" [The myth of '56, the place of memory], in *Élet és Irodalom* [Life and literature] (Budapest), 21 October 2005, pp. 3–9.

9. Cf. the speculations by Charles Gati in *Failed Illusions: Moscow, Washington, Budapest and the 1956 Hungarian Revolt* (Stanford, 2006); *Historia* (April 2006); and *Népszabadság*, 20 May 2006. In this respect I accept the theses of Csaba Békés, *Európából*; Rainer, *Nagy*; and Borhi, *Magyarország*.

10. Thomas Nipperdey, *Nachdenken über die deutsche Geschichte* [Reflections on German history] (Munich, 1986), p. 19.

11. Cf. Péter N. Nagy, "Vanrá remény, hogy volt '56" [There is still hope there was a '56], *Népszabadság*, 22 October 2005, p. 3.

12. Edmund Burke, *Reflections on the Revolution in France* (1790).

Bibliography

The preceding chapters are based primarily on books, essays, and documents in Hungarian, cited in detail in the endnotes.

Some important Hungarian collections deserve special mention: the Yearbooks (Évkönyvek) of the 1956 Institute and of the Historical Bureau of the Hungarian State Security; the minutes of the Central Committee of the Hungarian Socialist Workers' Party; the Press of the Revolution (A forradalom sajtója); *The Voice of the Revolution*, broadcasts in Hungary, 23 October–4 November 1956 (*A forradalom hangja*); two manuals (*Kézikönyv*) of the 1956 Institute about the chronology and the reprisals; the three document collections from Moscow: the Yeltsin Dossier, Missing Pages (Hiányzó lapok), Decision in the Kremlin (Döntés a Kremlben); *The Truth about the Nagy Affair* (preface by Albert Camus) (London, 1959).

Aczél, Tamás, and Tibor Méray. *The Revolt of the Mind*. London, 1959.

Alföldy, Géza. *Ungarn 1956*. 2nd ed. Heidelberg, 1998.

Andrew, Christopher, and Oleg Gordievsky. *KGB: The Inside Story*. London, 1990.

Arbatow, Georgi. *Das System*. Frankfurt am Main, 1993.

Bain, Leslie B. *The Reluctant Satellites*. New York, 1960.

Baráth, Magdolna, ed. *Szovjet nagyköveti iratok Magyarországról* [Secret reports by Soviet ambassadors on Hungary], *1953–1956*. Budapest, 2002.

Baráth, Magdolna, and Sipos Levente, eds. *A snagovi foglyok—Nagy Imre és társai Romániában* [The prisoners of Snagov—Imre Nagy and his group in Romania]. Budapest, 2006.

Bass, Robert, and Elizabeth Marbury, eds. *The Soviet-Yugoslav Controversy, 1948–1958*. New York, 1959.

Baudy, Nicolas. *Jeunesse d'octobre: Témoins et combattants de la revolution hongroise*. Paris, 1957.

Békés, Csaba. *Az 1956-os magyar forradalom a világpolitikában* [The Hungarian Revolution in world politics]. Budapest, 1996.

———. *Európából Európába* [From Europe to Europe]. Budapest, 2004.

Benz, Wolfgang, ed. *Dimensionen des Völkermordes*. Munich, 1991.

Bibó, István. *Válogatott tanulmányok* [Selected studies]. Vols. 1–4. Budapest, 1986–90.

———. *1956*. Edited by Gábor Szigethy. Budapest, 2003.

Bindorffer, Györgyi, and Pál Gyenes, eds. *Pesti Utca 1956: Válogatás fegyveres felkelők emlékezéseiből* [Pest Street 1956: Selections from the memories of armed insurgents]. Budapest, 1994.

Bispinck, Hendrik, et al., eds. *Aufstände im Ostblock* [Uprisings in the Eastern Bloc]. Berlin, 2004.

Borbándi, Gyula. *Magyarok az Angol Kertben: A Szabad Európa Rádió története* [Hungarians in the English Garden: The history of the RFE]. Budapest, 1996.

Borhi, László. *Magyarország a hidegháborúban* [Hungary in the Cold War]. Budapest, 2005.

Bozóky, Éva. *Zord idk nyomában* [Tracing the history of hard times]. Budapest, 1998.

Braham, Randolph L. *The Politics of Genocide: The Holocaust in Hungary.* New York, 1994.

Brix, Emil, and Hannes Stekl. *Der Kampf um das Gedächtnis* [The battle for the memory]. Vienna, 1997.

Djilas, Milovan. *Conversations with Stalin.* New York, 1962.

Doder, Dusko. *The Yugoslavs.* New York, 1978.

Donáth, Ferenc. *A márciusi Fronttól Monorig* [From the March front to Monor]. Budapest, 1992.

Ember, Judit. *Menedékjog 1956: A Nagy Imre-csoport elrablása* [Right of asylum 1956: The kidnapping of the Imre Nagy group]. Budapest, 1989.

Eörsi, István. *Emlékezés a régi szép időkre* [Recalling the good old times]. Budapest, 1988.

Eörsi, László. *A Tüzoltó utcai fegyveres csoport a forradalomban* [The armed group of Tüzoltó Street in the revolution]. Budapest, 1993.

———. *Ferencváros 1956: A kerület fegyveres csoportjai* [Ferencváros 1956: The armed groups in the ninth district]. Budapest, 1997.

———. *Corvinisták 1956: A VIII. kerület fegyveres csoportjai* [The Corvinists 1956: the armed groups in the eighth district]. Budapest, 2001.

———. *A Széna tériek 1956* [The Széna Squareists 1956]. Budapest, 2004.

Farkas, Vladimir. *Nincs mentség, Az ÁVH alezredes voltam* [No excuse, I was a lieutenant colonel in the ÁVH]. Budapest, 1990.

Fazekas, György. *Forróősz Budapesten* [Fiery fall in Budapest]. Budapest, 1989.

Fehér, Ferenc, and Ágnes Heller. *Hungary 1956 Revisited: The Message of a Revolution—a Quarter of a Century After.* London, 1983.

Fejtő, François. *A History of the People's Democracies: Eastern Europe since Stalin.* Harmondsworth, Middlesex, 1974.

Földes, László. *A második vonalban* [In the second line]. Budapest, 1984.

Fryer, Peter. *Hungarian Tragedy.* London, 1956.

Furet, François. *The Passing of an Illusion: The Idea of Communism in the Twentieth Century.* Translated by Deborah Furet. Chicago, 1999.

Futaky, István, ed. *Ungarn: Ein kommunistisches Wunderland? Küss die Hand, Genossin* [Hungary: A Communist wonderland? Kiss the hand, comrade]. Hamburg, 1983.

Gasteyger, Curt. *Die feindlichen Brüder* [The hostile brothers]. Bern, 1960.

Gati, Charles. *Hungary and the Soviet Bloc.* Durham, 1986.

——. *Failed Illusions: Moscow, Washington, Budapest, and the 1956 Hungarian Revolt.* Stanford, 2006.

György, Péter. *Néma hagyomány* [Silent tradition]. Budapest, 2000.

Gyurkó, László. *Arcképvázlat történelmi háttérrel* [Portrait sketch with historical background]. Budapest, 1982.

——. *1956.* Budapest, 1996.

Hay, Eva. *Auf beiden Seiten der Barrikaden* [On both sides of the barricades]. Leipzig, 1994.

Hay, Julius [Gyula Háy]. *Born 1900: Memoirs.* London, 1974.

Hegedüs, András. *A történelem és a hatalom igézetében* [Under the spell of history and power]. Budapest, 1988.

——. *Satelliten nach Stalins Tod* [The Satellites after Stalin's death]. Edited by Manfred Wilke. Berlin, 2000.

Hodos, Hermann George. *Schauprozesse* [Show trials]. Frankfurt am Main, 1998.

Hoensch, Jörg K. *A History of Modern Hungary, 1867–1986.* Translated by Kim Traynor. London, 1988.

——. *Ungarn—Geschichte, Politik, Wirtschaft* [Hungary—history, politics, administration]. Hanover, 1991.

Horváth, Miklós. *1956 hadikrónikája* [Military chronicle of 1956]. Budapest, 2003.

Hungaricus [Sándor Fekete]. *A magyar nemzeti-demokratikus forradalom néhány tanulságáról* [About some lessons of the Hungarian national-democratic revolution]. Budapest, 1988.

Huszár, Tibor. *István Bibó.* Budapest, 1989.

——. *Kádár János politikai életrajza* [János Kádár's political biography], 2 vols. Budapest, 2001–3.

——. *Beszélgetések Nyers Rezsővel* [Conversations with Rezső Nyers]. Budapest, 2004.

——, ed. *Kedves, jó Kádár elvtárs! Válogatás Kádár János levelezéséből 1954–1989* [My dear comrade Kádár! Extracts from the correspondence of János Kádár, 1954–1989]. Budapest, 2002.

Kanyó, András, ed. *Kádár János:Végakarat* [János Kádár: Last will]. Budapest, 1989.

Kecskeméti, Paul. *The Unexpected Revolution: Social Forces in the Hungarian Uprising.* Stanford, 1961.

Kemény, István, and Bill Lomax, eds. *Magyar munkástanácsok 1956-ban: Dokumentumok* [Hungarian workers' councils in 1956: Documents]. Paris, 1986.

Kenedi, János. *Kis állambiztonsági olvasókönyv* [Little state security reader]. Budapest, 1996.

Kern, Friedrich. *Österreich: Offene Grenze der Menschlichkeit* [Austria: Open border of humanity]. Vienna, 1959.

Király, Béla. *Honvédségből Néphadsereg: Személyes visszaemlékezések, 1944–1956* [From Honvéd Army to People's Army: Personal recollections, 1944–1956]. Paris, 1986.

Kiss, József, Zoltán Ripp, and István Vida, eds. *Top Secret: Magyar-Jugoszlav kapcsolatok 1956* [Hungarian-Yugoslav contacts, 1956]. Reprint. Budapest, 1995.

———. *Top Secret: Magyar-Jugoszlav kapcsolatok 1956–1959* [Hungarian-Yugoslav contacts, 1956–1959]. Budapest, 1997.

Kissinger, Henry. *Diplomacy.* New York, 1994.

Kiszely, Gábor. *ÁVH—Egy terrorszervezet története* [ÁVH—the history of a terror organization]. Budapest, 2000.

Kő, András, and Lambert J. Nagy. *Kossuth tér 1956* [Kossuth Square, 1956]. Budapest, 2001.

Kopácsi, Sándor. *Életfogytiglan* [Life sentence]. Budapest, 1989.

Kopátsy, Sándor. *Kádár és kora* [Kádár and his times]. Budapest, 2002.

Kornis, Mihály. *Sóhajok hídja* [Bridge of sighs]. Budapest, 1997.

Körösi, Zsuzsanna, and Péter Pál Tóth, eds. *Pártok 1956* [Parties, 1956]. Budapest, 1997.

Körösi, Zsuzsanna, and Adrienne Molnár. *Mit einem Geheimnis leben: Die Schicksale der Kinder der Verurteilten von 1956* [Living with a secret: The lot of the condemned people's children]. Herne, 2005.

Kövér, György. *Géza Losonczy, 1917–1957.* Budapest, 1998.

Kozák, Gyula, ed. *"Szuronyok hegyén nem lehet dolgozni," Válogatás 1956-os munkástanács-vezetők visszaemlékezéseiből* [Selections from the reminiscences of the workers' council leaders, 1956]. Budapest, 1993.

Kryuchkov, Vladimir. *Personal matters* [in Russian]. Moscow, 2003.

———. *Personality and Power* [in Russian]. Moscow, 2004.

Kyle, Keith. *Suez.* London, 1991.

Lasky, Melvin J., ed. *The Hungarian Revolution: A White Book.* New York, 1957.

Lendvai, Paul. *Der Medienkrieg* [Media war]. Frankfurt, 1981.

———. *Antisemitismus ohne Juden; Entwicklungen und Tendenzen in Osteuropa* [Anti-Semitism without Jews: Developments and tendencies in East Europe]. Vienna, 1982.

———. *The Hungarians.* Translated by Ann Major. Princeton, 2003.

———. *Auf schwarzen Listen* [Black listed]. Enl. ed. Vienna, 2004.

Lengyel, László. *A rendszerváltó elit tündöklése és bukása* [Splendor and downfall of the system-changing elite]. Budapest, 1996.

Lipcsey, Ildikó, ed. *Magyar-Román kapcsolatok 1956–1958: Dokumentumok* [Hungarian-Romanian relations, 1956–1958: Documents]. Budapest, 2004.

Litván, György. *Októberek üzenete* [The message of Octobers]. Budapest, 1996.

Litván, György, and János Bak, eds. *The Hungarian Revolution of 1956: Reform, Revolt, and Repression, 1953–1963*. London, 1996.

Lomax, Bill. *Hungary 1956*. London, 1976.

Marosán, György. *A tanuk még élnek* [The witnesses are still alive]. Budapest, 1989.

———. *Fel kellett állnom* [I had to stand up]. Budapest, 1989.

Méray, Tibor. *Thirteen Days That Shook the Kremlin: Imre Nagy and the Hungarian Revolution*. New York, 1959.

———. *Nagy Imre élete és halála* [The life and death of Imre Nagy]. Budapest, 1989.

Miőunovio, Veljko. *Moscow Diary*. Translated by David Floyd. With an introduction by George Kennan. London, 1980.

Mikes, George. *The Hungarian Revolution*. London, 1957.

Molnár, Miklós. *Budapest 1956: A History of the Hungarian Revolution*. London, 1971.

———. *A Short History of the Hungarian Communist Party*. Boulder, Colo., 1978.

———. *De Béla Kun à János Kádár*. Paris, 1985.

Nagy, András. *A Bang-Jensen ügy* [The Bang-Jensen affair]. Budapest, 2005.

Nagy, Imre. *Politisches Testament*. Munich, 1959; Paris, 1984.

———. *Snagovi jegyzetek 1956–1957* [Notes from Snagov, 1956–1957]. Edited by István Vida. Budapest, 2006.

Paetzke, Hans-Henning. *Andersdenkende in Ungarn* [Dissenters in Hungary]. Frankfurt am Main, 1986.

Pongrátz, Gergely. *Corvin Köz 1956* [Corvin Passage, 1956]. Debrecen, 1982. Reprinted 2004.

Portisch, Hugo. *Österreich II*. Vienna, 1996.

Pünkösti, Árpád. *Rákosi*. 2 vols. Budapest, 1992–1996.

Rácz, Árpád, ed. *Ki volt Kádár?* [Who was Kádár?]. Budapest, 2001.

Rainer, János M. *Nagy Imre: Politikai életrajz* [Imre Nagy: A political biography]. Vol. 1: *1896–1953*. Vol. 2: *1953–1958*. Budapest, 1996–1999.

———. *Ötvenhat után* [After 1956]. Budapest, 2003.

Rákosi, Mátyás. *Visszaemlékezések* [Memoirs]. Vols. 1–2: *1940–1956*. Budapest, 1997.

Rauchensteiner, Manfried. *Spätherbst 1956: Die Neutralität auf dem Prüfstand* [Late fall 1956: Neutrality put to the test]. Vienna, 1981.

Révész, Sándor. *Egyetlen élet: Gimes Miklós története* [A single life: The story of Miklós Gimes]. Budapest, 1999.

Ripp, Zoltán. *A pártvezetés végnapjai* [The last days of the party leadership]. Budapest, 1997.

————. *1956 Forradalom és szabadságharc Magyarországon* [1956: Revolution and war of independence in Hungary]. Budapest, 2002.

Romsics, Ignác. *Magyarország története a XX. Században* [Hungary's history in the twentieth century]. Budapest, 1999.

Savarius, Vincent [Béla Szász]. *Freiwillige für den Galgen: Die Geschichte eines Schauprozesses* [Volunteers for the gallows: The story of a show trial]. Cologne, 1963.

Schmidl, Erwin A, ed. *Die Ungarnkrise 1956 und Österreich* [The Hungarian crisis and Austria]. Vienna, 2003.

Shawcross, William. *Crime and Compromise: János Kádár and the Politics of Hungary since the Revolution.* New York, 1974.

Shevchenko, Arkady N. *Breaking with Moscow.* New York, 1985.

Standeisky, Éva. *Az írók és a hatalom (1956–1963)* [Writers and state power (1956–1963)]. Budapest, 1996.

Stanek, Eduard. *Flüchtlinge in Österreich, 1945–1984* [Refugees in Austria, 1945–1984]. Vienna, 1985.

Szabó, Miklós. *Foglalkozásuk: Emigráns* [Their Profession: Emigrants]. Budapest, 1958.

————. *Politikai kultúra Magyarországon 1896–1986* [Political culture in Hungary, 1896–1986]. Budapest, 1988.

Szabó, Zoltán. *Terepfelverés* [Terrain survey]. Bern, 1987.

Szakasits, Klára. *Fent és lent 1945–1950* [Up and down, 1945–1950]. Budapest, 1985.

Szűcs, Miklós. *Ezredes voltam 1956-ban a vezérkarnál* [I was a colonel in 1956 at the general staff]. Budapest, 1989.

Tischler, János. *Lengyelország és Magyarország 1956-ban és 1981-ben* [Poland and Hungary 1956 and 1981). Pécs, 2003.

Tóbiás, Áron, ed. *In memoriam: Nagy Imre.* Budapest, 1989.

Tőkés, L. Rudolf. *Hungary's Negotiated Revolution.* Cambridge, 1996.

United Nations Report of the Special Committee on the Problem of Hungary. New York, 1957.

Urban, George R. *Radio Free Europe and the Pursuit of Democracy.* New Haven, 1997.

————, ed. *Stalinism—Its Impact on Russia and the World.* London, 1982.

Váli, A. Ferenc. *Rift and Revolt in Hungary.* Cambridge, 1961.

Varga, László. *Az elhagyott tömeg* [The abandoned masses]. Budapest, 1994.

————, ed. *Kádár János a bírái előtt* [János Kádár before his judges]. Budapest, 2001.

Vas, Zoltán. *Betiltott könyvem* [My banned book]. Budapest, 1990.

Vásárhelyi, Miklós. *Ellenzékben* [In opposition]. Budapest, 1989.

Wittner, Mária. *Ellenőrizve* [Monitored]. Edited by Péter Tamaska. Budapest, 2002.

Yakovlev, Alexander N. *A Century of Violence in Soviet Russia.* Translated by Anthony Austin. New Haven, 2002.

Index